Beyond the Bottom Line

Socially Innovative Business Owners

Jack Quarter

Q

Quorum Books

Westport, Connecticut • London

Library of Congress Cataloging-in-Publication Data

Quarter, Jack.
    Beyond the bottom line : socially innovative business owners / Jack Quarter.
        p. cm.
    Includes bibliographical references and index.
    ISBN 1-56720-414-7 (alk. paper)
    1. Social responsibility of business—Case studies.   2. Industrial management—
Social aspects—Case studies.   3. Industrial management—Employee participation—
Case studies.   4. Businesspeople—Attitudes—Case studies.   5. Business ethics—
Case studies.   I. Title.
HD60 .Q37 2000
658.4'08—dc21   00-032815

British Library Cataloguing-in-Publication Data is available.

Library of Congress Catalog Card Number: 00-032815
ISBN: 1-56720-414-7

First published in 2000

Quorum Books, 88 Post Road West, Westport, CT 06881
An imprint of Greenwood Publishing Group, Inc.
www.quorumbooks.com

Printed in the United States of America

The paper used in this book complies with the
Permanent Paper Standard issued by the National
Information Standards Organization (Z39.48-1984)

10 9 8 7 6 5 4 3 2 1

To Hugh Oliver

Contents

Introduction

Businesspeople are a privileged group, who have attempted to protect their advantages against movements for social justice. Rather than being the leaders of such movements, they tend to be the object of them, as suggested by class-based theories. Nevertheless, there are businesspeople who have departed from tradition and have either thrown their support behind movements for social justice or have taken a leadership role in them. Generally, this is done apart from their business, but in exceptional cases, their business is used as a laboratory for social innovation. They are not only business entrepreneurs, but social entrepreneurs—that is, innovators and social risk-takers who devote themselves and their businesses to achieving and promoting their ideals. This group is the subject of this book.

Even though there is an element of philanthropy in these initiatives, in that they are motivated by benevolence and humanitarianism, it would be inappropriate to describe this group in that manner. This point requires some elaboration, because it is important to demonstrate how the socially innovative businesspeople who are the subject of this book differ from typical philanthropists. Take, for example, Andrew Carnegie, the emigrant from Scotland who became a wealthy U.S. steel magnate in the latter half of the nineteenth century and a leading proponent of philanthropy as a duty of the wealthy. The post-retirement Carnegie was guided by his motto that "he who dies rich dies disgraced" (Carnegie 1901, 43). By 1913, he had given away $332 million, an astonishing sum for that time, including the endowment of 2,500 libraries in the U.S., Canada, and the U.K. (Wall 1992). Among his benefactors were the Andrew Carnegie Relief Fund, established in 1901 to provide financial assistance for his former employees in need, and the Carnegie Endowment for Peace, a cause to which he devoted much energy in his final years.

But in spite of his exceptional generosity and his unusual philosophy that led him to view his wealth as "trust funds" that he administered "to produce the most beneficial results for the community" (Carnegie 1901, 15), Carnegie was uncritical of the system in which he operated. Rather, in his *Gospel of Wealth* (originally published in 1889), he argued: "We accept and welcome, therefore, as conditions to which we must accommodate ourselves, great inequality of the environment . . . as being not only beneficial, but essential to the future progress of the race" (Carnegie 1901, 4). Moreover, Carnegie's manner was patronizing. He believed that "the man of wealth" was "the mere trustee and agent for his poorer brethren, bringing to their service his superior wisdom, experience, and ability to administer, doing for them better than they would or could do for themselves" (Carnegie 1901, 15).

Although there have been other wealthy people who have been exceptionally generous (for example, Henry Ford, Will Kellogg, Ted Turner, George Soros, Robert Bosch, Brooke Astor, and the Rockefeller, Heinz, Duke, McArthur, and Pew families), most wealth is passed on to family heirs. Therefore, even though there is a positive social impact from the give-back by the wealthy to the community, it would seem inappropriate to characterize philanthropy as a movement for social justice.

By comparison, the businesspeople who are the subject of this book have actively contributed to movements to create a more just workplace and society. Their actions are based upon a social vision that they implemented in their business and also promoted in society. Their efforts at applying their philosophy to their business also differentiate this group from traditional philanthropists. In spite of their generosity, Carnegie and other leading philanthropists have had relatively conventional business practices. Carnegie, for example, was not renowned for the benevolent treatment of his employees; his reputation was particularly tarnished by the huge strike in 1892 at Homestead Steel (one of his companies) that resulted in bloodshed from which he was unable to disassociate himself (Wall 1992).

In other words, philanthropy has generally been associated with two distinct roles: one involving a conventional set of practices for earning wealth, and another relatively distinct role for disbursing it. In reflecting upon this dilemma, George Soros, a contemporary financier and philanthropist who has been exceptionally generous in promoting an "open society" in Eastern Europe (Slater 1996; Soros 1995), states frankly that: "I have been successful in playing by the rules of the game" (Soros 1997a). Soros argues that it is not the role of businesspeople like himself to create the rules of the game, but that of government and society. Although Soros is concerned about the diminished social-welfare role of government in ameliorating the inequalities produced by the market (Soros 1997b), he takes a conventional view of the investor's role, and dismisses social investment strategies as both ineffective and inappropriate. He states, "I recognize the power of the markets and I don't fight against it" (Soros 1997a).

It is not simply philanthropists such as Soros and Carnegie who have separated their contribution to society from their business role, but also socialists such as Fredrich Engels and William Morris. For about 20 years, while Engels operated and, subsequently, became a partner in the family firm of Ermen and Engels (a company that manufactured sewing thread and had about 800 employees) and lived a lifestyle that could best be described as "bourgeois" (including memberships in the most prestigious clubs in Manchester), he wrote manuscripts, many of them in collaboration with Karl Marx, that created the foundations of modern communism (McLellan 1977). In spite of writings and related political activities, Engels engaged in relatively conventional business practices until he retired from the family firm at age 50 (in 1870) in order to move to London where he and Marx could work more closely.

William Morris, another leading figure in nineteenth-century socialist circles, owned a successful business, Morris and Co., which produced stained glass and other artistic products (Vallance 1909). At the same time, he was a leading social activist, who in 1885, led a group that organized the Socialist League (of which he became the first chair). He believed that society's problems were so severe that they could be solved only through revolution.

There are others who could be included in this tradition that combines a relatively conventional role for business with a distinct commitment for social justice issues. An outstanding example is Leland Stanford, the nineteenth-century railroad "robber baron" and benefactor of Stanford University, who in his latter years developed a fundamental critique of the system that made him wealthy, and as a senator representing California, introduced legislation that was intended to incorporate into law the legal basis for worker cooperatives (that is, democratically managed employee-owned firms) (Altenberg 1990). Another example is Cyrus Eaton, the industrialist who late in his life returned to his home town of Pugwash, Nova Scotia, to establish a Thinkers Lodge and series of conferences that led to a loose network of elite intellectuals who lobbied for disarmament (Gleisser 1965), and who shared in the Nobel Peace Prize in 1995 (Knox 1995). Like philanthropists, these businesspeople had one set of rules for their business life and another for actualizing their social ideals.

In the eleven case studies that follow in chapters 2 through 10, there has been greater unity between the ideals that are espoused and the associated business practices, in that the ideals have been integrated into the business. In other words, these social innovators have attempted to depart from the rules of the game in how they conduct their business. But as the case studies will illustrate, there is a complexity in departing from the rules; for a business to succeed, it has to compete effectively in the market and this presents a major constraint upon its practice. Below are case studies listed by chapter numbers and divided into two broad groupings: innovations in industrial and economic democracy and community innovations.

Industrial and Economic Democracy
2. The John Lewis Partnership (U.K.)
3. The Scott Bader Commonwealth (U.K.)
4. Endenburg Electric (the Netherlands)
5. Allied Plywood (U.S.)
6. The Baxi Partnership (U.K.)
6. Tullis Russell (U.K.)
7. Harpell's Press (Canada)

Community Innovation
7. Harpell's Press (Canada)
8. The Body Shop (U.K.)
9. Inmate Enterprises (U.S.)
9. K. T. Footwear (New Zealand)
10. Wilkhahn (Germany)

   The first seven case studies deal with industrial and economic democracy, including various models for the transformation of a conventionally owned firm. These involve placing an owner's shares into a trust that controls the firm; establishing a worker cooperative; or converting the firm to employee share-ownership. These case studies also deal with innovative efforts at involving the employees in decision making, not simply within the work unit but also at all levels of the organization, including the board of directors. The final five case studies (the seventh case study falls into both categories) involve innovations that change the relationship between the corporation and the surrounding community—sustainable development, support for movements for social justice, or assistance for an oppressed group through involving them in the business. The case studies are from six countries: the U.K., the U.S., Canada, the Netherlands, Germany, and New Zealand.

   The businesses range in size from a large corporation with 40,000 employees to a very small enterprise with about 20. Most of the innovators are men. Most come from a privileged background, but some are from poor families and one is a member of a racial minority. All the businesses are currently functioning, even though in several cases the architects of the innovation have died. The case studies explore the owners' aspirations, the current practices of the business, and the extent to which the owners' aspirations have been achieved.

   It is useful to put this phenomenon within a historical perspective if only to understand that it is not simply recent, but also something that businesspeople have struggled with in the past. Therefore, the first chapter begins with Robert Owen, the nineteenth-century British industrialist who is arguably the originator of this tradition. This first chapter discusses Owen and refers briefly to some other examples to establish the historical significance of this tradition. From this discussion, a series of propositions using organizational change and social movement theory are developed and applied in the concluding chapter to an analysis of the case studies. Also in the concluding chapter, a framework is presented that seeks to explain the behavior of such businesspeople, and to interpret its meaning as a social phenomenon.

   The contributions of the businessespeople discussed in this book are noteworthy in their own right. But given the temper of our times in which crass self-interest is seen as a virtue and in which many businesspeople are accumulating vast amounts of wealth with little or no concern for the social consequences of their actions, this phenomenon is of even greater significance.

1

Robert Owen: The Historical Tradition

There are relatively few businesspeople who use their firms to develop and promote innovative practices that contribute to movements for social justice. The prototype and giant of this tradition was Robert Owen, the British industrialist who achieved such fame for his social views and his social innovations that there is an academic field of study referred to as Owenism or Owenite Socialism that, to this day, involves an international group of scholars. Owen serves as an important historical antecedent to the eleven case studies of more contemporary businesspeople that follow. As noted in the Introduction, after the discussion of Owen, a series of propositions using organizational change and social movement theory will be presented. These will be used in the concluding chapter to analyze the case studies.

ROBERT OWEN

In 1771, Robert Owen was born in a small town in Wales, the fourth of five children in a working-class family. From early childhood he was precocious, and by age 7, he had become the assistant master in the local school. At age 10, he moved to London where he lived with his older brother and for four years apprenticed in a linen-draper shop. At that time, the cotton industry was booming, spurred on by such inventions as the steam engine and spinning jenny. At age 15, Owen left London for Manchester, where for the next 14 years, he established his reputation as a skilled manager in the cotton industry, and engaged in a series of partnerships with leading industrialists of the time that made him wealthy.

At about this time, through a fortuitous contact in Manchester, Owen met and later fell in love with Caroline Dale, the eldest daughter of David Dale, the principal owner of the New Lanark cotton-spinning mills. Under Dale's direction,

New Lanark (a short drive from Glasgow, on the banks of the River Clyde) had become an internationally recognized factory-community with a standard of health and schooling far superior to the norms of that period. This statement must be put in perspective, for the norms of that period were primitive by modern standards, and permitted six-year-old children to work a lengthy day in a grimy factory. Owen admired Dale, a devoutly religious Presbyterian, for his generosity to charities and for benevolence to his employees. For example, when the first cotton mill at New Lanark burned down, Dale continued to pay his employees' wages until production resumed. Owen knew of New Lanark, which attracted visitors from all over the world, and through his relationship with Caroline Dale he had the opportunity to visit the community in 1798. A year later, he returned with two partners and purchased the mills for the relatively low price of £60,000 from Dale, who was ill, growing old, and lacking a male heir to take over the business. Dale was less eager to part with his daughter, but relented shortly after the sale of the mills.

Although there were some indications during his Manchester stay of Owen's interest in social reform (for example, memberships in the Board of Health and the Literary and Philosophical Society), New Lanark represented a turning point in his life (Cole 1969). Owen's early work at New Lanark was embedded within a reformist value system that would appeal to any forward-looking businessperson. He introduced practices to improve efficiency and increase profits. He was a highly skilled manager, dealing with such problems as absenteeism, poor productivity, and theft through improved systems of organization and individual feedback to the workers regarding their performance. Unlike other mill owners, however, he shunned physical punishment. Instead, he opted for such behavioral motivators as the "Silent Monitor," a four-sided block of wood that hung next to each worker's machine and displayed a color reflecting performance. The mills of New Lanark were consistently profitable during the period Owen managed them (1799–1825), and permitted him to amass considerable personal wealth (Robertson 1971).

But Owen's reforms went beyond what was needed to make New Lanark (its 2,000 workers making it one of the largest industrial establishments of the time) into an efficient business. Although Owen was a great admirer of Dale, he referred to New Lanark (prior to his involvement) as having "vicious and inferior conditions" (Owen 1857, 79). Owen's first measures were to fix age 10 as the youngest at which he would employ any child, and to ban the importation of pauper apprentices, a significant part of New Lanark's labor force. He also went about improving physical conditions by having one story added to each house; having the streets cleaned of dung; starting a company store where food and clothing could be purchased cheaply; levying stiff fines to end drunkenness; and initiating a general community fund (to which all workers contributed one-sixteenth of their wages) to provide free medical care and support for the sick.

Owen's initiatives at New Lanark have been described as philanthropic in that they were motivated in part by kindness and concern for the residents' welfare who, in the beginning at least, viewed his unusual ideas with suspicion. However, it would be misleading to portray Owen as a philanthropist (in the typical use of the term) because his benevolence was part of a grander scheme designed to prove that the problems of society could be overcome through improvements to the social environment. Education, and particularly education beginning from infancy (one year of age at New Lanark), was central to Owen's thinking. He established the first known school for infants and a night school for the employees of the mills. In his 1813 book, *A New View of Society,* he wrote that: "The governing powers of all countries should establish rational plans for the education and general formation of the characters of their subjects. These plans must be devised to train children from their earliest infancy in good habits of every description" (Owen 1969, 106).

Owen held such great conviction about the power of education that he believed that a well-formulated plan had the potential to transform society. He stated: "Any general character, from the best to the worst, from the most ignorant to the most enlightened, may be given to any community, even to the world at large, by the application of proper means" (Owen 1969, 101). Owen's ideas not only represented a radical form of environmentalism in an era that attributed an individual's social class to heredity, but were based upon a humanitarian ideal that departed fundamentally from the thinking of the day. As Owenite scholar Sidney Pollard says: "His is not the humanism of the Renaissance, or even that of the Enlightenment, which proceeded on the powerful, if always unspoken, assumption that the full development to the rounded and free human being was thinkable only in terms of a privileged minority. What was new and revolutionary in Owen was the belief, made possible for the first time in history by precisely the economic revolution in which he played such a striking part in his younger years, that the right to a full humanity was to be available to all, even to the humble peasant and cotton spinner and street sweeper" (1971, x). Defying the prevalent wisdom of his day, Owen declared that: "The infants of any one class in the world may be readily formed into the men of any other class" (Owen 1969, 174). New Lanark, where Owen went about improving the living conditions in the community, became a laboratory to prove his theory.

At first, Owen's plan at New Lanark to build community centers that would also be used for educational purposes ran into problems, because his partners viewed it as an unnecessary expenditure. But his contacts within British society served him well. When his social innovations became more salient, he was able to attract a set of partners (educators and intellectuals such as Jeremy Bentham) who shared most of his opinions about the importance of education, and were therefore willing to support the necessary investment. Central to this scheme was the Institute for the Formation of Character, which included schools for children at work in the mills, public halls, community rooms, and a nursery school. In line with progressive educators who were to follow, Owen believed that schooling should be enjoyable—a fundamental departure from the punitive practices of his day. All children learned basic subjects, and girls learned to knit and sew. There was a great emphasis on dance, music, and physical exercise; even religion, of which Owen was a strong critic, was taught to satisfy some of his partners. Owen was achieving great fame for his innovations at New Lanark, and in a 10-year period, the Visitors' Book was signed by 20,000 people, including leading figures from Britain and other parts of the world. With respect to his educational innovations, Margaret Cole, one of Owen's many biographers, writes: "These ideas were astonishingly modern; so much so, in fact, that New Lanark between 1816 and 1826 might also be regarded as an epitome of the progress made in English education during the following hundred years" (1969, 79).

Owen then started to turn greater attention to the conditions outside of New Lanark, and again his proposals demonstrated an insight that was generations ahead of his time. In his book *A New View of Society,* he demanded a universal state educational system, colleges for training teachers, a ministry of education, a nationwide census of employment and wages, and a system of state-aided public works during economic downturns. He convinced Sir Robert Peel to introduce legislation that included such provisions as making 10 the minimum age for factory employment; reducing the working day for those under 18 to a maximum of 10.5 hours (not including time for meals and instruction); a prohibition on work between 9 P.M. and 5 A.M.; schooling during the first four years of factory life; and inspectors to be appointed and paid for by the Justices of the Peace. Three years later, the legislation was passed in a watered-down form, so much so that Owen disassociated himself from it; nevertheless, it helped to pave the way for further industrial reform.

As he devoted greater attention to issues outside of New Lanark and generated proposals that were arguably revolutionary, Owen started to lose favor with the British elite. When he proposed to settle the poor in "Villages of Co-operation"—self-supporting agricultural communities based on communal living—he was refused a hearing in the House of Commons. Owen's Report to the County of New Lanark in 1820 went further and became the blueprint for Owenite Socialism. Owen argued that labor was the source of wealth and, therefore, it must be rewarded properly. The central problem facing society was the lack of "employment at wages sufficient to support the family of a working man" (Owen 1969, 201).

Owen earned an international reputation both for his reforms at New Lanark and for his writings. Although he maintained a substantial stake in New Lanark until 1828, in effect, he had ceased to be a businessman and had become the symbol of social movements, with a strong following among both the British working class and social reformers in the U.S. and Europe. The word "symbol" is used deliberately, since Owen did not seek to lead a social movement in the same manner as he directed New Lanark. Rather, his ideas had such broad appeal that various social movements embraced them.

As a result of continuing interference from his business partners in New Lanark's curriculum, Owen looked to the U.S., and in 1825 set up a commune in

New Harmony, Indiana. Within three years it had failed, largely because of his poor leadership, costing Owen much of his personal fortune. Undeterred, he subsequently proposed to the general leading the Mexican revolution, Santa Anna, that he be given the opportunity to pursue his social experiments in Texas. In essence, Owen (nearing age 60) was losing the practical edge that had made him so successful as a social reformer, and was becoming a millennial thinker. Until his death at age 87, he spent most of his time lecturing and writing, and he embraced spiritualism. Yet even in the latter part of his life, he was able to pull off such major accomplishments as organizing labor bazaars (mutual associations in which the participants exchanged services with each other); organizing the Grand National Consolidated Trades Union that for a brief period united the British labor movement; serving as the governor of an Owenite community called Queenwood; and completing the first volume of his autobiography in the final year of his life.

There was a significance to Robert Owen's work that extended beyond him as an individual—social movements had grown around him that were inspired by his egalitarian and humanitarian ideas and his work at New Lanark. No less a critic of Owen's "utopianism" than Fredrich Engels would admit, with admiration, that "every real advance in England on behalf of the workers links itself to the name of Robert Owen" (1959, 80). The British cooperative movement, which traces its formal beginnings to Rochdale in 1844, associates itself with Owen, as does the labor movement and the movements for educational reform and early childhood education. G. D. H. Cole concludes his biography of Owen by stating: "When the workers were sinking under the despair bred by evil factory conditions, his faith and hope raised them up to strike the first concerted blow for economic freedom. Not for nothing do many movements look back to him as their founder or source of first inspiration" (1966, 321).

POST-OWEN AND THE UTOPIAN TRADITION

There are at least three ways in which Owen acted out his social objectives. First, he was a humanitarian who dedicated his fortune to the service of others. Even though he was left without any significant wealth after New Harmony, the aging Owen was able to live comfortably, supported in part by his children. Second, he was a social critic, visionary, and advocate for many causes that did not directly involve his business interests. In the eyes of others, his success in business gave credibility to his ideas and political initiatives. Third, his bold innovations at New Lanark were empirical proof that a better environment leads to better people and that class divisions and their associated problems are not an inevitable derivative of human nature but can be remedied through social innovation and legislation.

Owen was only one of a group of social innovators at that period: Charles Fourier and Henri Saint-Simon also sought to demonstrate that the social misery and the gross social inequalities produced by the Industrial Revolution could be ameliorated through such solutions as model communities based on socialist principles. Within this tradition, ideals are not only visualized and espoused, but they also become part of the lived experience, both collective and individual. Owen's approach was labeled as utopian socialism by Marx and Engels (Cohen 1967). The label utopian is in part disparaging in that it implies a lack of realism, impracticality, and, by implication, suggests that the ideals are unattainable. Engels, as noted, acknowledged the contribution of Robert Owen and the utopian socialist tradition, but was also critical of it, referring to it as a "mishmash" lacking any scientific basis (Engels 1959). For Marx and Engels, the existing social conditions placed such major constraints on human agency that, with the exception of periods of crisis, a utopian agenda was doomed to failure. Ironically, Marx and Engels also projected a utopian vision, but they did not dwell on the details. Rather than attempting to demonstrate that it was possible to create communist models within capitalism, they channeled their energies into trying to prove why contradictions within the system would lead to crises that would increase the likelihood of communism coming about. While they did not discount the importance of human agency, and indeed put much of their energy into political organizing, in balance, they viewed agency as being of lesser importance than the utopians. Moreover, the type of agency they favored was action designed to organize a communist revolution during periods of crisis, as reflected in *The Communist Manifesto* of 1848, where they exhort "Working men of all countries, unite!" (Marx and Engels 1968, 121).

This debate between the utopians and Marxists parallels a broader discussion in the social sciences between social determinism and human agency (Hook 1958; Mannheim 1953; O'Sullivan, 1990). The critical issue in this discussion is attempting to reconcile the human desire to transcend and influence the organization of society, with society's powerful impact on shaping behavior. Both the utopians and Marxists acknowledged the important effect of the existing social conditions upon the potential for change. Owen, as noted, believed in an extreme form of environmentalism. But paradoxically, he, like other utopians, also believed that by organizing innovative projects in the workplace and community, it would be possible to demonstrate that more equitable social conditions could be created. The utopian philosophy reflected an optimism (perhaps a naive optimism) that positive examples would inspire movements for social change to transcend the social conditions that shaped them. In essence, utopianism is more a theory of action than a scientific theory.

It should also be emphasized that utopianism and socialism are not to be equated. The desire of striving for ideal solutions to social problems has been utilized by Christians (the social gospel), reform-minded liberals, anarchists, behavioral scientists such as B. F. Skinner, and other intellectuals ranging from Plato to Thomas More, whose influential book *Utopia* (published in 1516) describes an ideal state consisting of a republic of philosophers. Even though these traditions differ, Manuel argues that a central element in utopian thought is the reduction of inequalities; "gross inequalities," he states, "are not counte-nanced" (1969, 375).

Utopianism also has deep roots in religious thought that goes back to the Biblical period. But Manuel (1969, 371) differentiates utopianism from religious millennia in that "it comes to pass not by an act of grace, but through human will and effort." Nevertheless, even for businesspeople who are inspired by utopian ideals, religious inspiration can be important. Among Quaker businesspeople, in particular, there is a strong utopian strain that has manifested itself in attempts to create an ideal workplace. For example, George Cadbury, the driving force behind the Cadbury chocolate dynasty, was a devout Quaker who also created a model factory-community when in 1879 he moved production from Birmingham to the countryside village of Bournville (The Bournville Village Trust). Cadbury operated on the principle that the working conditions of the employees should not be compromised for the sake of profit. The firm was distinguished by high wages, a pension fund endowed by the company, medical and dental services, and an impressive array of sports facilities, that is, a progressive form of social welfare (Stranz 1973). Comparisons with Birmingham showed that after 20 years, Bournville experienced much lower rates of infant mortality and death from other causes. The Cadbury family has followed the traditions that George Cadbury established, and in the U.K., has led in promoting ethical standards for business.

Joseph Rowntree, another successful Quaker businessman and chocolate pro-ducer, engaged in similar practices with respect to his employees (Vernon, 1958). Rowntree's son, Seebohm (a company director until he became chairman in 1923), took the family's philosophy a step further and used his influence as an advisor to British prime minister, David Lloyd George (prime minister from 1916 to 1922), to encourage much of the social welfare legislation of the day (Briggs 1961). Rowntree promoted works councils for industry as a means of overcoming top-down decision making. (Rowntree & Co. introduced one during the First World War.)

Although the utopian tradition is a significant strain among Quaker businesses, it is by no means confined to that religion. For example, in 1923 James Eagan, a devout Presbyterian in Birmingham, Alabama, who was influenced by the social gospel, transferred his ownership of the American Cast Iron Pipe Company into a trust out of concern for the welfare of his employees, most of whom were poor Blacks (Cleghorn 1995).

Therefore, the utopian tradition is grounded in a variety of perspectives that have inspired its proponents to visualize, implement, and promote their ideals. The common features in these perspectives are the desire to achieve greater justice in society and the workplace, and the optimistic belief that this goal can be achieved through the creation of positive models. Utopianism is a theory of action based on the assumption that humans can find ideal solutions to the problems of the day.

Although the utopian orientation still exists, over the years it has fallen out of favor, in part because, as suggested by sociologist Daniel Bell's End of Ideology critique (Bell 1960), communist revolutions have failed to achieve their ideals. However, the essence of utopianism—visualizing ideal solutions and demonstrating that they can be realized—continues.

The term utopianism has been supplanted by such labels as visionary, arguably less extreme in connotation. With respect to business, "visionary" has become an accolade for business leaders who work for the betterment of their company and the community (Liebig 1994; Spayde 1995). But visionary leadership can also be associated with objectives that are personal, individual, and even spiritual, as well as with social goals that are often conventional, as for example, improving company performance through managerial innovations. For that reason, a different term, socially innovative, will be used in reference to the businesspeople who are the subject of this study. The term socially innovative, unlike visionary, does not have an individualistic connotation, and is associated to a greater extent with pragmatic criteria, which differentiates it from utopianism. Unlike utopianism, socially innovative does not necessarily address issues of social justice; for the purposes of this study, however, this aspect of the term will be assumed.

AN INTERPRETIVE FRAMEWORK

With respect to socially innovative businesspeople, the same issue arises that was part of the debate between utopian socialism and Marxism: to what extent do the social conditions within which a business operates place constraints upon experiments for human betterment within the workplace? Or put more positively, under what circumstances are such experiments most likely to be sustained within the innovator's firm and become associated with movements in which others attempt to emulate these ideals?

Initially, the analysis will focus on Robert Owen in order to develop a series of propositions to be applied in the concluding chapter. The analysis of Owen will start with his innovations at New Lanark and proceed to the broader social movements with which he is associated.

Owen was able to proceed with his work at New Lanark because he and his partners owned the factory-community and he was the principal manager. His privileged status as a major investor and manager sanctioned his right to make changes to the mills and the community. To a degree, he also required the cooperation of the residents of the community. At first there was some resistance, but from 1807 (after he paid full wages during the temporary closure of the mills), he won their full cooperation. As a result of their ownership rights, however, Owen's various partners were in a stronger position to challenge his innovations, and they did present problems for him. His first two sets of partners took a narrow business view of New Lanark and questioned some of the expenditures on the community. His third set of partners shared Owen's ideals; he had differences, however, on religious teachings with those who were Quakers.

New Lanark was ideally suited for Owen's innovations because his father-in-law, David Dale, had already established a tradition for philanthropy. In fact, there are some who suggest that Owen understated the contribution of Dale. McLaren (1983, 22) refers to New Lanark as "a very famous institution before Owen took it over in 1799. If evidence of this is needed, one only has to look at the Visitors Book starting in 1795 to see that Dale's New Lanark had already become something of a showpiece." Although Dale was a devout Christian who tried to put his beliefs into practice, and Owen was an atheist and a critic of religion, they admired each other. Dale's reputation as a leading businessman in Scotland enhanced Owen's status, and until Dale's death in 1806, Owen was probably sheltered from criticism to a degree. Owen was also protected because the mills were highly profitable both during Dale's tenure and after Owen started introducing his innovations (Robertson 1971). Owen's skill as a hands-on manager, prior to and during his involvement in New Lanark, enhanced his credibility. Although his reformist intentions were apparent from the beginning, he admitted that his goal was also "to produce the greatest ultimate profit to the proprietors" (cited in Donnachie and Hewitt 1993, 63).

For all of these reasons, Owen was in a strong position to innovate within New Lanark. However, his reputation did not simply come from what he was doing at New Lanark, but from convincing others that the experiments he was undertaking had a more general importance. His powerful intellect and his charismatic leadership qualities were important contributions in this regard. Like charismatic leaders in general, Owen presented an appealing vision of the future (Yukl 1981). Through his experiments at New Lanark and subsequently at New Harmony, he attempted to prove that the problems associated with capitalism and industrialization could be overcome by building model communities. In his early work at New Lanark, Owen provided evidence of the effectiveness of his innovations, but his experiment in communitarian socialism at New Harmony was a failure. By then, however, Owen had earned his reputation and the New Harmony setback did not change it.

Owen's early work at New Lanark and his ability to organize support for child labor legislation can be interpreted within a resource mobilization perspective (Jenkins 1983; Morris and McClurg Mueller, 1992). To gain political support, he used his privileged status within society, including his connections with others in the British elite, and his charismatic leadership qualities. However, as Owen became more radical in his thought and veered from a reformist, philanthropic agenda to one that had revolutionary intent, the British elite ostracized him. In that respect, he might be contrasted to Seebohm Rowntree, who was able to use his privileged status as a leading industrialist and the connections he had among the British elite to influence the introduction of important social welfare legislation by the British Liberal Party under the leadership of Lloyd George.

As Owen's star waned among the British elite, it rose among the social movements that were forming to address similar issues. These included the cooperative movement, the communitarian movement, the labor movement, and educational reform movements, particularly early childhood education. While these movements lacked the same power as the British elite with which Owen had originally been associated, they were nevertheless growing in influence. From a resource mobilization perspective, they were challenging movements that were altering the balance of power in society (Gamson 1975; McCarthy 1977; McCarthy and Zald 1973).

These movements embraced Owen, elevating him to an icon. One can only speculate why this occurred. Initially, Owen's status was based largely upon his work at New Lanark. However, as his work progressed, his status was no longer dependent upon proprietorship, but rather upon his penetrating insights and, even more so, upon the boldness with which he challenged the injustices of British society. This made him appealing to like-minded social movement activists. One might also speculate that the anomaly of a successful industrialist critiquing the very premises that were the foundation of staggering social inequalities added to Owen's appeal. In a society in which the lines based upon class were tightly drawn, Owen was highly unusual in that he moved from a working-class background to become a successful industrialist, and then cast aside that role to become a social innovator and a vociferous critic of the status quo. Even though Owen's experiment in communitarian socialism was unsuccessful and he lost his wealth in that effort, his reputation was sufficiently robust to withstand any setbacks.

Nevertheless, it is ironic that Owen was elevated to an icon, since he was an iconoclastic thinker who challenged the most sacred truths of society. Moreover, in his relationship to these social movements, he was not a leader in the same sense as at New Lanark. These movements were so broad and pervasive that others who were making major contributions were not necessarily aware of Owen. During his lifetime, there were many intellectuals addressing the exploitive conditions of the Industrial Revolution, and there were many activists participating in the same movements for social justice in which Owen was involved. For example, German cooperative pioneers such as Hermann Schulze Delitzsch and Friedrich Wilhelm Raiffeisen were working independently without any apparent awareness of Owen (Hasselmann 1971). That is not to say that the work of Owen or of other social innovators was without consequence. Social innovators are important, but they inevitably operate within a culture that influences them and which they, in turn, influence. During the period when Owenism was at its zenith, the predominant norms of British society were in the process of change and Owen was one influence—and an important influence—upon that process.

From this discussion of Owen, a series of propositions can be formulated. These will be reconsidered, following the presentation of case studies, in the concluding chapter of this work. First, the likelihood that businesspeople will succeed in introducing innovations into the workplace will depend on such factors as control over the firm; their leadership qualities in convincing their employees of the value of their innovations; and their ability to gain the support of such key players as management, union leaders, and investors, the support of these key players being critical to sustaining the innovation. These factors were in place at

New Lanark: when Owen had difficulties with partners, he found others who shared his aspirations.

Second, once the innovator ceases to be involved, several factors influence the likelihood that that the innovation will be sustained: 1. the commitment of other key players; 2. market factors that affect the performance of the company; and 3. the extent to which the innovation departs from existing norms—the assumption being that the greater the departure, the more vulnerable the innovation, unless the predominant norms also change.

This second proposition, although not specifically discussed above in the context of Owen and New Lanark, is based on the following events. Owen sold the controlling interest in the mills in 1825 to Charles and Henry Walker, sons of one of his partners. As Quakers, they shared Owen's ideals and continued the policies that he had initiated. A report of government inspectors in 1833 notes "a most extraordinary degree of attention devoted to the education of children" (cited in Donnachie and Hewitt 1993, 149). However, unlike Owen, the Walkers were not innovators and eventually New Lanark's educational system became the norm rather than the exception. In 1875, New Lanark's school was transferred into the state system. The mills at New Lanark, once among the largest cotton manufacturers in Britain, also declined in significance until their closure in 1968. New Lanark is now a historical site that is being restored as a living, working community by the New Lanark Conservation Trust. Therefore, the pattern at New Lanark fits, in part, the Weberian thesis that over time there is a tendency for innovation brought about by charismatic leaders to become part of organizational routines (Weber 1947; Zald and Ash 1966). However, New Lanark also departs from the Weberian thesis in that the innovations initiated by Owen inspired like-minded social movements to transform the predominant norms. Had Owen not succeeded in turning over New Lanark to businesspeople who shared his ideals, it is unlikely that his innovations would have survived as long as they did. That was the case at the American Cast Iron Pipe Company (mentioned previously) where, after the death of the innovator James Eagan, management succeeded in reinterpreting his intentions (Cleghorn 1995).

The third proposition pertains to the relationship between an innovation in a particular firm and social movements. Related social movements, as noted, embraced Owen's innovations at New Lanark. In the case studies that follow, the businesspeople also have aspirations beyond their firm. Some engage specifically in helping to organize social movements and other affiliate with existing movement organizations. It is proposed that with respect to social movements, a similar dynamic exists as in organizations, in that there is a tendency on the part of elite social groups to minimize the impact upon predominant norms (Zald and Ash 1966). Excepting for periods of crisis, the strongest movements are likely to be those whose objectives can be easily integrated within the predominant norms. Movements that pose a more fundamental challenge (non-normative in the view of Piven and Cloward [1992]) are more likely to be weak and have less impact.

With respect to Owen, it is noteworthy that movements having a great influence on the predominant norms used some aspects of his ideas (for example, educational reform), whereas movements that had a minimal influence used other aspects (for example, communitarian socialism). The educational reforms that occurred during the nineteenth century were major, but they could be subsumed by the capitalist system. Owen's blueprint for socialist communities, however, departed so fundamentally from capitalism, that it could become the predominant model only through a massive transformation in society. Although experiments of this sort have continued (for example, the Hutterite communities and the Israeli kibbutzim), they are on the margins rather than part of the predominant model.

The fourth proposition is based upon the role of the state in relation to social movements. The state is often justifiably characterized as a conservative influence in opposition to social movements challenging the predominant norms. This point is made strongly by Marxists who view the state as representing class-based interests in opposition to counter-hegemonic social forces (Carroll 1997). In her study of major political revolutions, Skocpol (1979) argues for a more autonomous role for the state that both influences the course of movements and responds to them. Since her work deals with political revolutions in which the predominant norms are in flux, it might not be generalizable to the movements in this book that are more specific and have occurred in relatively stable liberal-democratic states. Nevertheless, Skocpol's analysis provides an explanation of the complex relationship between social movements and the state.

During his innovations at New Lanark, Robert Owen operated quite independently of the state. However, as he shifted his goals from New Lanark to society at large, he became more interested in influencing government, for example, in lobbying for legislation to restrict child labor and to regulate the conditions of work in the factories. Owen's blueprint for society is outlined in his report prepared for the county of New Lanark in 1820. As noted, he also wanted the state to intervene in creating a public education system, teachers' colleges, and public works in economic downturns. Most of his proposals became realities, though not all during his lifetime. Essentially, the state responded to pressure from social movements that were influenced to a degree by Owen's thinking. This would support the view that a liberal-democratic society is responsive to social movements (Jenkins 1983), albeit the degree to which it is responsive varies according to such factors as the class interests of the movement, its political strength, tactics (Gamson 1975), and the ease with which its objectives can be incorporated within the predominant norms.

This analysis also suggests that the state has an important role in sanctioning innovation and incorporating it through legislation into the predominant norms. Such legislation creates a frame of reference for social innovators such as Owen and the businesspeople discussed in this book, and it can also pose a challenge for their work in that they seek changes in the legislative framework.

CONCLUSION

After eleven case studies are presented in the succeeding chapters, they will be analyzed in relation to these propositions in the concluding chapter of this work. The propositions will also be reconsidered in the process; discussion of the propositions will focus upon both the sustainability of these innovations within companies and the innovations' impact upon society. In addition, a model will be presented that seeks to explain the behavior of socially innovative business-people and the meaning of their work. In line with the preceding discussion of utopianism, the model will be based upon a theory of social action that balances the inherent desire of humans to rise above the conditions in which they live with the obvious constraints of those conditions. This model takes into account both human agency and social conditioning as they pertain to the socially innovative businesspeople who are the subject of this study. Its objective is to interpret the meaning of these innovators' projects, both for their companies and for society. In so doing, it will be argued that the individualistic ethic that has sustained these businesspeople in their innovations stands in the path of understanding the value of their contributions.

2

The John Lewis Partnership

The John Lewis Partnership is one of the most successful retailing businesses in Britain. In 1995, its network of high-street department stores and the Waitrose supermarket chain together with some smaller subsidiaries employed 41,100 and yielded profits of £150 million against revenues of £2.82 billion[1] (John Lewis Partnership 1996). Although customers know John Lewis through its quality of service, few are aware of this company's history, its innovative social structure, and its highly unusual founder.

The company was started in 1864 in London by John Lewis, a merchant, who liked to be known as John Lewis of Oxford St. At age 19, his son Spedan (John Spedan Lewis) entered the business, became a partner two years later (in 1906), and started a process of social innovation that transformed John Lewis into a unique corporation. Spedan Lewis's mission was sparked by the realization that his father, his younger brother Oswald, and himself were drawing more from the business than the 300 employees. "Too much for three—too little for 300," was his succinct summary of the problem (Lewis 1948, 7). "There on the one side was my father and the other side his staff—my father with over a hundred separate pieces of property that he never saw and that were nothing but a bother to him . . . the staff with an employment that was extremely insecure and that gave them a living so meagre that they were far less happy than they could have been" (Lewis 1948, 18). "As I turned these things over in my mind," Lewis reflected, "it occurred to me that, if a very much larger proportion of the income from the business had gone to the other people who were likewise giving their own working lives to it, the business itself would have been vastly more efficient and my father's life would have been really far happier." (Lewis 1948, 16).

This realization (which Spedan refers to in his books, *Partnership for All* [1948] and *Fairer Shares* [1954]) became a catalyst for the pioneering innovations that he brought to the company, innovations that became his life's work. Much of the thinking that led to these bold innovations occurred during a two-year recuperative period following a serious riding accident in 1909 that necessitated two major operations. The cornerstone of the innovations were two irrevocable settlements of trust: the first in 1929, a year following the death of his father, whom Lewis feared would have opposed the arrangement had he found out about it, and the second in 1950, when Lewis at age 65 finalized the arrangement that he had created in the first settlement. Previous to the 1929 settlement, Lewis had bought out the holding of his brother Oswald, thereby leaving himself in exclusive control of the company upon his father's death.

Although the settlements were quite complex, Lewis essentially made a gift of his property in the company (estimated conservatively at about £1 million in 1929) to a Trust (the John Lewis Partnership Trust Ltd.) that was set up for this purpose. The trust serves as a holding company for the John Lewis Partnership plc (that is, a public limited company) through which the business operates. For his property in the company, Lewis received deferred bonds that paid no interest. About one-fifth of the capital represented in these bonds went to Lewis to develop the Leckford Estate (his home). Lewis, who was a knowledgeable botanist, had Leckford developed into a prosperous farming enterprise, and, in 1946, gave it along with other property that he owned to the Partnership.

By placing his property into the Trust, Lewis wanted to see the workers in the company become the beneficiaries of its profits; however, he did not want to make them an outright gift of the company, because he was concerned that they might sell their share and pocket the money. He was conscious of a Boston company, Filene Brothers, in which the workers sold their controlling interest acquired through profit-sharing, and he was afraid that something similar could happen to John Lewis. Referring to the Filene Brothers incident, Lewis expressed a lack of confidence in the wisdom of his employees upon whose behalf he was acting: "I cannot see what else was to be expected. We should have a completely different world if . . . the rank and file of a retail drapery business had such wisdom and self-control as the Filene scheme required of them" (Lewis 1948, 72). Therefore, to guard against such an eventuality, Lewis transferred the ownership in the company from himself to the Trust (not the individual workers). The Trust was to become the custodian of the property on behalf of the workers, both current and future.

In the first settlement in 1929, Lewis controlled the voting stock in the Trust, and in the 1950 settlement, the voting stock was controlled by trustees (60 percent by the "chairman" of the Partnership and 40 percent by three other trustees elected by a central council representing the partners of the company). The procedures were specified in a detailed constitution that Lewis created. All workers on permanent contract (including part-time employees) became partners (currently 35,000 of the 41,100 employees). As partners, they became the beneficiaries of the stock held in the Trust and, therefore, the recipients of the company's dividends. In other words, through being the beneficiaries of the Trust, the partners assumed the right to the net income of the company that normally goes to shareholders. Moreover, through this approach, Lewis was able to neutralize the potential influence that the holders of voting shares normally have within a corporation. By locking the voting stock into the Trust and by surrendering his control of it (as he did in 1950), Lewis was in effect creating a company that had no shareholders, that was immune from the threat of external takeover, and that was intended to function for the benefit of its employees as long as it could meet the measure of the market.

Considering the overall dynamic of capitalism that sanctifies the rights of shareholders, this ownership arrangement represented a fundamental departure from the predominant norms. In effect, Lewis had converted a major department store in the U.K. from a conventional capitalist corporation to social property owned by no one. Lewis was not the first to create such an arrangement. In 1888 in Jena, Germany, Ernst Abbe bought up all of the outstanding shares in the firm Carl Zeiss (following the death of his partner and the founder after whom the company was named) and donated them to a trust that became the holding company (Oakeshott and Schmid 1990; Volkmann 1966). Carl Zeiss has evolved into a giant multinational under this arrangement. Similarly, as mentioned in chapter 1, James Eagan used this same arrangement in 1923 at the American Cast Iron Pipe Company in Birmingham, Alabama (Cleghorn 1995). However, Lewis not only donated the company's stock to a trust (as did some others before him), but also worked through a detailed organizational redesign (to be discussed) that gave the employees opportunities for participation in decision making. Moreover, in his books and other writings, he carefully developed a rationale for his Partnership model and engaged in other movement activities to promote his innovation.

By the standards of the First World War and the period immediately following it when this plan was put in place, Lewis's ideas for decision making were highly innovative. But within Western Europe, the predominant norms for employee involvement in decision making have changed, and that part of Lewis's work is less striking at present. Whereas Lewis was unrestrained in rearranging the ownership and ensuring that the employees were beneficiaries of the dividends that normally would be paid to shareholders, his paternalistic attitudes as reflected in his lack of confidence in his employees' abilities made him more cautious in his approach to decision making. Nevertheless, he referred to his employees as partners, and accorded them the right of one vote each as would be expected in a democratic workplace (Ellerman 1990). But, as will be discussed, he limited the areas in which that right could be exercised. Even though he opened up opportunities for employee participation, he did not want to challenge the sovereignty of management.

In 1955 after appointing his successor Bernard Miller, Lewis (age 70) stepped down as chairman of the company, leaving behind the legacy to which he had devoted his life. The creation of the Partnership was not simply a dispassionate task; it was for him a lifelong mission to which he dedicated his considerable energies with a fervor that bordered on religiosity. He was an indefatigable worker who employed three secretaries, typically working into the evening hours and on weekends (Lynn 1985). It is said that even in the bath, he would dictate to a secretary who stood outside with the door ajar. For Lewis, his life, including his social life, was the Partnership, both creating it and, subsequently, writing about it. Throughout, he was supported by his wife Sarah, who was the vice chairperson until her death in 1953. Reflecting upon Lewis some years later, Sir Bernard Miller (as he was to become) wrote: "Spedan will be thought of as a twentieth-century Robert Owen. I think that he will always be recognized as at least as important in the twentieth century as Robert Owen was in the 19th" (Miller 1985, 43).

Before casting Lewis into a type of industrial sainthood, it is necessary to undertake a more detailed assessment of his work and his complex relationship to the Partnership, where he is now known respectfully as "the Founder," and also as a "difficult person" by the dwindling group who knew him personally. This assessment will be considered under the following headings: remuneration, industrial democracy, and movement.

REMUNERATION

From the beginning of his involvement, Lewis sought to improve the pitiful earnings of the company's employees. Although his attitude was in part idealistic, it was also pragmatic: he felt that poor pay led to inefficiency. His attitude was also paternalistic in that, as a man of wealth, he felt some obligation to improve the condition of those in his employment, even though it is not clear that he identified with their plight. Throughout his writings, Lewis shows an enlightened concern about inequalities in wealth and their consequences. "Our world of millionaires and slums is more and more volcanic," he wrote. "The have-nots are becoming more and more conscious of what there is to have, and in all countries they are an overwhelming majority. . . . The remedy may be a fairer sharing of the proceeds" (Lewis 1954, 3–4). However, in addressing the issue "What is fair?" Lewis argues that "mere equality is not the answer. . . . Wide differences of earnings seem necessary if possessors of uncommon ability are to . . . develop and exert it as the common good requires. . . . But the present differences are far too great" (Lewis 1954, 4).

In other words, Lewis was not seeking to achieve an equal distribution of wealth, but to establish a livable minimum and to narrow the gap between the lowest and highest paid. "What really matters," he argued, "is that the lowest incomes shall not be too low. The first step is surely to abolish real poverty, the lack of means for a healthy life in decent surroundings. This will mean adopting the principle of a living wage" (Lewis 1954, 36). To put these principles into practice, the John Lewis Partnership has adopted the following policy: work is remunerated at the "market rate." To ensure that differences do not become excessive, the constitution specifies that the ratio of the highest to the lowest paid should not exceed 25 to 1 and that the highest-paid partner should not have a salary greater than the after-taxation equivalent of £5,000 in London "in 1900." Currently, the chairman of the company (the highest paid) has an annual salary of about £300,000. Although the pay ratio Lewis introduced was not revolutionary, by modern standards it represents a significant departure from norms in which the earnings of CEOs of large corporations have ballooned to 157 times that of the average employee (Thurow 1996).

In addition, Lewis established a system of "Family Allowances to partners who have dependents and for whose services the current 'market rate' does not in the judgment of the Partnership suffice for a decent standard of living for such a household" (Lewis 1954, 143). Although the formal system of family allowances is no longer in practice because of provisions through the welfare state, requests from employees in need are still considered in confidence by a special committee.

Salaries are augmented by each partner's share of the annual profits. Lewis was reluctant to use the term "profit sharing" because he recognized that it referred to "a system of business in which profit is shared between workers and owners of capital" (Lewis 1948, 43). The ownership arrangements at the John Lewis Partnership are analogous to a nonprofit corporation. Given that there are no external shareholders who have a prior claim on profits and, after taking account of the company's needs, their sole recipients are the partners. Lewis argued for the term Partnership Benefit, later changed to Partnership Bonus. Each year the board of directors decides what portion of the profits should be retained in order to develop the business. In that respect, the board is acting not only on behalf of the current employees but also of future generations. Since the John Lewis Partnership cannot finance itself through public share offerings, it relies on retained earnings both to satisfy its financial needs, as well as to provide an adequate capital base should it need to borrow from financial institutions. Although the portion of each year's profits retained in the company depends upon the circumstances prevailing at the time, the general pattern in recent years is that about four-sevenths has been retained. Consistent with Lewis's views, profits paid out as bonuses are distributed in proportion to salary: those who earn higher salaries receive a larger annual bonus than those who earn less. Although Lewis initiated this principle as a basis for sharing profits, he was certainly not prompted by self-interest, because he himself did not accept any remuneration from the company. It was simply a policy that he felt was appropriate for distributing the wealth ("fairer shares," as he stated in his 1954 book).

Lewis's bonus system dates back to 1920, when he introduced it at Peter Jones, the second department store that his father purchased. It came under Spedan's control in 1916 after a falling-out with his father that caused Spedan to exchange his stake in John Lewis for control of Peter Jones (Poole 1992). Peter Jones had been losing money ever since it was purchased by his father in 1905, and Spedan, already managing the store part-time, viewed it as an opportunity to test out his theories of management free of his father's interference. He came into conflict with the shareholders, who were demanding dividends in spite of the company's financial problems. At the 1918 general meeting, he stated: "Believe me, in the next twenty or thirty years if you want a really sound industrial concern, you will have to admit your employees to a far larger share of the total earnings than before. The days when a lot of shareholders could stay at home doing nothing and take a very large proportion of the earnings of a business are all over" (Lewis 1918a, 4). Just before making his statement to the shareholders, Lewis had issued a letter to the employees of Peter Jones. Titled "To My Fellow-Employees of Peter Jones, Ltd.," in it he announced his intentions about profit sharing: "Once we are making profit enough to pay all our dividends and to provide proper reserve funds against a rainy day, all further profit will belong to the staff" (Lewis 1918b, 3).

The bonus was originally paid in the form of a share promise (a deferred share) because Lewis was concerned about the cash drain on a company that was still financially fragile. The bonus was subsequently revised and changed to a preferred share with a fixed rate of interest of 5 percent. Because increases in interest rates were leading to decreased share values, and because the employees were in need of more immediate compensation, this arrangement was unsatisfactory. Therefore, since 1970, the bonus has been paid in cash. Moreover, it has been paid consistently with the exception of the war years (when payment was delayed) and from 1948 to 1953 (when the company experienced financial difficulties, in part due to the wartime bomb destruction of its main department store in London). During the past 20 years, the Partnership Bonus (as it is currently labeled) has constituted a substantial share of each employee's remuneration, averaging about 17 percent of base salary, or the equivalent of nearly nine weeks' pay. The bonus, which (under British law for profit-related pay) is for the larger part free of tax, has ranged from a high of 24 percent in 1979, 1987, and 1988, to a low of 8 percent in 1993, when profits slumped during the recession. In 1995, the bonus was 15 percent.

In addition to salaries and the Partnership Bonus, the John Lewis Partnership has a well-developed system of benefits that includes a pension plan started in 1941, which is entirely paid for by the company rather than the more usual practice of having the employees contribute; paid leave of up to six months for partners completing 25 years of service; discounts of from 12 to 25 percent (depending upon the years of service) at the department stores, and 12 percent at the supermarkets; as well as standard sick leave and health care benefits. Since 1931, the Partnership has provided an in-house medical service, comprising at present 18 full- or part-time doctors and 50 nurses, physiotherapists, and chiropodists. Perhaps the most impressive benefits are the heavily subsidized amenities and social activities that, in the words of Spedan Lewis, help to make the Partnership into a "community" that in some respects resembles "the Religious Orders of the Middle Ages" (Lewis 1948, 29). The subsidies include: tickets for plays, operas, ballets, films, and concerts; clubs and societies, such as the Partnership Sailing Club, which owns five cruising yachts and a fleet of dinghies; the Music and Dramatic Society and the Chess Club (one of Spedan Lewis's passions); and residential country clubs (including a castle), with fishing, hunting, and golfing facilities, available to members and their families. Through these subsidies, the Partnership is able to make available facilities for which lower-paid members lack the resources. Such facilities also provide the opportunity for people who work together to become involved in each other's social lives.

The remuneration policies of the John Lewis Partnership attempt to realize Spedan Lewis's objectives of ensuring that employees receive a "living wage" and of reducing, to a degree, inequalities typical of the business world. There was one study undertaken in 1987 suggesting that employees at John Lewis are paid at the high end of market relative to other major retailing firms in Britain (Bradley and Taylor, 1992), but the current practice is to pay at the market rate.

INDUSTRIAL DEMOCRACY

Although Spedan Lewis was capable of thoughtfulness and kindness, the people with whom he worked in management also viewed him as a controlling individual for whom fear, including the fear of dismissal from the firm, could be an instrument to achieve his goals. Therefore, it is ironic that Spedan Lewis would claim to be a pioneer of industrial democracy. Paul May, who was deputy chairman of the company from 1955 to 1970 and whose son Stephen became a member of senior management, likened Spedan Lewis to "a rather awesome headmaster, and in those days headmasters were people you were very frightened of" (May 1985, 59).

Lewis was a tall, charismatic man who had sharply defined facial features and who was known to fly into temper tantrums when he was frustrated. Martyn Lloyd-Davies, who served in many senior management positions before retiring in 1984 from the Partnership, felt that Spedan Lewis never left any doubt as to who was the boss: "While he talked at length about industrial democracy, let us have no illusions: democracy stopped at him. If you want a pen picture of an autocrat, that was him" (Lloyd-Davies 1985, 91).

In spite of his autocratic manner, from 1912, Lewis was introducing mechanisms for employee participation in decision making that were leading edge for that period. He was aware of the nineteenth-century experiments in worker cooperatives, and he felt that one of their failings was weak management. In that judgment, he appeared to be influenced by the critiques of the Fabian writers Beatrice Potter and Sydney Webb, whom he cites in his books, as well as by his aristocratic disposition that lacked respect for the judgment of "rank-and-file" workers (an expression that he used with regularity). "If the subordinate members had constantly or occasionally the power to change the occupant of the principal post," he argued, "that partnership might be back at the position in which so many attempts to establish producer cooperation have come to disaster, the position in which the managed have power to change their managers and fail to use that power sensibly" (Lewis 1954, 165–66). However, Lewis was also cognizant of managerial abuse of power: "If the managers are too powerful, the managed are oppressed . . . if their own power is too small and that of the managed is too great, the general community will be served too badly" (Lewis 1954, 101). The solution he sought was that "between managers and managed, power is sufficiently divided" (Lewis 1954, 102).

As such, the detailed constitution that Lewis wrote for the Partnership sets out a systematic series of checks and balances that permits management to govern without feeling vulnerable, yet recognizes the influence of rank-and-file employees. He referred to the system as a "constitutional monarchy," in which management is secure in its role—as distinct from an "ultra-democratic republic" that permits employees to select and dismiss management. As the term constitutional monarchy implies, the weight of authority is clearly with senior management.

The principal authority in the Partnership is the "chairman," who serves as both the chief executive and the head of the board of directors. To protect the chairman against the rank and file (a matter that concerned Lewis greatly), the holder of the office is granted "life-tenure (until age 70)," provided that he or she upholds the constitution of the Partnership (as subsequently discussed). As such, the John Lewis Partnership has had, since its inception in 1929, only four chairmen: Spedan Lewis, Sir Bernard Miller, Spedan's nephew Peter Lewis, and, since 1993, Stuart Hampson. In line with the monarch analogy, the chairman is normally appointed by the outgoing holder of the office. Since the company prefers to have long-serving holders of the office, the practice has been to skip a generation in each appointment.

In his role as chief executive, the chairman selects a senior management team (directors of trading, finance, personnel) with whom he works closely to develop policy. A tradition of strong graduate recruitment for senior management was established by Spedan Lewis in the late 1920s, well in advance of other retail companies. Research suggests that the Partnership's senior management is highly committed to the philosophy of the company and tends to function as a relatively coherent team (Flanders, Pomeranz, Woodward 1968). Unlike other corporations, the John Lewis Partnership's management does not have to satisfy external shareholders who might demand higher profits; nor does it have to be concerned about external takeovers, since all of the voting shares are held in trust. These circumstances have made it much easier for management to plan for the future, as emphasized by Stephen May, a member of the senior management team:

Too much of the time of too many companies is spent being concerned about the share price and looking over their shoulder worrying about a takeover; making decisions for three months ahead rather than making long-term strategic decisions. We have a huge advantage (a critic might say that we have a compensating disadvantage) in that there are no shareholders to punish us for our incompetence. I believe that is not a weakness because the internal disciplines upon us are strong from our own workforce.

The internal disciplines to which May refers are the mechanisms within the Partnership for managerial accountability. The primary mechanism is the central council, consisting of about 130 members, which can be likened to the parliament of the Partnership. The front bench of the council consists of senior management (appointed by the chairman) who are required to make annual reports and to be answerable to the other members elected annually through secret ballot by the partners. At present, nearly half of the elected members are "rank and file," and the remainder are either branch or department managers. The council is free to discuss any issue that it chooses, but it has traditionally focused on such welfare issues as pay, pensions, discounts, and, more recently, Sunday shopping. To allow it some independence from managerial control, the council is guaranteed an annual income of 1 percent of the total paysheet (£3.7 million in 1995) and has total discretion over the use of the funds. These funds support the work of the council, which normally meets six times a year, as well as the standing committees (Ways and Means, Pay and Allowances, Claims and Retirement) that help the council achieve its goals.

The council also has an important role in electing the representatives of other parts of the governance—namely, three trustees of the constitution (the others being the chairman and deputy chairman) and five directors of the central board (the other five being appointed by the chairman, who together with his deputy are ex-officio members). If three members of the central board elected by the council request it, the central council has the right to be consulted on any decision to close a branch, or even a department involving twelve or more partners. Any alterations to the constitution require the agreement of the central council.

The council's most publicized power is its right to depose the chairman. Should two-thirds of the council support a resolution that the chairman is unfit to hold office (no reasons are required), the trustees elected by the council acquire the majority voting power in the Trust and must vote in accordance with the council's wishes. Under such circumstances—which have yet to occur and might be seen as analogous to the U.S. Congress voting to impeach a president—the chairman's control over the majority of the voting shares in the Trust ceases and the trustees elected by the council assume the majority control. This authority of council reflects Spedan Lewis's desire to find a balance between providing management with the security to manage, yet not the absolute right to do whatever it likes. In effect, council retains a negative sanction that it can apply in a very extreme case rather than a positive role in the chairman's selection. Graham Smith, a department manager who is in his fourth year on central council, says: "Within the context of modern democracy, it doesn't seem like the right way of doing things. I can only say that the Partnership works pretty well." Likewise, Spedan Lewis recognized that the selection process for the chief executive could be more democratic, but he argued against it: "That degree of democracy is only practicable where the margin for error with impunity is enormously wider than in competitive business. Navigation would be impossible if the captains of ships had to comply with majority votes of the ship's company" (Lewis 1954, 132).

In addition to the central council, partners of the John Lewis Partnership elect representatives to branch councils (40 in total) for each of the department stores and other sizable work units. These councils deal with issues relating to the branch and may also comment upon issues that are under consideration by the central council.

The councils, both central and branch, have a strong representation from management and look to management for a lot of their direction. Even the representatives that council elects to the central board tend to be from senior and middle management, thereby ensuring that the board is effectively management's voice. Nevertheless, council's resolutions are not treated lightly. The chairman has never turned down a recommendation from central council, and if the managing director of a branch is not prepared to go along with a local council's recommendation, then the matter must be referred to the central director responsible for that matter.

Although the John Lewis Partnership has made a big effort to involve rank-and-file employees in the governance, and has three-day introductory workshops for newly elected representatives, a substantial minority remain apathetic. For example, about one-third of the partners do not even vote in elections. Geri Cox, who is in her second year on the central council and is a sales assistant at the Peter Jones store in London, criticizes those who refuse to participate: "A lot of people do feel that the council is ineffective. I think that is because they haven't participated. There is a give and take in everything. If you are there, you have to balance the good for everyone concerned, taking account of the good of the business."

Given the control that Lewis accorded to management, it is questionable whether the John Lewis Partnership can be described as an industrial democracy. In their status as partners, employees have a type of membership that accords them one vote each. This arrangement, which makes partnership analogous to citizenship in a political democracy, represents an important departure from corporate conventions that allocate voting rights in accordance with shares, or on the basis of property. However, there are obvious limits on the domains over which employee right to vote can be exercised, and particularly in selecting the chairman. Therefore, it would be more appropriate to use the term "partial participation" (Pateman 1970) to describe the decision-making model at the John Lewis Partnership. Employees have opportunities for participation, and in giving feedback and in communicating their concerns, but management develops the company policies and makes the final decisions. Therefore, given the predominant role of management in the council, it might be viewed as more of a communication forum than a governing body. Graham Smith emphasizes the importance of having the senior management in the council communicate with the other members: "At the last council meeting, the director of trading was on his feet answering questions for one hour and 20 minutes after submitting an extensive report on his activities for the past year. It is very informative and it also provides the members with a high degree of knowledge of the business."

A similar flow of information occurs outside the council in "constituency meetings" within departments where council representatives brief other employees. The minutes of the central and branch councils together with the financial reports are published and circulated widely throughout the Partnership (a practice that Spedan Lewis initiated when he took over the management of the Peter Jones department store in 1914).

Among the committees in the John Lewis Partnership, the most meaningful for the employees are the "committees for communication," first introduced in 1912 by Spedan Lewis. Unlike the formal governance, these committees are confined to nonmanagement personnel. Although the committees can discuss whatever they like, they are primarily a mechanism for employees to express their concerns about their working conditions (for example, the timing of lunch breaks, the need for air conditioning) and to ensure that these concerns reach management. There is at least one of these committees in every branch (with a minimum of one representative for every 36 partners), and normally they have from 12 to 15 members elected by secret ballot. The Partnership appoints four people whose job is to chair these committees. From their inception, Lewis ensured that the minutes of committees for communication were anonymous and therefore protected the participants from reprisals by management. He argued that "reasonable freedom of speech and general publicity, far from undermining discipline and sapping authority, have the contrary effect. Only those who are incompetent to exercise authority, or who wish to abuse it, need be afraid of reasonable freedom of speech and proper publicity" (Lewis 1948, 56–57).

The minutes of these committees are published in the *Chronicle* magazines of each branch of the Partnership, together with a reply or comment from executive officials associated with expressed concerns. Partners are also encouraged to write letters to either the *Chronicle* in their branch or *The Gazette,* the weekly magazine of the Partnership, first published in 1918. As with the minutes of the committees for communication, the tradition is to publish letters to *The Gazette* anonymously to ensure freedom of expression. It is rare that letters are not published. Spedan Lewis placed great value on an independent press within the Partnership, arguing that "If democracy is to be genuine, then journalism must have a very high degree of such freedom of speech" (Lewis 1948, 396). Journalism, he felt, would "bridge the gulf that in large-scale teamwork develops between managers and the managed" (Lewis 1954, 11). Symbolic of the importance attached to journalism is the fact that the general editor is viewed as a senior management official.

Both the committees for communication and the letters to *The Gazette* are intended to create two-way communication between management and other employees. The minutes are sent to the partnership's chairman and the partners' counsellor, a senior management official who serves as an independent ombudsman for the company. Created in 1944, this position was for many years ahead of any similar roles now commonplace in government. The partners' counsel is one of five senior management positions classified as the "critical side"—that is, people who review and comment upon the actions of the executive. Part of the function of the critical side is to facilitate communication within the Partnership, and to ensure that individual members feel free to express their concerns and that these concerns are attended to properly. There is, however, an obvious contradiction in having a company ombudsman and other "critical side" officials as senior management rather than as rank-and-file employee representatives. Again, this reflected Lewis's concern about granting too much influence to employees.

The formal communication mechanisms of the Partnership may be viewed as a bridge between the governance and the grievance process. Given that only a minority of the employees is unionized, the grievances of individual members are dealt with internally. If a grievance cannot be settled directly, then it is taken to a registrar who, as the local representative of central management, works in confidence to assist the employee with his or her concern. The registrar is not beholden to the managing director of a branch, but rather reports directly to the chief registrar, another of the senior management positions on the critical side. When a grievance cannot be settled in this manner, the employee has the right to petition the central council, which sets up a tribunal to hear the case and to make a recommendation that may include an award for damages, and that can only be overturned by a veto of the chairman. These petitions may involve dismissals as well as other types of grievances. In the case of dismissals, if the employee has passed a five-year review, the partners' counsel can exercise a veto and the matter is then referred to the chairman for a final decision. Spedan Lewis, who wrote these procedures into the constitution of the Partnership, argued that, with respect to petitions from members, the council is "a tribunal independent of the executive" (Lewis 1954, 93).

MOVEMENT

Although Lewis was interested in other businesses adopting the Partnership model, he focused his energies on his own firm rather than attempting to build a movement. As his innovations became known, he was courted by the Industrial Co-partnership Association, a group of progressive business leaders desiring to promote a more equitable role for workers in industry. At first Lewis resisted. In a 1928 letter to the Association, he excused himself by saying: "My own system is so sensational in its character that, if I were not very careful to avoid publicity, it would, I believe, receive so much attention that it would come to the notice of my father, who is over ninety, and he would be grievously distressed" (Lewis 1928, 1). Subsequently, he declined to make a financial contribution to the Association because "as I give up to my co-partners the whole of my own income, it is them you must look to for any corresponding contribution" (Lewis 1929, 1).

Lewis did join the Association in the 1930s, began to play an active role at meetings and conferences, and eventually became a vice president. However, he recognized that the arrangements of the John Lewis Partnership were quite radical relative to the mandate of the Association. In a letter to the Association's secretary in 1931, he emphasized this point:

It (the John Lewis Partnership) is *not* a scheme of "co"-partnership. It is based, on the contrary, upon the ideas that interest upon capital is in theory indefensible but in practice too convenient to be abandoned for the present and probably for a long time to come; and that capital should receive no more than a moderate, fixed rent together with a reasonable, fixed reward for having taken any particular risk; and that, subject to these charges only, every profit-making enterprise should be conducted wholly for the benefit of its workers of all grades (Lewis 1931, 1).

Lewis's point of view on this matter mirrored the principles of the cooperative movement, as originally stated by the Rochdale Pioneers (Macpherson 1979), but he did not acknowledge it as such.

Lewis declined to become involved in party politics, opting instead for "neutrality" (Lewis 1954, 198). In essence, he pursued his objectives largely as a loner, assuming somewhat naively, that if he created an ideal model, it would act as a lodestone to attract other businesspeople. He was, after all, a highly successful entrepreneur who was used to marching to his own tune and to having others follow.

Lewis did promote the Partnership in his two books, published in 1948 and 1954, as well as in his other writings, arguing that the model he had developed "should suffice for any enterprise of any possible size and complexity, no matter how large and various its operations or how widely its branches were scattered over the world" (Lewis 1948, 313). Although he did not present a comprehensive social analysis, he did attempt to situate the Partnership in the Cold-War atmosphere of the 1950s, referring to it on the cover of his 1954 book as "perhaps the only alternative to communism." He viewed the Partnership as representing a "fresh path" that would rejuvenate British industry (Lewis 1954, 12). But he also recognized that the market and overall culture of capitalism place constraints upon socially innovative business practices, including his own.

It is quite tragic that on retirement in 1955, Lewis was unable to stand back from his creation. Consequently, by 1960 (at age 75), he had become embittered and disillusioned. When senior management at the Partnership did not seek his advice on a regular basis, as he seemed to expect, he openly criticized the chairman Bernard Miller (his hand-picked successor). In spite of efforts by Miller to mollify him, he went so far as to request that the central council grant him up to 25 percent of the space in each issue of *The Gazette* to make his views known.

When his request was turned down by an 81 to 6 vote, his bitterness increased (Lewis 1960a, 677–78).

Lewis was also disappointed with the lack of take-up of the Partnership model. A 1957 letter to Miller indicates that he still held out hope: "There seems to me to be still a real chance that I may live to see our experiment burst into a sudden blaze. But in the meantime it has been something of a disappointment" (Lewis 1957, 1). By 1960, the disillusionment was apparent: "The experiment embodied in the John Lewis Partnership has come too late to have perhaps some value," he stated in one of his many letters to *The Gazette* (Lewis 1960b, 448). Max Baker, one of the senior management team who worked closely with Lewis, recalled: "It was a vision that inspired him and he sacrificed a lot for it, not least his own family. . . . He thought that he would blaze a trail that others would be inspired to follow. It didn't happen and he died (in 1963) a bitterly disappointed man" (Baker 1985, 114).

CONCLUSION

Since the mid-1950s, the John Lewis Partnership has been a consistently profitable company. Studies carried out by economists (Bradley and Estrin, 1986, 1988; and Bradley and Taylor, 1992) suggest that during the 1970s and 1980s, the performance of the Partnership compared very favorably to the leading retailers in the U.K. on a range of measures. Bradley and Taylor (1992, 138) summarize the data as follows:

The John Lewis Partnership was a major business success during the 1970s and 1980s, judged by financial and economic data. It ranks high or top in profitability and productivity, and shows no significant evidence of under-investment, over-borrowing or under-liquidity. . . . The overall business performance is directly comparable with the market leaders in both the food and non-food retailing sectors in which the Partnership operates. Thus the Partnership's experience casts doubt on the generally pessimistic conclusions of traditional performance models which imply that commercial performance is likely to suffer because of the absence of capital market discipline and the impact of employees on decision-making. The Partnership's achievement is all the more notable when we consider that it emerged from the Second World War in poor shape and performed badly relative to the retail sector as a whole in the early 1950s. The subsequent long-term recovery was exceptionally strong.

The John Lewis Partnership does not guarantee protection for its employees against the nonperformance of duties. However, it is a firm that is immune from external takeover (a major source of job insecurity in the modern world), and the company has a tradition of protecting its employees against redundancies (as in the closing of a store or a department within a store) by investing in retraining and providing support until the persons affected find jobs. Consequently, the Partnership has a low employee turnover relative to the norms in the industry. In addition, in its department stores where 80 percent of employees are full-time, its ratio of part-time to full-time is low relative to industry norms. The combination of these factors means that the Partnership has a relatively stable, knowledgeable work force that is generally satisfied with their conditions of work (Flanders, Pomeranz, Woodward 1968).

As noted, the Partnership's decision-making structure is a form of partial participation. In the main, the central council provides a venue for senior management to have their proposals vetted and to receive feedback on their activities. It is one of the mechanisms for accountability and communication between management and the rank and file. Other mechanisms are the branch councils, committees for communication, and the magazines (*The Gazette* and *Chronicle* in each branch).

The dominant role of senior management within the Partnership stems from the tradition that Spedan Lewis established (that is, a "constitutional monarchy" rather than a "democratic republic"). When he created the Partnership, Lewis did not ask his employees whether he was doing something that they desired. Like a patron responsible for his underlings, he did what he thought was best, and by any objective standard, he acted with extraordinary generosity, benevolence, and foresight. Moreover, to ensure that the tradition of the benevolent patron continued, he handpicked his successor and gave subsequent holders of the office the right to do the same. For years, there has been a compact between management and the rank and file instead of the adversarial relationship that existed at the company in 1920 when the employees went on strike and were fired from the firm by Spedan Lewis's father. This compact has led to a denial of the employment relationship and the differing interests of management and the rank and file, as evidenced by the substitution of the term employee by partner. The justification for this substitution is the argument that the employees are co-owners of the company and are therefore self-employed.

In part, this argument is tenable. If one views ownership as a bundle of rights, as proposed by American economist David Ellerman (1990), then the partners at John Lewis possess the right to share the net income, as do business owners in general, as well as the right to one vote in electing representatives to the company's governance. However, the latter right is partial because the partners do not participate directly in either electing representatives to the central board or in the selection of the chairman. They can, through their representatives on council, dismiss the chairman, a point to be borne in mind by a chairman appointing a successor. Moreover, the partners do not, as is typical for owners, benefit from the net value of the company because the arrangement Spedan Lewis created ensures that the Partnership is held in trust for future generations. That arrangement came about because the Partnership was started through a gift by Lewis to the Trust, and without any financial investment from the partners, as is usual in the start-up of a business. Therefore, the partners have partial ownership rights.

In addition to having partial ownership rights, the partners are also involved in an employment relationship. It seems odd to argue that employees can be involved in both an ownership and employment relationship within the same

Beyond the Bottom Line

firm, but that is the case for employee-owned companies and worker cooperatives in general, and is recognized in law in countries such as Canada (Quarter
and Hannah 1989; Quarter 1995). In at least two firms (the Beef Terminal in
1979 and Harpell's Press in 1982) where management attempted to decertify a
bargaining unit by arguing that the workers were owners, the labor relations
board rejected that argument and emphasized that the workers (albeit owners in
part) were also in an employment relationship.

At the John Lewis Partnership, management hires the other employees and
may, under certain conditions, dismiss them. Management decides what the
employees earn and allocates a portion of pay for performance of duties. These
are manifestations of the employment relationship that exist alongside the partial
ownership relationship. The question that must be asked is whether the compact
between management and other employees, arising in part from the ownership
trust arrangement, prevents the rank and file from asserting their interests as
forcibly as they might otherwise do. At the John Lewis Partnership, the union
representing only a small portion of the employees has a nominal role. The conditions of employment flow from the decisions taken by management, as guided
by feedback from employee representatives in the central council and other
employee input bodies.

The John Lewis Partnership leads to many questions that merit further consideration. Perhaps the most perplexing is the lack of interest by other family
firms in this model.[2] In part, that may be because the John Lewis Partnership was
set up through an endowment (Cornforth et al. 1988) from Spedan Lewis, and
generally the owners of family firms expect to be compensated fully by a purchaser, including their employees. However, the trust arrangement that Lewis
made does not require an outright gift and does have the potential for adoption
by family firms that want to sell to their employees (see chapter 4, Endenburg
Electric), and thereby protect the firm against external takeover.

In addition to family firms converting to employee ownership, Lewis's trust
arrangement could also be adopted in a company that is starting up. However,
where a company is not yet established (in contrast to John Lewis in 1929), placing the shares into a trust may hinder the ability to borrow money when it is
badly needed. The mechanisms for communication and decision making that
Lewis created are also generalizable and could be implemented without transferring ownership to the employees.

Lewis's disappointment at the lack of response to his pioneering efforts
reflects a naiveté and perhaps even blindness to how radical his innovations
were. In the words of Geri Cox, the sales assistant at the Peter Jones department
store where Lewis began his experiments in 1914:

Everybody knows about Spedan Lewis; he gets mentioned in conversations. But if I had
money like that, I wouldn't have given it away. He must have been mad! If you had what
he had, would you have given it all away in an experiment?

THE JOHN LEWIS PARTNERSHIP

1864   John Lewis opens drapery shop in London.

1885   John Lewis's son, John Spedan Lewis, is born.

1906   On his 21st birthday, and two years after starting employment there, Spedan Lewis becomes a partner (one quarter share) in the family firm.

1909   Spedan Lewis suffers a serious riding accident that incapacitates him for two years. During the recuperation period, it is believed that he conceived of much of the plan for the John Lewis Partnership.

1914   Spedan Lewis is given control of the Peter Jones store owned by his father and begins introducing much of the plan for the Partnership.

1926   Spedan Lewis purchases the holding of his brother Oswald.

1928   Spedan Lewis publishes the 268-page Partnership's constitution, the same year that his father dies.

1929   Lewis places the company's shares into a trust. The John Lewis Partnership is created with all full-time employees as partners who are entitled to participation rights in decision making and a share of the annual profits. Lewis receives no further fee or dividend for his work in the company. The initial trust is viewed as experimental.

1946   Lewis transfers his personal estate to the Partnership.

1948   Lewis writes *Partnership for All,* his first book on the Partnership.

1950   Lewis finalizes the trust arrangement and surrenders control of the corporation to the John Lewis Partnership Trust Limited.

1954   Lewis publishes *Fairer Shares,* his second book about the Partnership.

1955   Lewis retires at age 70 and nominates Bernard Miller to succeed him as chairman.

1963   John Spedan Lewis dies at age 77, bitterly disappointed at the lack of take-up of his innovation.

1995   As the largest department store chain in the U.K., the John Lewis Partnership employs 41,100 and has annual sales of £2.82 billion.

NOTES

Unless otherwise cited, the quotes in this chapter from the following members of the John Lewis Partnership are from interviews conducted in March 1995: Stephen May, General Inspector; Geri Cox, Sales Assistant at Peter Jones, Ltd.; and Graham Smith, Department Manager at Peter Jones, Ltd. Lorna Poole, the Chief Archivist, provided invaluable assistance in researching background materials; and Robert Forsythe, the Press Officer, and Ruth Bonner of the Press Office helped to coordinate my activities.

1. In May 2000, £1 purchased about U.S.$1.58.

2. In the U.K., the John Lewis Partnership model has directly influenced at least two conversions of family firms—the Baxi Partnership in Preston, a heating manufacturing firm in 1983 (see chapter 6), and in 1996 the John Oldrid Partnership in Boston, a department store. Information about the John Oldrid Partnership Trust Ltd. was from interviews with Adrian Isaac and Steve Fowler, and at the Baxi Partnership from an interview with Phil Baxendale.

3

The Scott Bader
Commonwealth

Scott Bader, an independent producer of synthetic resins and polymers, is head-quartered in the village of Wollaston in the Northampton area of England. The company was started in 1920 by an unusual Swiss emigrant to England, who is described in the *New Dictionary of National Biography* as a "reincarnated Robert Owen" (Corina 1996). Like Owen, Ernest Bader was both a skilled businessman and an imaginative social pioneer who attempted to transform the way in which business was structured. Essentially, Bader, without any financial compensation, surrendered the ownership of the business that he and his family had developed to an arrangement called the Scott Bader Commonwealth structured around the novel idea of common ownership. Moreover, he attempted in his later years to build a movement of like-minded firms (the Industrial Common Ownership Movement). In 1976, at age 85, he sat in the gallery of the British House of Commons during the second reading of the Industrial Common Ownership Bill, and heard himself referred to as "a saint of a man" (Hoe 1978, 209). Even though his formal education ended at age 12, he received an honorary doctorate from the University of Birmingham. His son Godric, who played a leading role in estab-lishing the Commonwealth and subsequently served as the managing director and chairman before assuming his honorary title of life president, said of his father: "He had a sense of destiny, of the importance of the idea that had come to him."

Ernest Bader was born in 1890 in Regensdorf, an hour's drive from Zurich.[1] He was the last of 13 children in an unstable family; his father was a farmer and a small businessman up and down on his luck. At age 21, Ernest set off for London, bearing the romantic memory of a beautiful English girl who had attended his mother's household school seven years earlier. Desiring to prove to his family that he could make a success of his life, and possessed of a high energy level that he could effectively channel into the task at hand, Ernest (who had worked as a clerk for a chemical company during his adolescence) set up Scott Bader as a chemical products import business in 1920. For financing, he used the £300 dowry of his wife Dora, whom he met for the first time shortly after his arrival in England. Scott Bader (Scott was the family name of his wife) started out as the agent for Swiss Celluloid, and then became the agent for the first oil-soluble synthetic resins (Albertols) that were to become the cornerstone of the paint industry. Business prospered, and eventually Ernest purchased a factory in East London to manufacture pigment pastes. When this factory was destroyed by German bombers in 1941, he moved it to Wollaston, where the business continued to grow.

The Wollaston site occupied a 44-acre estate, the centerpiece of which was a huge eighteenth-century manor house. In 20 years, Ernest had moved from being a self-employed importer of chemical products to the chief executive of a rapidly growing manufacturing enterprise, and the lord of an impressive country manor.

Nothing would foretell the turn that Bader would take in the post-war period, a turn that would lead him to channel his energies into becoming a social pioneer and "prophet"—to use the label ascribed to him by E. F. Schumacher, the author of *Small Is Beautiful* (Schumacher 1978, xiii). Up to that point, Bader's relationship with his employees was not the kind one would anticipate of an advocate of industrial democracy. He was a harsh, demanding boss who readily resorted to intimidation and emotional outbursts to inspire fear in his insecure work force. He exuded a sense of power of which others were very conscious. In the words of his biographer Susanna Hoe: "Ernest was always a man to be master in his own house. He developed a policy of divide and rule over the years which was to keep the upper echelons of his staff forever on their toes" (Hoe 1978, 55). One reason that his staff feared him is because he was known as an "impulsive sacker" (fire people first and ask questions later). The company's lore includes his attempts at firing people who, unknown to him, were not even employed by Scott Bader.

During the period in which he focused upon building up his business (1920–1945), Ernest Bader was a hard-driving entrepreneur. However, in many respects, he was a nonconformist; he was also capable of kindness and generosity and sometimes displayed striking examples of humanitarianism. Both he and his wife were fervent Christians who not only participated in mainstream Christian congregations but also experimented with Mazdaznan (an offshoot of Zoroastrianism) and, subsequently, the Quaker religion. Toward the end of the First World War, Bader joined a community of conscientious objectors in Stanford-Le-Hope, near London. His conversion to pacifism was in part a reaction to his military service in Switzerland. He maintained his commitment to pacifism for the rest of his life, formally joining the Quaker's Society of Friends at the end of the Second World War, and later becoming an activist in the nuclear disarmament movement. The Baders also got caught up with the philosophy of naturism, whereby they attempted to live in harmony with the natural world. They were principled vegetarians who objected to the killing of animals and who planted their own orchards. They were known to frolic outdoors in the nude, not as an act of sexuality, but to achieve oneness with nature. As a Christian duty, they felt that they should do without children, opting instead to create a home for orphaned and abandoned babies of the First World War. They adopted three children, one of whom was black, before having two children of their own, including Godric Bader. In the latter part of his life, Bader dedicated himself to building alliances with leaders of the developing world, and involving himself and Scott Bader in international development, to which the company has given with exceptional generosity.

The dualism in Ernest Bader's personality was apparent to people with whom he worked closely. In a tribute to him when he died in 1982 (at age 91), John Anagnostelis, a former Scott Bader Commonwealth secretary, stated:

> Most people who got near to him saw Ernest as a puzzle and an enigma, a mixture of good and evil, of rage and pacifism, of generosity and meanness. [He was] the visionary founder, dreaming up the whole edifice, but lacking the skill and mostly the patience of bricklaying, detailed planning and solving routine, humdrum problems of everyday life. One of his most creative gifts was the ability to select people who could build on and contribute to the realization of this vision. At the same time he interfered with their functions, persecuted them, and when he could, he got rid of them. His impact on the British and international industrial scene was important enough to overshadow the rages and ills he inflicted on people close to him (Anagnostelis 1982, 6–7).

Mick Jones, who is the current Commonwealth secretary, shared a similar view: "We all have mixed memories of him, both good and bad, and we will all miss him one way or another (Jones 1982, 1).

THE SCOTT BADER COMMONWEALTH

In 1945, Ernest Bader, then age 55, was full of vitality and about to embark upon his project of converting Scott Bader from the conventionally structured limited company that he had directed to common ownership in which it would become social property not directly owned by anyone and with a governing structure allowing for employee participation at all levels of decision making. In effect, after devoting himself from 1920 to 1945 to building a successful but conventionally organized chemical-production business, Bader set out on a second career as a social innovator—a career that for his remaining years he would also pursue with great devotion. As he embarked on this new project, the nonconformist side of Bader, which he had expressed in such social issues as pacifism and in his religious views, came to the fore.

Bader proceeded cautiously at first, knowing that he desired to draw his business practices in line with his religious and social convictions, but lacking a clear vision as to how that might be done. In a letter to his employees dated November 4, 1943, Bader broached the idea of the "Common Wealth" (a term that was said to have originated with Peter Plokhoy in 1659) and "the formation of a Community," of which his employees would be members. In the early formulation of these ideas, Bader talked of a Christian community (named the Scott Bader Fellowship) that would undertake "beneficial work" in the surrounding village (Bader 1943). In his various statements on the Fellowship (the forerunner to the Commonwealth), Bader made frequent reference to "social responsibility," an in-phrase among forward-looking businesspeople in the 1990s. To finance the Fellowship, the Bader family agreed to turn over the dividends that they would normally receive as the shareholders of the company to a Fellowship Fund. The employees, who were already recipients of an annual bonus based on a share of the company's profits, were also invited to contribute. Although the ownership of the company remained under the control of the Baders, a Fellowship committee was elected by the employees to deal with such issues as pay, work conditions, and administration of the Fund. In the tradition of Christian Socialism and with a strong concern for social justice, Bader wrote: "The differences between rich and poor, top-dog and under-dog, must disappear once and for all, and give way to a common endeavor for the general good of mankind. The worker must understand the value of money and economy, and not allow his energies to be dissipated in drink, tobacco and gambling. The rich, too, need a puritan revival. That is what our Fellowship stands for" (Bader 1947, 6).

Lacking a formal education, and handicapped in expressing himself because English was not his mother tongue, Bader issued statements through the company newsletter (at that time called the *Catalyst*) to dialogue with others and to reformulate his position, which was attracting increasing interest. In one of these statements, which he referred to as a "sermon" because it was liberally sprinkled with religious terminology and had a messianic tone to it, he states: "I would plead that Britain must produce a social economy of its own, quite different from both Russian communism and American capitalism. *Someone* [emphasis mine] has called this 'The Third Way'" (Bader 1948, 4).

However, interest in the Fellowship waned because the company employees felt uncomfortable with the Saturday prayer meetings and with demands for a commitment to pacifism (an unpopular idea at the end of the war). Also, in spite of the structures put in place for greater participation in decision making, Ernest Bader's autocratic style of management remained unchanged. In response to some dismissals in 1948, the employees went on strike, a major embarrassment for an advocate of democratic decision making. Although denouncing the strike as "a communist attempt to get hold of factory control" (Hoe 1978, 102), in the end he relented, recognized the union, and rehired the people that he had previously fired.

In spite of this setback, Ernest Bader proceeded with his idea of a Commonwealth and renounced the Bader family's ownership of the company.

Like Spedan Lewis (founder of the John Lewis Partnership) and Harold Farmer (of the now defunct Farmer & Sons), whom he befriended at the time, Bader set up a dual company structure: a holding company for the stock and an operating company through which business was transacted. This arrangement proved practical insofar as the transfer of the family's stock to the Commonwealth and structuring it as a charitable trust meant that the family did not have to pay death duties (a costly tax in the U.K. that would have necessitated additional financing if it had to be paid). The transfer of ownership from the family to the trust was done in two stages: in 1951, the company's share capital was increased from a value of £10,000 to £50,000 by capitalizing the reserve. Under this arrangement, the Bader family, primarily Ernest and Dora, held 10,000 50-pence shares, and the Scott Bader Commonwealth held 90,000. More importantly, however, the Bader family retained its control of the company, because its shares represented the controlling votes for the election of directors and for modifying the constitution. In 1963, the remainder of the stock was donated to the Scott Bader Commonwealth, and a seven-person board of trustees, consisting of four internal representatives and three from society at large, assumed responsibility for it.

The common ownership arrangement that Bader created is often referred to as worker ownership. Because the employees have some rights associated with ownership, there is a justification for that interpretation. However, it should be emphasized that the Baders did not give the company stock to individual employees and the employees were not the shareholders. E. F. Schumacher stresses that point: "It would be better to think of such a transfer as *effecting* the extinction of private ownership rather than the establishment of collective ownership. . . . In truth, ownership has been replaced by specific rights and responsibilities in the administration of assets. While no one has acquired any property, Mr. Bader and his family have nonetheless deprived themselves of their property" (1973, 278–79). Therefore, technically speaking, the shares held in the Commonwealth, a company limited by guarantee, are owned by no one. The employees invest nothing when they join, and they take nothing with them when they depart. Unlike a typical employee-owned firm, the members of the Scott Bader Commonwealth have no entitlement to a share of the net value. However, as members of the Commonwealth (a right that flows from their labor role), they have one vote each with respect to the affairs of the business and, as will be discussed, opportunities are available at all levels of the organization, including the board of directors. As members, they are also entitled to a share of the firm's annual net income or profits. In other words, the common ownership arrangement Bader created granted the employees voting and net income rights (two rights normally associated with ownership), but not an entitlement to the net value or the equity in the firm. In the event of a sale of the company, the beneficiaries would be charitable causes, not the employees. Therefore, by creating the Commonwealth, Bader was converting the company from the ownership of his family to a form of social property. The company would continue to transact business as long as it met the measure of the market. To safeguard the company's stability, a matter that concerned Bader, the constitution specified that the board of trustees was required to intervene should the company run at a loss; in addition, any changes to the constitution required the trustees' approval.

Ernest Bader viewed common ownership as a third way between capitalism and communism, both of which he referred to as "war-based" societies. Instead of ownership in the conventional sense, he talked of "trusteeship," a concept popularized by India's revolutionary leader Mohatma Gandhi (Hoe 1978). Bader also drew some sustenance from the tradition among Quaker business families such as Cadbury and Rowntree, who had made their employee and community interests a priority. The Eight Foundations of a True Social Order (published by the Quakers in 1918), although silent on the concept of common ownership per se, does recognize that ownership arrangements are important to human well-being. For example, the Quaker Foundations state that: "The ownership of material things, such as land and capital, should be so regulated as best to minister to the needs and development of man" (cited in Hoe 1978, 218).

The preamble to the Commonwealth's constitution in 1951 makes reference to the "well-known testimony of the Quakers" (Scott Bader 1987, 2). It also makes it evident that Bader's intentions were not simply to tinker with conventional business practice, but to seek a fundamental transformation in industry. Although the grammar is flawed, the intent is clear:

By establishing common ownership in industry we mean such a fundamental reconstruction so that undertakings are communally owned and co-operatively run, and show that teamwork which is neither collectivism nor individualism, depending on leadership founded on approval rather than dictation within a framework of freedom of conscience and obedience to God. This involves a self-divestment of privilege and power on the part of the present employers and shareholders, and on the part of the employees the acceptance of their full share of responsibility for the policy, efficiency and general welfare of the undertaking (Scott Bader 1987, 2).

In creating the Commonwealth, Bader was therefore attempting to strike a bargain: his part was the "self-divestment of privilege and power" associated with ownership; and the employees' part was the "acceptance of their full share of responsibility." In addition to the endowment of the Commonwealth, the concrete manifestations of Bader's contribution were a corporate governance that gave employees the opportunity to influence the decisions of the company, security of employment unless their own democratically elected council agreed to their dismissal (referred to as a certificate of mutual security), and up to six months' sick leave at full pay. The company also attempted to reduce its income disparities by establishing a 4-to-1 pay ratio of highest to lowest. The employees' part of the bargain was set down in a Code of Practice that outlined their responsibilities to the company and community, including such matters as: participating in the affairs of the Commonwealth; attempting to protect each other's jobs through (if necessary) accepting reductions in earnings; eschewing second jobs; not profiting off others; not producing weapons of war; and protecting the natural environment by avoiding both the negligent discharge of pollutants and the waste of natural resources (Scott Bader 1987).

In transferring his holdings to the Commonwealth, Bader made little provision for either himself or his family. As Brian Elgood, one of Scott Bader's international business managers and an employee of the company since 1964, notes: "He treated the community with a great deal more generosity than he treated his family." He not only gave his company to the Commonwealth but also his home, Wollaston Hall, where he and his wife continued to live in one section. Ernest Bader's vows of poverty were so pure that when he died in 1982 at age 91 (his wife Dora died three years earlier), his family had to sell his personal belongings in order to pay his bills and wind up the estate. As for providing for his family, Godric Bader remarked that "He never thought about it." For Ernest, his life from 1945 onward was the Commonwealth. When he donated the founders' shares in 1963, there was (according to research undertaken by Blum [1968]) ambivalence among the employees, only about one-third favoring the transfer. However, Ernest Bader, now recognized both nationally and internationally for creating the Commonwealth, was driven by the pursuit of his vision and by social reinforcement from movement activists throughout the world. "He wanted to matter," says Godric Bader, seeking to understand the perplexing question as to why his father acted as he did. Moreover, to ensure that the dream did not end with him, Ernest urged Godric to "carry on," and in anticipation that the dream would be realized, he impulsively promised his son in one conversation "you're going to get knighted." For Godric, pursuit of the dream, which he shared with his father, was sufficient motivation.

INDUSTRIAL DEMOCRACY

While Ernest Bader did not blink an eye when it came to giving away his property, he did balk at transferring managerial control. When the Commonwealth was set up in 1951, the founders retained the right to appoint the board of directors, albeit subject to the approval of the community council. After the Commonwealth began, Ernest remained managing director and chairman of the board. In 1957, in an obvious move to retain the family's control, he appointed Godric to replace him as managing director and his nephew Brian Parkyn as deputy managing director. Ernest continued as chairman, a post that he held until 1965, when he was given the honorary title of founder president. When the founders' shares were transferred to the Commonwealth in 1963, Ernest had it written into the constitution that he would be entitled to hold the office of company chairman for life and that "Godric Ernest Scott Bader" was entitled to succeed him and could also remain chairman for life (Scott Bader 1987). The chairman also retained the right to appoint and remove the directors of the company.

During Godric's tenure as managing director, which lasted until 1971, Ernest continued to participate actively in company affairs, insensitively berating his son at public meetings and actively interfering with his plans for managing the company. Godric, who is a gentle person with strong democratic instincts, had great difficulty coping with his dominating father.

The conflict between father and son reached a head when the constitution was amended in 1971, the changes including the elimination of the family's privileged status in the company's top positions. This was also the occasion of Ernest's 80th birthday, an event that was honored by the community with the presentation of a polyester-resin bust. As an expression of his bitterness about the new constitution, Ernest later destroyed the gift and brought the ashes to a public meeting of the Commonwealth, where he presented them to his son, saying, "This is what I think of your rotten new constitution." Nor did Ernest stop there. He launched a diatribe in the company's newsletter and explored with lawyers whether he could sell the company and give the proceeds to charity. Although his behavior was quite erratic, for the most part it was tolerated because, in the words of Scott Bader's technology manager, Alan Green, "He was the head of the family; the family tends not to go against the father." There were limits to the Commonwealth's tolerance, however, and at a high point of Ernest's vitriolic behavior, he was censured by the community at a public meeting.

It is ironic that Ernest Bader created the basis for a democratic governance, because his own instincts were quite the opposite. The governance has many checks and balances, almost as if Ernest Bader recognized how difficult it would be to hold management accountable. There are two basic corporate entities—the Scott Bader Commonwealth (the charitable trust that holds the shares) and Scott Bader Company Ltd. (the operating company through which business is conducted). In theory, the holding company or Commonwealth is the supreme governing body, in that the shares of the company are held within it and it accords membership to employees (voting rights being derived from membership). The Commonwealth has a veto over executive and board appointments, in that nominees for these positions have to be granted Commonwealth membership before their appointments are approved. The board of the Commonwealth, consisting of six people elected by the members of the organization, plus the chairman of the company and a representative of the surrounding community, is therefore referred to in the constitution as the "board of management." However, other than the specific duties of according membership and of administering charitable donations, the constitution defines the Commonwealth board's powers in very vague terms: [to] "exercize a philosophical oversight of the community" (Scott Bader 1987, 16). Ian Alexander, a former chairman, acknowledges the problem: "In all honesty, I feel that the role of the Commonwealth board has not been strong or dominant. It is the board of the holding company; that sounds strong and powerful. Its main power is through the power of membership." As such, Alexander favors combining the Commonwealth board with the board of trustees, a body that also tends to be inactive.

In referring to the operating company board as the "main board," Alexander is expressing a widely held viewpoint within the company. This viewpoint is based on the premise that the so-called bread-and-butter issues take precedence over values or the so-called missionary objectives of the Commonwealth. Mick Jones, the Commonwealth's secretary and only paid staff person, acknowledges the secondary role of the Commonwealth, but he feels that it need not be so: "In legal terms, the board of the Scott Bader Commonwealth is the board of the holding company, but in practice it doesn't behave as the board of the holding company. And for very good reasons, because I think it would be wrong for the Commonwealth board to interfere in the running of the business. But there are occasions when maybe they should, or at least have input."

Symbolic of the superior status of the company board, its members are paid £4,500 a year, whereas the members of the Commonwealth board, as trustees of an organization with charitable status, cannot be paid. The elected members of the company board are trained for their role, whereas there is little training for the Commonwealth board. The managing director (the chief executive officer) and the chairman of the company both sit on the company board, whereas only the chairman is on the Commonwealth board.

Both of these boards are mechanisms whereby the employees of Scott Bader can participate in decision making and interface with management in developing company policies. But in spite of these mechanisms, senior management at Scott Bader has exercised a strong hand in directing the company. Even though four of the eight members of the company board are elected by the employees (the others being two outsiders chosen by the board, the managing director, and the company chair), management has tended to control the direction of Scott Bader. Brian Elgood argues that by making the company board nonexecutive (the managing director being the only executive member), the influence of senior management on company policy has been increased because "the senior management team has to do all of the proposing to the board." Consequently, the primary function of employee representatives on the company board is to provide feedback to company executives on their proposals. Employees also have an opportunity to react to management proposals through the community council, a 14-person body with representatives elected on a geographic basis. With the exception of grievances, for which it is the final decision maker, the community council is advisory to the company board, and within that mandate generally provides feedback on a broad range of employment issues such as salary, benefits, and conditions of work.

In the past, there have been attempts to organize unions to address workplace issues and, in 1948, the Chemical Workers Union did succeed in forming a local branch during the strike against the company. However, out of respect for the Commonwealth, the secretary of the Chemical Workers, Bob Edwards (who joined Scott Bader's board of trustees in 1963) agreed that rather than have the union intervene, Scott Bader would be allowed to settle internally both its pay rates and its disputes with its employees. The assumption behind this strategy was that the employees at Scott Bader were not employees in the conventional sense. When the Chemical Workers were taken over by the Transport and General Workers Union, some employees of the company retained their affiliation, but the union has continued to dissociate itself from collective bargaining. Therefore, the functions normally handled by a union have been dealt with internally, primarily through the community council. Roger Scott, an employee-member of both the council and the company board, argues that the role of the council differs from a union because it does not enter into formal negotiations with management and, in particular, does not adopt an adversarial stance typical of collective bargaining: "We act as oil to smooth the wheels; we try and remove friction between management and the work force," he states, "by passing information in both directions." Austin Shelton, the current chair of the community council, acknowledges the limitations of the council: "Let's be fair, they [management] hold the purse strings. You have to be a very strong person on the community council to really stand up. I take a good many points to the managing director that I feel uncomfortable about and, generally speaking, they are dealt with."

Research on Scott Bader, undertaken in 1960 and 1989, indicates that in spite of the opportunities for worker participation in decision making, "a substantial majority . . . remain[ed] low or non-participants" (Hadley and Goldsmith 1995, 183). That research also indicates that active participants are drawn primarily from the management and technicians in the company, and that the production and clerical workers tend to be relatively uninvolved. In the Hadley and Goldsmith research, the main reasons that employees give for not participating is "the abuse or potential abuse of power by management" (1995, 182). They argue that since 1971, when Godric Bader stepped aside as managing director and subsequent managing directors were recruited externally, a "managerialist" culture has developed that has drawn the company "closer to the predominant models of organization prevailing in conventional industry" (Hadley and Goldsmith 1995, 185).

The current managing director, Ian Henderson, agrees with the Hadley/Goldsmith thesis and notes that in 1989, when he left British Petroleum (where he was a divisional manager) to assume his position at Scott Bader, "I came in from the outside as a managerialist," believing "that there were benefits from the Scott Bader system that could be afforded—if you were successful." In other words, support for the values and decision-making structures depends on the company's success—or, stated differently, there is a dichotomy between the business operations and the values system, a dichotomy implicit in the differing mandates of the company and Commonwealth boards. Henderson asks, with an engaging frankness: "Are we happy that elected people (that is, employees elected to the board) can be in a majority and determine things on a non-executive board of the company? You've got to empower and trust the managers." The solution he foresees is "a much simpler structure: one supervisory governing system (in which the existing representational mechanism is sandwiched into one) and one executive governing system. I'd like to see qualified employee representatives being elected, and I'd like to see them alongside mature industrial people. Participation and empowerment," he feels, "must devolve to the shop floor."

Under Henderson's leadership, Scott Bader has further developed its foreign subsidiary holdings, which now include companies in France, Sweden, the U.S., Dubai, and South Africa. The subsidiaries (also in the U.K.) are part of a redefined operating company called the Scott Bader Group. Of the Group's 650 employees, only 300 now work in Wollaston, and 50 more in the other U.K. locations. Scott Bader has been able to accomplish this expansion with minimal borrowing (with a 1995 debt-to-equity ratio of only 10 percent) because it has been consistently profitable over the years and each year the company has retained a high percent (typically 90 percent) of its earnings (Scott Bader 1996).[2]

This high rate of retention is possible because of Scott Bader's common ownership structure; the company does not have to pay dividends to external shareholders (normally about 40 percent of profits), nor is it concerned about an external takeover to which a conventionally owned company with high reserves might be prone. Common ownership has forced Scott Bader to be self-reliant by limiting its ability to finance growth externally. Equity investments are not possible in a common ownership arrangement, and the collateral available for bank loans is less than for a conventionally owned company with a similar balance sheet. Therefore, Scott Bader has by necessity been conservative about financing, relying largely on its cash reserves; it utilized the reserves which it accumulated during the 1980s to expand in the early 1990s when bargains were available because of the recession. As a result of this expansion, in the past 10 years annual turnover has nearly doubled to £99 million and exports have increased to 29 percent of sales.

GROWING DISSATISFACTION

The changeover from a domestic to a multinational firm with only about half of its labor force in Wollaston has placed strains on the already fragile Commonwealth structure, because those working in the subsidiaries outside of the U.K. are in a traditional employee arrangement with the company. In 1982, Scott Bader had an unfortunate experience with a subsidiary acquisition. It took over Synthetic Resins Ltd. (SRL), a Liverpool subsidiary of Unilever and a producer of polyesters that Scott Bader wanted to add to its products; but, rather than simply strip SRL of its assets and close it down (as would usually be done in such a takeover), Scott Bader attempted to keep the Liverpool operation going, even though it was losing money. However, after three years, it was decided that the losses could no longer be sustained and the membership voted to close down the company. Dick Matthews, who was on the board at the time, expressed the discomfort that many of the members experienced: "There I was, a working lad, making a decision to close them down. I never thought I had to go on that board and make that decision. In a conventional company you can blame the so-called

bosses; but we only have ourselves to blame." Stuart Reeves, Scott Bader's information officer, notes that the closure "left a very bad feeling with lots of people
here. We felt that we had done a dirty on them." He adds, "Commercial takeovers
have to be handled very carefully because we're supposed to have this different
attitude to worker/management relations."

The SRL buyout reflects the constraints that market forces place on a company like Scott Bader. On the one hand, there is a commitment to a philosophy
that differs from conventional capitalist firms. But on the other hand, Scott
Bader could not continue indefinitely to absorb the losses of its subsidiary. Yet
in spite of the soul searching after SRL, the transition from a locally based firm
in Wollaston to a multinational with subsidiaries has proceeded without much
resistance from the employees. To understand why, one has to go back to the
major benefit that employees at Scott Bader perceived themselves as deriving
from the conversion of the firm. For most (particularly the factory workers, clerical staff, and junior managers), it was job security (Hadley and Goldsmith
1995). Godric Bader agrees: "Common ownership didn't matter that much to
the employees. What did matter is that they couldn't be chucked out. They had
what's called a certificate of mutual security, which is more important than
money. That they did understand: if they were accepted as Commonwealth
members, they would have a job for life." The Scott Bader operation at
Wollaston has had a low staff turnover rate (3 percent in 1995) and, as a result,
there are many employees with lengthy tenure in the firm. The members of the
Commonwealth supported the shift to a multinational firm, because it was perceived as making Scott Bader more competitive, therefore enhancing their job
security.

While labor policies recommended by management at Scott Bader are scruti-
nized carefully by the employees, the same is not true of the purchase of subsidiaries. Brian Elgood states: "It is relatively easy to go and buy a company in
Dubai, but to agree on pay rates can be labyrinthine and lengthy."

Giving senior management and the company board the exclusive right to make
decisions about acquiring other firms represented a change of policy for Scott
Bader. For example, in 1978, when the company acquired a U.K. firm, Strand
Glass, the recommendation was approved by a vote of the members at an extraordinary general meeting. The decision to close SRL was also approved at a general
meeting.[3] More recently, the employees have come to accept that acquisitions are
the exclusive domain of senior management and the company board, and no
longer of the entire community. As already mentioned, this change of practice is
related to a widely held view among employees that the company is being
strengthened by becoming a multinational. Ian Henderson was headhunted by
Scott Bader largely because of his international experience; in order to hire him,
the reference in the constitution to a seven-to-one ratio (originally four to one)
between the highest and lowest paid salaries was eliminated. Derek Muir, the
chairman who was hired in 1995, was also headhunted because he had extensive
managerial experience in a multinational corporation. Neither he nor Henderson

had any experience in managing a company with Scott Bader's decision-making structures.[4]

The risks associated with becoming a larger firm were anticipated in Scott Bader's constitution, which originally specified that the firm's maximum size be 250 employees, a figure amended in 1971 to 350. "Perhaps the company should not have grown so much," says Godric Bader, "so that it could have been more readily managed by the work force." But on further reflection, he notes: "With the enormous pressure in the chemical industry and the incredible competition, it wasn't possible to maintain the viability. I felt that the employees' jobs were important and finding people who were committed to what we were trying to do was virtually impossible. You need people who have experience in managing across country boundaries. We haven't been able to train people for that." Again, the highly competitive market in which the firm operated became a major influence upon policy decisions.

At the same time as Scott Bader has been expanding internationally, there has grown a feeling of insecurity among employees in the Wollaston part of the firm, who fear that work will go overseas. Among Wollaston employees, there has also been a high level of dissatisfaction with senior management (as indicated by two recent social audits). In response to falling profit margins, management introduced a series of labor policies to reduce the size of the work force at Wollaston and, at the same time, to increase productivity. The policies include a voluntary early retirement plan with a generous buyout package; a lowering of the mandatory retirement age from 65 to 60, which was supported by the community council but was resented by older employees; a flextime program that cut into overtime pay; and performance-related pay.

Ian Henderson defends management's right to manage: "My feeling is that Godric Bader's tenure was one where his idealism was misinterpreted as weakness. There was a swinging of the power away from management towards the work force, and so that you had elements of egalitarianism and freedom to act that were not in the interests of the development of the business. In the last decade, we've been trying to get the pendulum to swing the other way."

Evidently then, the tensions between the success of the business and the values system, tensions that were implicit in the separation between the Commonwealth and the operating company when the conversion first occurred in 1951, continue to this day. As the company has grown and imported professional managers with the skills to operate in an international environment, the tensions between values and business have been exacerbated. Andrew Gunn, the Scott Bader Group's finance director and corporate secretary (and also the only practicing Quaker aside from Godric Bader), disagrees with this separation:

I will stress it is very damaging to see the company board as looking after the business and the Commonwealth board as looking after the values. Because values equal good and business equals bad, this therefore encourages people to look at the Commonwealth board as a good set of guys and the company board as a bad set of guys. But the company board not only has the responsibility of looking after the business but in the constitution it has the responsibility for carrying on the business within the values.

Historically, the challenge for Scott Bader has been to create the synthesis to which Gunn refers.

CONCLUSION

In addition to converting his firm to common ownership, Ernest Bader attempted to build a movement of firms that shared his ideals. In 1958, together with Harold Farmer of the firm Farmer & Sons, he formed the Society for Democratic Integration in Industry, known as Demintry. Like Scott Bader, Demintry attempted to form a value base for industry by arguing that "the fundamental ethical ideas taught by all the great religions could only retain their power if they are applied in the economic life" (cited in Blum 1968, 45). The member organizations of Demintry had a variety of arrangements, from common ownership firms like Scott Bader to conventionally owned companies with profit sharing and participatory management. Among the latter was Best & Lloyd, a Birmingham manufacturer of light fittings, whose principal owner and managing director at that time, Robert Best, paid to the employees the profits normally reserved for shareholders, and also set up a group discussion system and managerial board with employee representatives. This approach was promoted by James Gillespie, a controversial consultant and the author of *Free Expression in Work,* who introduced his anarchist views about industry (Gillespie 1965) to family firms such as Best & Lloyd, L. G. Harris & Company Ltd., and Aston, Chain and Hook, that were primarily of Quaker origin.[5] Although welcoming copartnership firms into Demintry, Ernest Bader was critical of the participatory arrangements at Best & Lloyd, arguing that "the approach seems rather too elementary inasmuch as quite ordinary matters belonging clearly to management are brought forward for discussion at the various group meetings" (Bader 1957, 3).

Because of its range of members, Demintry did not formally advocate common ownership. However, the link between democracy and ownership was made clear in the organization's principles, which advocated that "ownership of the business must be vested in some organ of the whole body to express democratic integration and a sense of belonging by all its members" (Blum 1968, 45).

In 1971, Demintry evolved into the Industrial Common Ownership Movement (ICOM), with Ernest Bader assuming the honorary role of founder president. ICOM was primarily a secular organization, and it was not committed to the religious and antimilitarist values that were so important to Bader. Shortly after it was formed, Bader resigned from ICOM when it failed to support a pacifist resolution that he introduced (Hoe 1978).

Although there were 1,400 British firms in 1995 registered under the Industrial Common Ownership Act,[6] Bader's expectations that Scott Bader would be the germ of a mass movement that would transform capitalism have not been realized. In the U.K., only two family firms have followed the same route as Scott Bader, a conversion to common ownership and the donation of the principal owners' equity to a related charitable trust. In 1978, a Northampton jeweller named Michael Jones converted the company bearing his name to a common ownership cooperative (Michael Jones Co-operative Ltd.) and donated his equity in the firm to a related charitable trust named Michael Jones Community Ltd., which continues to this day to support worthwhile causes in the local community. A devoutly religious man, Michael Jones belonged to a small group of Christian businesspeople that included Ernest Bader.[7]

In 1965, another Bader acquaintance, Connor Wilson, the founder of Airflow Development, a manufacturer and distributor of ventilation and heating products, donated his equity in the company (about 75 percent of the shares) to Airflow Community Ltd., a charitable trust similar to the Scott Bader Commonwealth, with its employees, currently about 300, as members. Connor Wilson's son Bryan, who was Airflow's marketing director before starting his own business in 1976, recalls that his father (who died in 1992 at age 80) was a devout Christian, pacifist, and "pink capitalist," who believed strongly that "the wealth of the business should be shared between the people who created it."[8]

Among family firms in the U.K., Michael Jones Jewellers and Airflow are the exceptions rather than the rule. Most examples of common ownership are very small start-ups. Because they lack the initial endowment of Scott Bader and the financing available to conventionally structured firms, they tend to grow slowly. Arguably, Ernest Bader's expectations regarding the potential of the common ownership movement were unrealistic and might be characterized as messianic. Indeed, at the signing ceremony to create the Commonwealth in 1951, the participants were reminded by Queen's Council Monroe that "invitation cards to the funeral of capitalism have not yet been sent out" (Hoe 1978, 119).

Although Scott Bader has fallen short of the utopian expectations envisaged for it, if it is viewed in relation to the norms of industry, a different assessment emerges. The company has grown steadily since 1951—from 161 employees and a turnover of £625,000 to 650 employees and a turnover of £99 million (Scott Bader 1996). Its annual profits during this period have increased from £72,000 to £1.86 million. Moreover, unlike other British firms in chemical production, which have either closed down or been bought out by large multinationals, Scott Bader has retained its independence and continues to grow. Its resin-based compounds, now involving two-thirds of its production, are used for boats, bridges, and building panels. Subsidiaries in the U.S. and France are converting the resins to moldings. Its polymers, either water-based or water and oil emulsions, involve the other one-third of production, and are used to make printing inks and adhesives. Ian Henderson states proudly: "We're here! Where is there an independent polymer and resin company employing 650 people anywhere in Europe? There is only one. The others have been gobbled up."

Evidently then, common ownership has proved effective in protecting Scott Bader and the jobs of its employees against outside predators. In the Wollaston area, where the economy has been hurt by the downsizing of its shoe-manufacturing industry, Scott Bader not only continues to employ people but has also about doubled since 1951 when the conversion occurred. However, job security is no longer the absolute that it was conceived to be at the creation of the Commonwealth. In 1978, 1980, and again in 1994, Scott Bader has introduced voluntary redundancy schemes to cope with downturns in business caused by raw material price increases over which the company has no control. The buyout packages, for which employees volunteered, were generous by industry norms—for example, permitting employees in their mid-50s with 20 years of service to leave with about two years' salary. To provide opportunities for younger workers, as noted, Scott Bader lowered its mandatory retirement age from 65 to 60. Despite these changes, and relative to the norms of modern industry where job security is becoming an antiquated concept, Scott Bader has provided a relatively dependable work environment, albeit less so than in 1951.

As noted, the ideal of a flat pay scale has also been subject to change. Yet the current ratio remains low by industry norms: pay for jobs in the bottom categories is above that for similar positions in other firms, whereas upper management salaries are lower. But there is concern among some employees that removal from the constitution of the reference to a specific pay ratio and the introduction of performance-related pay reflect a continued shift in the direction of industry norms. Dick Sharp, a production worker and a member of the Commonwealth board, says "my greatest fear is that an annual pay raise will disappear and the only increases will be performance pay." However, to date, Scott Bader has maintained a superior standard.

Scott Bader's pension, too, is at the allowable maximum. In addition, the company pays for supplementary medical insurance; sick leave at full pay for up to six months; a one-month "sabbatical" trip after 25 years' service with all expenses paid; subsidized meals in the Commonwealth Centre; and a subsidized indoor pool on the estate. Historically, Scott Bader has attempted to build a community where its employees share not only their workplace but also their recreational activities; but, in recent years, it has become increasingly difficult to get people involved. The Commonwealth Centre, located on the estate and once the hub of community life, is used much less than in the past.

With respect to employment issues, Scott Bader might be viewed as an excellent place to work. But the firm was not converted to common ownership simply to become another employer. The objectives were to change the relationship to the community and, even of more importance, to change the relationship between employee and manager. As a member of the community, Scott Bader has consistently donated 5 percent of its pre-tax profits to various causes. In Britain, the company has given generously to organizations assisting the homeless and the disabled. Internationally, it has supported development work in South Africa, Zimbabwe, and Malawi. Some of the projects to which Scott Bader contributes are individually determined by employees, who are given annual vouchers of up to £200 to make donations.

Compared to conventional business standards in which community contributions for socially responsible corporations are typically about one percent of profits, and the overall norm is much lower, Scott Bader's contribution has been exemplary. But judged by the ideals set forth in the constitution and demanded by Ernest Bader, the company has been wanting. Few members of the Commonwealth share Ernest Bader's commitments either to pacifism or to building a common-ownership movement. Scott Bader is, first of all, their workplace and not a mission that they promote.

In part, this might be because the decision to convert Scott Bader to common ownership did not come from the employees or even from pressure that they exerted on Ernest Bader. Whereas improvements in the work conditions were important to Scott Bader's employees, there was no demand on their part to become owners of the company. Moreover, the concept of ownership that Ernest Bader created was unfamiliar to them. Membership in the Commonwealth does not entitle them to any share of the company (the most tangible sign of ownership). Profit sharing at Scott Bader was originally conceived of as a bonus to reward the staff for their contribution to the company— that is, a labor dividend serving as an adjustment to the annual wage. More recently, the profit-sharing arrangements have been revised so that a portion is in the form of profit-related pay distributed in proportion to salary level and a portion is a year-end bonus, paid to everyone equally. In neither its current nor original form is profit sharing a payment to shareholders, as in a more conventional ownership arrangement.

The most tangible symbol of ownership at Scott Bader is the voting right. All members of the Commonwealth have one vote in the affairs of the business and are entitled to elect their representatives to the governance. Compared to the norms of industry, the opportunities for participation (for example, in the election of employee representatives to the board of directors) are exemplary. But again, in relation to its ideals, Scott Bader has fallen short. There is a sizable group of employees who don't participate, and among those who do, there is concern that the balance of power has tilted too much to the executives of the operating company. Moreover, with the shift to a multinational company, employees are apprehensive that executive authority will increase even further and that the decision-making processes will resemble those of a conventional corporation. Yet there is an irony surrounding this concern that must be noted: the shift to a multinational has had the tacit support of the employees, because it is perceived as enhancing job security by diversifying production and making the company more competitive.

By industrial standards, Scott Bader has been a good employer, but the ideals of common ownership have not led to the fundamental redefinition of the employee-management relationship that was originally anticipated. The workers at Scott Bader tend to think of themselves primarily as employees, and more so than in the past when they were more likely to view themselves as co-owners or trustees. Compared to workers in a more conventional firm, the employees of Scott Bader are provided with financial information, which is shared openly, and are highly knowledgeable about company policies. They have the opportunity to either present their views or be represented in general meetings, the community council, and the boards of both the operating company and the Commonwealth. Therefore, the employees of Scott Bader may have been able to strengthen their employment conditions beyond what would be possible in a typical collective-bargaining process. Through the arrangement at Scott Bader, they can participate in a range of issues that extend beyond the typical collective-bargaining process. For example, to enhance the security of their employment, the employees have voted to approve very high rates of retention of company profits (90 percent) relative to conventional corporations. The Scott Bader experience, therefore, provides no support for the theory that democratic worker-owned firms degenerate because the employees are only interested in short-term gain and not in reinvesting in the firm (Webb and Webb, 1921).

In reflecting upon the plight of Scott Bader at this point, Godric Bader (who, at age 73, remains the embodiment of the dream and the conscience of the company) is working on revitalizing the ideals of the founders. He is fond of quoting Otto Sik, the former deputy prime minister of Czechoslovakia, who, in reference to common ownership, mused: "This isn't possible for either blue-collar working people or even less traditional managers to understand; it is for poets and artists." In retrospect, Godric Bader suggests that instead of total common ownership or trusteeship, it might have been preferable to combine that arrangement with direct ownership by the employees. "That way," he believes, "people would have felt that they have a bit of a stake."

Godric Bader's comments reflect the stock-taking that is quietly occurring at Scott Bader 45 years after the conversion. The bullish confidence and optimism that common ownership would become a movement to which large numbers of businesses would gravitate as an alternative to capitalism and communism no longer exists. There is still a recognition of Scott Bader's distinctiveness, as reflected in its ownership arrangements, its decision-making processes, and its relationship to movements for social justice in the U.K. and internationally. But even within Scott Bader itself, there has been a significant erosion of the ideals in the direction of practices that are more in line with conventional norms.

Therefore, the Scott Bader experience seems to support the thesis that, over time, innovative organizations become more conservative (Weber 1947; Zald and Ash 1966). This shift may also be viewed in generational terms (Mannheim 1952). As the employees associated with the conversion come to retirement, and a new generation becomes involved that lacks contact with the founder and the ideals of the original conversion, it is likely that the conservative shift will continue—unless the predominant norms for industry also change.

Among the current members of the Commonwealth, there is widespread concern about what the future holds for Ernest Bader's dream. Andrew Gunn, the company's director of finance and a strong advocate of common ownership, states: "It was a remarkable gift. Those who received the gift have been struggling since then to live up to it."

THE SCOTT BADER COMMONWEALTH

1890   Ernest Bader is born in Regensdorf, Switzerland, the last of 13 children.

1911   Bader immigrates to London.

1920   Scott Bader is started as a chemical products import business. The firm's name is taken from the surnames of Bader and his wife, Dora Scott.

1941   Scott Bader's factory in London is destroyed by German bombs. Production is shifted to Wollaston, where Bader purchased a 44-acre estate.

1943   Bader first broaches the idea of the "Common Wealth" with his employees.

1951   Ernest Bader donates 90 percent of the family stock to a trust and creates the Scott Bader Commonwealth as a common-ownership firm. Bader still retains control of the voting shares.

1957   Ernest Bader appoints his son Godric as managing director and continues as chairman until 1965.

1963   The remaining stock is donated to the trust and placed under the control of a board of trustees. The donation also includes the family home. The constitution specifies that Ernest Bader is chairman for life and is to be succeeded in that role by his son Godric.

1965   Ernest Bader retires as chairman and receives the title of founder president.

1971   Godric Bader ends the family's privileged status in the firm and steps down as managing director.

1982   Ernest Bader dies at age 91.

1995   Scott Bader is the last of the independent chemical producers in the U.K., with 650 employees and annual sales of £99 million. Godric Bader, at age 73, has a titular role of life president.

NOTES

Unless otherwise cited, the quotes from employees of Scott Bader were from interviews by the author conducted in March 1995. Those interviewed were: Ian Alexander, Godric Bader, Simon Clarke, Brian Elgood, Alan Green, Andrew Gunn, Ian Henderson, Mick Jones, Eddie Lancaster, Derek Muir, Stuart Reeves, Roger Scott, Dick Sharp, Austin Shelton, Mossy Waters, and Phil Webb. The quote from Dick Matthews was taken from *Products of Principle*, BBC, 1986.

1. The background information on Ernest Bader comes from an interview with his son, Godric; interviews with other employees of the company; the biography by Susanna Hoe, *The Man Who Gave His Company Away: A Biography of Ernest Bader, Founder of the Scott Bader Commonwealth* (Wollaston, U.K.: Scott Bader, 1978); the book by Fred Blum, *Work and Community: The Scott Bader Commonwealth and the Quest for a New Social Order* (London: Routledge & Kegan Paul, 1968); and Ernest Bader's writings and correspondence.

2. Historically, the employees of the company have voted to approve the managing director's recommendation that their profit-sharing entitlement be limited to only 5 percent of the year-end profits—less than the 20 percent maximum allowed in the constitution. Also in accordance with the constitution, the percent of year-end profits for profit sharing must be at least matched by donations to charitable causes in both the U.K. and abroad.

3. From the interview with Godric Bader and confirmed in interviews with other employees.

4. Muir was a nonexecutive director of Tullis Russell, a paper maker headquartered in Scotland, which has since become employee owned (see chapter 6).

5. Information was obtained from an interview by the author with John Best in March 1995.

6. Personal communication with ICOM, March 1995.

7. Interview by the author with Michael Jones, March 1995.

8. Phone interview with Bryan Wilson, April 1995.

4

Endenburg Electric

Gerard Endenburg's pioneering innovations at Endenburg Electric in Rotterdam flow from the same tradition as the Scott Bader Commonwealth. Like Ernest Bader, Endenburg is a Quaker, and even more so someone educated as such from childhood. Having that background and the democratic practices associated with it allowed Gerard Endenburg to create an innovative system of decision making called sociocracy within his own firm and, subsequently, in other organizations in the Netherlands and internationally. Whereas Bader converted his firm to the Scott Bader Commonwealth and encouraged others to adopt that model when he helped to found the Industrial Common Ownership Movement, he lacked a process for transforming a conventionally organized workplace to a democratic arrangement. When he established the Commonwealth by using a top-down approach that reflected his style of management, he assumed that his employees would take advantage of the opportunity. This has happened to a degree, but not to the extent that was hoped for originally. Moreover, greater control has gradually shifted toward management.

Endenburg, by comparison, has not only created an end point, a democratic workplace that he refers to as sociocracy, but has also pioneered a process for converting his firm and other conventionally structured organizations to that approach. That process, organized through the Sociocratic Center that he directs, has been the focus of his efforts since the mid-1980s.

Sociocracy is defined around four basic rules: 1. decision making by consent, meaning the absence of "reasoned objection"; 2. "circles" where people with common work objectives make decisions regarding policy; 3. the interlinking of circles within an organization, by which is meant communication between circles facilitated by the shared representation of the circle leader and a minimum of two other representatives; and 4. within circles, the election by consent of representatives and other functionaries and after an open discussion (Reijmer and Romme 1994).

The ground rules and other practices introduced by Endenburg are adaptations of concepts that have been tried elsewhere. Consent and the decision-making circle are adaptations of Quaker processes; interlinking and the election of functionaries and of management are found in cooperatives and other types of mutual societies; and the ownership arrangement of a dual company structure involving a foundation for the shares and a limited company for the operating firm is similar to the Scott Bader Commonwealth and the John Lewis Partnership. Endenburg's contribution is in synthesizing these ideas, grounding their rationale in cybernetics, establishing a legislative framework for them, and encouraging other companies to adopt this approach by engaging in such movement activities as his writings and his work as director of the Sociocratic Center (Sociocratisch *Centrum*).

BACKGROUND

Endenburg Electric (officially *Endenburg Elektrotechniek B.V.*) is a Rotterdam firm founded in 1950 by Gerard Endenburg's parents. With about 110 employees and Fl.14 million[1] of annual revenues, it specializes in the design, production, and installation of electronic components for ships, buildings, and utilities.[2]

Gerard Endenburg, who is an electrical engineer, began working for the business in 1961 and became the managing director in 1968. Endenburg was quite pragmatic in his attitude to the business, and under his management it expanded rapidly. Nevertheless, his primary interest was changing the relationships of work, and beginning in 1970, when he embarked on the process of introducing sociocracy, Endenburg viewed the business as a "laboratory" where he could experiment. One of his first strictures was to place a ceiling on the size of the business, which he felt was necessary to change the work relationships.

Endenburg came from an unusual background. His parents were highly idealistic people who lived a communal lifestyle. They were pacifists, vegetarians, and abstainers, and they embraced the principle of free love. In the latter part of the Second World War, the elder Endenburg, like many other men in the western part of the Netherlands, was taken away by the Germans and placed in a concentration camp. About eleven at the time, Gerard Endenburg was left to support his mother and infant sister in the impoverishment resulting from the destruction of Rotterdam by German bombers. This he did by whatever method was available, including theft and foraging from rubble. "I had a pistol, a grenade, and an automatic rifle," Endenburg recalls—ironic in light of his pacifist values. "Once the war was over, returning to school was strange."

Endenburg attended a Quaker boarding school, where he was influenced by the teachers Kees Boeke and his wife Betty Cadbury (of the famous British chocolate-producing family). The school emphasized learning to live together, and Boeke (whom Endenburg views as his mentor) introduced him to the concept of sociocracy. Previously, Endenburg had attended a more conventional school, but he rebelled against its restrictive teaching practices. Interestingly, although Endenburg had reservations about conventional organizations, he learned to work within them. Prior to entering the family business and earning an MA in electrical engineering, he worked at Phillips, the huge Dutch conglomerate. He also taught radar technology in the Dutch army, where he became interested in cybernetics, a system that he utilized in his conceptualization of sociocracy.

Endenburg has published his ideas in three books, the most influential being *Sociocracy: The Organization of Decision Making,* translated into English in 1988. Although he has served as the general manager of Endenburg Electric since the mid-60s (his successor Piet Slieker was appointed in 1995), in recent years the focus of his work has been the promotion of sociocracy, which he has accomplished as the director of the Sociocratic Center, an organization founded in 1978 and now employing 15 people. Endenburg views himself as a social engineer who applies engineering principles to organizations, a process that he has undertaken through the use of analogues for translating problems from one discipline to another. One of the analogues in his writings is the bicycle, a symbol of Dutch culture of which he is very proud.

INTRODUCING SOCIOCRACY

From 1972 (when his father died and he purchased his mother's holding in the company) to 1984, Gerard Endenburg had exclusive control over Endenburg Electric. He had already started introducing sociocratic principles, but recognized that his ownership placed constraints upon the potential to transform the social relationships of the company. In his writings, Endenburg does not dwell on his critique of conventional ownership arrangements, but he is nevertheless forthright in his views: "Power is in the hands of the owners. The object of the organization is to make profits for the owners, who in many cases know nothing about the organizations they own. This authoritarian character, which manifests itself, for example, in the opposition of employer and employee, calls forth a reaction against the system as a whole" (Endenburg 1988, 198).

Endenburg, whose company was unionized and who has had a good working relationship with organized labor, had reservations about an adversarial relationship between employer and employee. "Unions," he argued, "were fighting against the absolute power of entrepreneurs. I can understand that, but at the same time, they were killing businesses." This battle was anathema to the idealistic world in which Endenburg grew up, a world that emphasized harmonious social relations. Therefore, an important step in changing this relationship was "to create a structure which disconnected ownership and absolute say." In 1984, to facilitate that end, Endenburg had his shares in the business independently evaluated, and then placed them in a foundation which, in effect, became the holding company for the operating firm and the owner of its stock. Based on the evaluation of the shares at Fl.1.2 million, the foundation made a loan to the business that was paid off over ten years from the operating profits.

Therefore, the conversion of Endenburg Electric was not an endowment (as was Scott Bader or the John Lewis Partnership), but a sale at fair value that was paid off over time. For the average owner of a small business without significant wealth, a sale at fair market value (such as that undertaken by Endenburg) might be more appealing than a gift. Nevertheless, like the John Lewis partnership and the Scott Bader Commonwealth, Endenburg Electric became a company not owned by anyone. The shares in the foundation reflect the value of the company; the shares have increased in value because the company has been consistently profitable. But because the shares are nonvoting, they are difficult to liquidate. Therefore, like these other companies, Endenburg Electric is immune from takeover and other shareholder pressures. To quote Piet Slieker, the general manager, "Our shares are in dead hands!" As long as the company can meet the measure of the market, its future is ensured.

Through neutralizing the power of the shareholders, Endenburg was able to eliminate one of the obstacles for introducing sociocracy. His objective was to create an environment in which "people would learn to guide their own situation." Interestingly, even though he was concerned about power relations as manifested in organizational hierarchy, Endenburg found it naive to talk about organizations without hierarchy. Rather, his concern was how to steer organizations so that they reflected the aspirations of the participants. "There is a certain sequence of rank both in the management organization and, for example, the circle organization. By applying the basic rules of sociocracy, however, the authoritarian power associated with rank is replaced by a power established and limited by means of the principle of consent" (Endenburg 1988, 63). Essentially, Endenburg, in line with Quaker thought, was attempting to find a way in which all members of an organization could participate in decisions without jeopardizing the ability to make decisions expeditiously and in a professional manner.

As noted, there are four basic rules of sociocracy (Endenburg 1988; Reijmer and Romme 1994), each of which will be discussed in turn.

Consent

Decision making by consent is the cornerstone of sociocracy. Consent, as defined by Endenburg, is a variation of consensus decision making, an approach that he was schooled in by Kees Boeke and which is central to Quaker philosophy. Annewiek Reijmer, an industrial psychologist who has worked in the Sociocratic Center for 10 years and is currently the head of the implementation circle, acknowledges the similarity between consent and consensus, but argues that the difference is important: "By consensus, I must convince you that I am in the right; by consent, you ask whether you can live with the decision." If one or more members of the group object to a decision, they are asked to provide their reasons. The other members of the group are expected to listen and respond to the objections until such time as the group is able to reach a decision with which all members can live. Not everyone is going to be happy, but in the end, they indicate to the other members whether the decision meets at least a minimum threshold of tolerance. The process of reaching that point is highly rationalized in that people who object are expected to state their reasons (hence the phrase "reasoned objection") and the others in the group are expected to respond in a rational manner. Reijmer indicates that "as a result, the group has to go slower than others using majority decision making." However, Gerard Endenburg emphasizes that the slower pace in formulating policies can lead to long-term gains in executing them because, as a result of the broad discussion and the pains taken to achieve consent, there is general agreement and support within the company.

One of the criticisms levelled against groups that use such processes is that it gives those in the minority a lot of influence over decisions. Endenburg emphasizes, however, that "consent is not a veto; in a veto, you can just say no. In sociocracy, when you say no, we ask why. You are part of the group, and the group is responsible for the realization of common aims. It is crazy for us to ignore you, and it is crazy for you to ignore us."

Endenburg's advocacy of consent is part of a critique of the limitations of democratic decision making with its emphasis on majority rule. In obtaining consent from all participants prior to making a decision, not only is tacit respect shown for each person but there is also an opportunity to incorporate minority opinions and thereby strengthen the group's position. The consent process encourages a dialogue in which the participants argue their position and attempt to arrive at an accommodation that all can accept. Unlike a majority-voting system, an attempt is made to avoid "winners and losers." Endenburg is blunt in his critique: "The democratic system is killing our society in the sense that it doesn't accommodate minority points of view. I am the majority; then get out of my way." He states further that: "The worth of a democracy can be measured in terms of the protection and the freedom given to minorities. If a democracy cannot manage this, it has become a demo-dictatorship" (Endenburg 1988, 231). Endenburg characterizes sociocracy as the next stage of a continuum whose prior points were autocracy and democracy. Whereas democracy is an improvement over autocracy, sociocracy "follows on from the democratic model" (Endenburg 1988, 8).

For people who have grown up with the majority rule of democracy, making decisions by consent can be frustrating. Hanny de Kruyf, head of the Sociocratic Center's education circle, acknowledges that "In the beginning people hesitate in saying that they have objections. It takes time to change behavior." The slow pace of dealing with each participant's concerns can also be problematic because the group cannot proceed until it finds a solution that everyone can live with. "It works," states Rudi Immers, who has been employed in the Installations Department at Endenburg Electric for four years, "but it is not easy because you are working with people. If one person cannot give his consent and the decision is held up, there's a discussion, and it can take lots of time to convince that person."

The sociocratic process of making decisions applies to policy issues, not implementation, which is viewed as the domain of management. Whereas the additional time to formulate policy may be seen as a drawback for businesses, this is partially offset by the support from members of the company when a decision is taken. In the best humanistic tradition, it is anticipated that giving people the opportunity to participate in the decision-making process will unleash their creativity. Endenburg believes that in most organizations "People are in doubt; they are afraid; they are not willing. They are looking to their boss, and have all kinds of other reasons not to be active. We have to be active to survive."

The Circle

The circle is an appropriate symbol for the sociocratic organization in that it signifies equivalence between participants—in contrast to the typical meeting arrangement with the leadership at the front looking down at the other participants. Through the circle, members of the organization with a common work objective come together to formulate policy for their unit. The circle does not replace management and the other administrative mechanisms of the organization; rather, it is superimposed upon them for the specific purpose of formulating policy. Circles occur at different levels of the organization. At Endenburg Electric, there are three distinct levels; the smaller Sociocratic Center has two. A large corporation or government department might have four or more levels.

About 90 percent of decisions are taken by the departmental circles that meet bimonthly to deal with the issues of their work unit. At Endenburg Electric, the departments are related both to the technical aspects of production (for example, manufacturing, technical installations, electronics) and to the administrative units (such as personnel and accounting), and they range in size from 6 to 25 (which is viewed as the maximum size for a circle). At the Sociocratic Center, the circles are for such functional groupings as education, publicity, and implementation, as well as for administration. Although the circles at the first level are related to work units, individuals in more than one work unit can be involved in related circles. Policies formulated by a first-level circle typically deal with issues exclusive to the domain of the work unit as opposed to the entire organization. Such policies are constrained by budget, which (at Endenburg Electric) is a Fl. 50,000 limit for each unit.

The general circle, or second-level circle, formulates policy for the entire company. It consists of senior management, department heads, and delegates elected by each department. At Endenburg Electric, this body usually has about 25 participants, typically the general manager and another senior management representative together with three representatives (the department head and two delegates) per first-level circle. There is, however, flexibility in the numbers, larger units choosing more delegates than smaller ones. In addition, for issues that are of importance to a particular unit, it can choose to send a larger number of delegates to the general circle. The general circle works closely with senior management to formulate company policy—for example, decisions about merging of departments, profit sharing, and long-term planning.

The top or third-level circle connects the organization with the external world. It consists of four external people (typically with backgrounds in such areas as finance, law, labor, and government), as well as the senior management from the general circle and two delegates from the general circle. The top circle is analogous to the board of directors in a conventional corporation. It oversees the organization, including planning for its future, and is responsible for administering shares in the foundation.

Interlinking of Circles

The objective of the sociocratic approach is for the circles to deal not only with the issues pertaining to their level of the organization but also to communicate with each other through representatives who overlap the various levels. Each circle is normally capped at 25 people so as to allow everyone the opportunity to participate. Therefore, in large organizations, there will be many circles reflecting the hierarchical arrangement. To ensure that there is communication not only within circles but also between circles, there is an interlinking (also referred to as a double linking) of circles. As such, the first-level circles (reflecting work units) have their leader and at least two representatives in the general circle. These representatives (including the first-level circle leader) are part of the decision making in the general circle and are responsible for communicating the concerns of their circle to the general circle, and for communicating the policies of the general circle to their departmental circles. Similarly, the general circle sends to the top circle the general manager and at least two representatives. They participate in decision making at the top circle and in intercommunication between these two levels of the organization. At each circle, meeting time is set aside to receive feedback from the representatives of circles at the other levels.

Through this interlinking of the circles, Endenburg has accepted the hierarchical structure of the organization, but has added mechanisms by which it can be steered. "Hierarchy remains," he states candidly, "but the interlocking circles provide a check against its excesses." He argues that "The double link means that you have a circle process between the circles, and information flows up and down. One of the problems is that when you bring information down (for example, from the general circle to the departmental circles), you have to translate it, and when you bring information up, you have to formulate it in a different way. The language changes as you go up and down the hierarchy."

Applying cybernetic principles, Endenburg reasons that the circle process consists of an operational component whereby management executes policy, a measuring or searching component whereby the results of a particular initiative are evaluated (usually according to some norm), and an instructional component whereby management is given feedback and the opportunity to restore equilibrium to the organization. This feedback process occurs within each circle and, through interlinking, between circles at different levels of the organization.

In common with other business executives, Endenburg accepts the utility of financial criteria as an important form of feedback. He expresses some ambivalence about the importance of profit, arguing that it "is no longer the primary purpose of the company" (Endenburg 1988, 200). But he also acknowledges that "profit is still a yardstick" (Endenburg 1988, 200), and therefore can serve as a useful standard for evaluating the operations of the company—or, if they are found wanting, for correcting them. He criticizes nonprofits for not undertaking careful evaluations of performance.

Since 1970, when he first started introducing sociocratic ideas into his company, he has shared both ongoing financial feedback for the company as a whole as well as for projects undertaken by units within the company. The importance of this information is underlined because a portion of each employee's annual compensation (typically about 8 percent) is derived from profit sharing, both short-term (based upon the performance of projects taken on by the employee's department) and annually (based upon performance of the company). For profit sharing related to projects (referred to as "short-term"), profit is distributed according to the number of hours an employee has worked (also taking into account the overhead). Losses are not deducted from pay, but must be overcome before subsequent project-related profits are distributed. For year-end profit sharing, the top circle decides upon the portion that will be distributed, after receiving feedback from the circles at the other levels. The profits are shared by all employees and capital suppliers according to a complex formula that takes account of their contribution to the sales of the company.

Although the interlinking of circles formalizes the sharing of information between different levels of the hierarchy and offers workers in the departments the opportunity to provide feedback to the general circle on policies affecting the entire company, the department circles do not have the same authority as the general circle. However, the general circle's recommendations are passed to the departments through their leaders and representatives on the general circle. Bert van der Eerden, who handles sales for the panel building/technical installations circle, believes that the interlinking of circles is a useful mechanism. "We get feedback at each meeting from our delegates to the general circle. If we disagree with their recommendations, we ask our representatives to the general circle to raise our concerns."

Recently, the panel-building unit had to deal with a recommendation from the general circle to merge its unit with electronics, because both units had insufficient contracts. The result would mean a reduction in the work force. "Delegates from the general circle brought the recommendation to the lower circles involved," van der Eerden states. "The people in the lower circles didn't want the merger, but did not raise any objections. There was insufficient work, and we felt that the merger was necessary, though we are not happy with it."

Although the departmental circles usually give their consent to the general circle's recommendations, this does not always happen. In 1976, for example, when several major shipyards in Rotterdam shut down, the company found itself in a crisis since the shipping industry accounted for more than one-third of its business (Reijmer and Romme 1994). As general manager, Gerard Endenburg recommended that 60 employees be laid off. However, one of the fitters in the company (Jan De Groot) objected, called a meeting of his circle, and recommended that the employees slated for layoff be given a few weeks to undertake a concentrated marketing effort. De Groot and the circle's chair were able to win the support of the general circle and, in response, the top circle agreed to utilize a portion of the company's reserve to finance the marketing effort. New projects were started, the company began to develop a more diversified customer base, and the layoffs were ultimately minimal.

Even though this incident stands out in the lore of the company, it does illustrate that the members of the lower circles are not passive recipients of information from the general circle. They are asked to give their feedback and sometimes take a different point of view which, because of the interlinking of the circles, can be easily communicated.

Election of Functionaries

The first three ground rules for sociocracy interact with the elections at different levels of the organization. In contrast to typical democratic practices (which generally utilize the secret ballot as a means of protecting each voter from coercion), sociocratic elections encourage the preferences of participants to be openly discussed. When an election is forthcoming, members of a circle are informed in writing.

For each circle, the balloting process includes not only the name of each person's nominee but also the name of the nominator. In the discussion that follows, the nominators are expected to give reasons for their choices. After a period of discussion, the chair of the circle sees whether there is consent from all participants for the choice with the most nominations. Participants in the circle who withhold their consent are asked to put forward their reasons. If those who object cannot be convinced, then the member of the circle with the next highest number of nominations is usually put forward, until such time as all members give consent. The elected person may not be the first choice of the majority, but it is someone with whom all members of the circle can live. Among the positions elected by a circle are the chair, who is a crucial choice because of the importance of arriving at consent; the secretary; and delegates to the other circles.

The sociocratic election process, while open, can present difficulties for members of a circle. "It is not always nice to hear something negative about yourself," says Arie Krijgsman, the head of the technical insulation department, "but in our system you have the opportunity to make the discussion worthwhile." Rudi Immers echoes this sentiment: "The selection process can be difficult and can affect people's ability to work together. They might not talk to each other and might even have conflict. We are all human and have feelings." Nevertheless, in spite of these reservations, Immers believes that the election process is a good one: "Every system has its difficulties, but the benefits in this system are greater than the drawbacks."

The election process pertains not only to the lower circles but also to the general manager who, like the others, is elected for a two-year term. Recently, Gerard Endenburg, who had served as the general manager since the mid-60s, indicated that he wanted to arrange for a successor. A support circle (or subcommittee) to the general circle was set up to define criteria and to establish a recruitment procedure. After an external search, which involved meetings with several candidates, the committee decided to look internally. The top and general circles held a joint meeting in which participants were asked to write their choice on a ballot. Piet Slieker, a company executive and an accountant by background, received the most support, but did not fit the original profile that emphasized a technical background in electronics. After a discussion and agreement by the meeting to redefine the position, the chair proposed Slieker. But, until there was a favorable psychological assessment of the candidate, two members withheld their consent. After the assessment was received, the top and general circles met again, and all participants gave their consent to the appointment.

Although the process places a lot of responsibility upon the circles to select people who are best for each position, it should be noted that the next higher circle fills some positions within a circle. In other words, the sociocratic process retains some hierarchical elements. For example, the general circle recommends department heads for the lower circles, and the top circle selects the general manager. However, in such cases, the recommendation is not finalized until feedback has been received from the circle for which the selection is being made.

MOVEMENT ACTIVITIES

Since the mid-80s, most of Gerard Endenburg's energies have gone into promoting sociocracy through the Sociocratic Center, where he has been the director. Sociocratic centers are being planned for the northern region of the Netherlands, U.S., Brazil, Germany, and Canada—areas where there has been interest in sociocracy. In the Netherlands, greater legitimacy was given to sociocracy when, in 1984, the government enacted legislation enabling a company to incorporate as a sociocratic corporation. On the surface, such a company (like Endenburg Electric) has a dual incorporation of a limited company (for the operating firm) and a foundation (for the holding company). However, the statutes follow the sociocratic model, and the company is referred to as a sociocratic corporation.

At this time, representatives of hundreds of organizations (private sector businesses, government agencies, and nonprofits) have attended workshops at the Sociocratic Center. The components of sociocracy most frequently adopted by these organizations are the circle, the interlinking of circles, making decisions by consent, and the system of compensation. About 40 companies have prepared statutes based upon sociocratic rules. To promote continuation of the change process, the Sociocratic Center also undertakes an annual social audit for firms with which it works. However, the fact that only two of these companies have owners who (like Endenburg) have been willing to place their shares in a foundation suggests the educational and consulting work of the Sociocratic Center has limitations.

One of the reasons why sociocracy is attractive to managers from conventionally structured organizations is that it can be grafted onto the existing structure. Sociocracy does not pretend to establish equality among all positions within an organization. Sociocratic practitioners work with hierarchical organizations by attempting to establish a process whereby all people, regardless of their position, have the opportunity to participate through the right to consent to policy decisions within their circle and through the interlinking of decision-making structures. The interlinking mechanism, as well as the related election process, is an obvious attempt to overcome the alienation of people in nonmanagerial functions by, at minimum, permitting them to participate directly in decisions related to their own unit and, through their representatives, at other levels of the organization. However, like all such endeavors, there are limits to what can be accomplished. Management is resistive, and often desires to hold onto its authority. At the same time employees, conditioned to a powerless role in decision making, have difficulty expressing themselves, even when given the opportunity to do so. Annewiek Reijmer acknowledges the problem: "In the beginning people act powerless. Then you say: 'You are complaining, do you have a proposal to deal with the problem?'" To facilitate participation, the facilitator goes around the circle encouraging people who never say anything to speak up. As Reijmer states: "We get people to try out their power."

But hierarchy per se works against people at the lower levels expressing themselves because they recognize that decision-making authority is vested elsewhere. The interlinking process creates two-way communication and it also creates representation, but as Rudi Immers states: "Most people find it difficult to criticize their boss. That would be true of this system or another."

CONCLUSION

The conversion of Endenburg Electric to sociocracy was largely Gerard Endenburg's initiative and was undertaken by him on behalf of his employees.

As with the other initiatives in this book, even though the conversion was moti-vated by idealism, it was still greeted with suspicion and mistrust. Bert van der Eerden, who started with the company in 1971 when Endenburg first introduced sociocratic ideas, recalls that "there was a lot of suspicion, and it continued for a while." Piet Slieker has similar recollections: "When Gerard Endenburg intro-duced sociocracy, some people said, 'I don't trust him!' or 'What's the hidden agenda behind this?'" Endenburg himself recalls the resistance, particularly from the company's two unions (the Catholic and Protestant CNV and the Socialist FNV), who balked at the idea of taking responsibility for the company.

Prior to its conversion to sociocracy, Endenburg Electric had a Works Council (Ondernemingsraad), as prescribed by Dutch law, in which all employees could vote for representatives who make recommendations about company policy. At first the two systems operated side by side, but the Dutch government allowed Endenburg Electric to set aside the Works Council and utilize the sociocratic sys-tem to represent employees.

There has been no thorough independent evaluation of sociocracy at Endenburg Electric or at other companies that have used this approach. At Endenburg Electric, it is acknowledged that the general circle functions effectively, but there is greater difficulty in maintaining the department-level circles, some of which tend to lapse into inactivity. That problem might not be due either to the concep-tualization of sociocracy or to the process used to implement it, but to such fac-tors as broader social conditioning and education, and the impact of organiza-tional hierarchy upon those in noncentral decision-making roles. These factors appear to temper experiments such as sociocracy. As with other innovations dis-cussed in this book, there is a struggle in achieving and sustaining the ideals.

In an effort to increase motivation, the management of Endenburg Electric is toying with the idea of employee share-ownership. This has already happened to some extent, because some employees have taken their share of profits in non-voting stock rather than cash, which has the advantage of being tax-free provided that it is left in the company for at least seven years. The company is now con-sidering making the allocation of nonvoting shares to employees as the normal practice for sharing profits. It is also considering giving a portion of the com-pany's reserves to the employees in the form of nonvoting shares because, as Piet Slieker states, "the employees' motivation will increase and they will feel that it is their company." Thus, despite the introduction of this extensive system of employee participation, and neutralizing the influence of capital by placing the owner's shares in a foundation, Endenburg Electric is still struggling with issues that affect other businesses—namely, motivating their employees and enhancing competitiveness in a changing industry. This struggle places a major constraint upon innovation and appears to have the greatest impact when innovation fun-damentally departs from existing norms.

Confronted with declining profit margins during the 1990s, the company is now looking at placing greater emphasis on knowledge creation as its primary service and reducing its involvement in electronics' production and installations. That type of change will require a more highly educated labor force than the company has at present and may be difficult to sell to some of the current work force. Piet Slieker, who will lead the company through this change, recognizes that it represents a challenge, and all the more so because, in accordance with the sociocratic model, the employees will have to consent. "The people who work in the company," Slieker says philosophically, "realize that it's a strange company. I think that's good."

As for Gerard Endenburg, his work will focus on directing the Sociocratic Center and in encouraging other organizations to adopt sociocracy. Combining both idealism and pragmatism, he remains determined to change the relationships of work, but he is constrained by his perceptions of what is possible. He has been working with sociocratic ideas for 26 years and feels that the ideas are applicable not only to the workplace but also to the family and to other social settings. At age 62, he is determined to proceed with the work that has motivated him through much of his life.

ENDENBURG ELECTRIC

1933   Gerard Endenburg is born in Rotterdam.

1943 to 1948   Endenburg attends Quaker boarding school that has a seminal influence upon his thinking.

1950   Endenburg Electric is founded by Gerard Endenburg's parents.

1968   After working in the business since 1961, Gerard Endenburg takes over as managing director.

1972   Following the death of his father, Endenburg assumes absolute control of the firm. He starts experimenting with sociocratic ideas.

1978   Endenburg founds the Sociocratic Center to promote sociocracy in other firms.

1984   Endenburg transfers his shares to a foundation that serves as the holding company for the operating firm. He is paid for the shares over 10 years from the company revenues.

1988   Endenburg's second of three books, *Sociocracy: The Organization of Decision Making,* is translated into English.

1995   Endenburg steps down as general manager of Endenburg Electric to concentrate his energies as director of the Sociocratic Center. Piet Slieker, a company manager, is appointed as his successor.

1995   Endenburg Electric has 110 employees and about Fl. 14 million in annual revenues.

NOTES

Unless otherwise specified, quotes from the following employees of Endenburg Electric and the Sociocratic Center are from interviews conducted by the author in February 1995: Gerard Endenburg, Bert van der Eerden, Rudi Immers, Arie Kriejgsman,

Hanny de Kruyf, Pieter vander Meché, Annewiek Reijmer, Hanny De Kruyf, and Piet Slieker. There are also quotes from Gerard Endenburg and Annewiek Reijmer's writings.

1. In May 2000, Fl. 1 purchased about U.S.$.40.

2. The background section on Endenburg is based upon interviews with Gerard Endenberg and other employees in the company, as well as his book, *Sociocracy: The Organization of Decision Making* (Rotterdam: The Sociocratic Center, 1988).

5

Allied Plywood

The Employee Stock Ownership Plan (or ESOP as it is known) has been widely used in the U.S. to convert family firms lacking a successor to employee ownership. This chapter will discuss the origins of the ESOP in the U.S. and will present a case study of Allied Plywood, a Washington, D.C. firm that in 1982 was converted to total employee ownership by its founders, Ed and Phyllis Sanders. Chapter 6 will discuss the variation of the ESOP used in the U.K., and some comparisons will be made to the U.S. model. Before looking at Allied Plywood, the philosophy behind the ESOP and the social movement surrounding it will be analyzed.

THE CAPITALIST MANIFESTO

The ESOP was pioneered in the U.S. by the late Louis Kelso, a corporate and finance lawyer who, together with Mortimer Adler and, subsequently, with his wife Patricia Hetter Kelso, authored a series of books that argued for a revival of capitalism through a more equitable distribution of wealth. Kelso's seminal work, *The Capitalist Manifesto* (coauthored with Adler in 1958), was presented as capitalism's response to *The Communist Manifesto* of more than a century earlier. Kelso and Adler were highly critical of communism, socialism, and even of the "mixed capitalist economy" (a phrase that they use to refer to current forms of capitalism in the West), and they set out a plan for the transition to a "fully capitalistic society" (Kelso and Adler 1958, 106–7).

On the surface, their analysis had the ingredients of a conservative revival but, ironically, it (like that of Marx and Engels) is grounded in an egalitarian ethos whose objective is to achieve a broad distribution of wealth. Whereas Marxism viewed private property as the root of inequality, Kelso argued that the problem is not private property per se, but the lack of access to it by the average worker. Essentially, Kelso attempted to stand Marxism on its head by demonstrating that its objective of a classless society could be achieved within a capitalist economy. "Capitalism and democracy together," *The Capitalist Manifesto* states, "create an approximation of the ideal classless society in which all men [a term used throughout the book] are citizens and all are capitalists, and which the good life that was possible only for the few in the pre-industrial plutocracies and slave economies of the past becomes equally possible for all" (Kelso and Adler 1958, 255). With a transition to a fully capitalistic society, Kelso and Adler envisaged a "freedom from labor" and a "freedom for leisure" that would permit people to work on building civilization without requiring extrinsic compensation (1958, 19). As these ideals were achieved, the role of the state would be reduced sharply. Although Kelso and associates refer to their goal as a fully capitalistic society and make a logical claim for their use of the term, they also project a society that represents a fundamental restructuring of capitalism as it is currently known.

There are two central points in Kelso's rationale. The first is that labor is of declining importance to generating wealth and, therefore, increasingly the beneficiaries of new wealth are the owners of capital. The second point (related to the first) is that the distribution of wealth is becoming less egalitarian. This criticism of capitalism has a lengthy history predating Kelso and, ironically, is a central theme of *The Communist Manifesto*. That Kelso is a strong proponent of capitalism, however, makes his criticism of monopoly control all the more compelling.

Noting that "90 percent of the wealth of the economy is concentrated in about 5 percent of the households" and that "one percent of all households own 65 to 70 percent of all marketable stocks" (Kelso and Adler 1958, 171), *The Capitalist Manifesto* was highly critical of government for introducing policies that promoted the concentration of ownership. "Instead of using the power of government to increase the number of owners of highly productive capital investments," *The Manifesto* stated, "we have used it to increase the present concentration of ownership" (1958, 202). *The Capitalist Manifesto* also argued that government should not be pushing welfare schemes, which Kelso and Adler referred to as being "governed by the principles of charity and expediency rather than justice" (1958, 196); instead, government should "broaden participation in the production of wealth *as a means of broadening the just distribution of income*" (emphasis theirs) (1958, 236).

Put differently, if capital were widely diffused throughout society and everyone could share in the dividends from its investment, then policies to redistribute income would be less necessary. In effect, the dividends associated with capital ("the wages of capital") would lead to a just distribution of income, and work-for-pay would become a less significant part of people's lives. To achieve this end, Kelso suggested that unions broaden their role and become "producer unions" to "represent their members both as labor workers and as capital workers" (Kelso and Hetter Kelso 1986, 162). In the latter role, they would bargain for an increased stake in capital or (to borrow a current cliché) an increased piece of the action.

The mechanism that Kelso and his associates adopted to achieve their objectives was "capital credit"—not to be confused with consumer credit. Whereas consumer credit entails loans for the purpose of purchasing consumer goods, capital credit involves loans for investment. If the investment is effective, it should lead to increased cash flow that, in turn, would pay off the loan and the associated interest. Therefore, capital credit may also be referred to as "self-liquidating debt."

The Capitalist Manifesto sets out a series of mechanisms whereby capital credit could be made readily available to the public, including low-interest loans by the central bank to finance expansion by businesses with ESOPs. *The Manifesto* drew an analogy to the Homestead Act of 1862, through which the U.S. government passed into private hands billions of acres of land. Instead of land, the distribution would be in the form of capital credit so that the *new wealth* (emphasis mine) created by society would be widely held rather than simply accrue to those who currently monopolized the control of capital. Kelso devoted less discussion to the redistribution of existing wealth, preferring to avoid advocating policies that would lead to conflict (class conflict) between the haves and have-nots. Nevertheless, *The Manifesto* does acknowledge the need for taxation policies and incentives to ensure that wealth in estates with large capital accumulations is transferred in such a way as to produce greater equality. However, the focus of Kelso's analysis was to distribute new wealth broadly through the liberal use of capital credit. Norman Kurland, a Washington attorney and longtime associate of Kelso, elevated access to capital credit to "a fundamental human right, without which economic sovereignty for all is virtually impossible" (1994, 69), and called for an "Industrial Homestead Act" with a package of proposals (adapted from *The Capitalist Manifesto*) that would make capital credit readily available for various forms of industrial development.

A handful of ESOPs were created between 1956 (when Kelso developed the first) and 1974 (when the U.S. government approved a series of tax changes to make ESOPs more attractive). The 1974 legislation, and subsequent amendments in 1984 and 1986, came from the initiative of Senator Russell Long, then the chair of the Senate Finance Committee, and a populist from Louisiana who became the leader in Congress for the ESOP movement. In speech after speech, he repeated the prophetic refrain that: "Unless we do something to change the way in which economic growth is financed, almost all of that new capital will be owned by the same 5 to 10 percent of the population that already owns more than 90 percent of the nation's capital assets" (Long 1984, 6). By the early 1980s, a network of movement organizations (the National Center for Employee Ownership, the ESOP Association, the Center for Economic and Social Justice, for example) began lobbying for improved ESOP legislation. In effect, the ESOP had become the focus of a social movement intended to reform capitalism.

THE ESOP

An ESOP is a benefit plan that is set up by a company for its employees. The ESOP, authorized under the Employee Retirement Income Security Act (ERISA) of 1974, has some similarities to a pension plan in that it contains deferred labor compensation that the beneficiaries (or employees) receive at retirement. But unlike a pension plan, the ESOP invests its assets primarily in the employer's stock rather than diversifying its holdings. Therefore, even though the ESOP operates at arm's length from the sponsoring company, its value (and therefore its benefit) to the employees is tied to the company's performance. In the basic plan, the employer makes defined contributions to the ESOP of either newly issued stock or of cash to purchase existing stock. These contributions, which are tax deductible for the employer, become the capital stake of each employee and of the employees as a group.

A variation of the basic ESOP plan, and one that is widely used, is the leveraged ESOP. In this arrangement, the ESOP borrows money from a lender and uses that loan to purchase a portion or, in some cases, all of the company's stock. The guarantees for the loan and the cash for the repayment come from the company, which passes these payments through the ESOP to the lender. The advantage to the company is that both the principal and interest portions of the loan are tax deductible. This tax benefit represents a significant financial gain, since normally, only the interest portion can be deducted. The company is also able to deduct from corporate income the dividends paid out on the stock held in an ESOP. And the lender, typically a bank, also receives a break in that 50 percent of the interest is free of tax (a subsidy ended in 1996).

As the ESOP pays off the lender, the shares that the company has issued to the trust are allocated to all full-time employees, usually in relation to their salaries. For employees to be entitled to their capital allocation, they must be vested in the plan, something that must begin no later than their third year of company service (although it can happen sooner). Vesting must be completed by the end of their seventh year, at which point the employees have a nonforfeitable right to the shares in their account. Employees normally retain their holding in the ESOP until retirement when the company buys them out. Employees receiving their money before retirement must either transfer it to a retirement plan or pay a 10 percent penalty in addition to their income tax.

If the company performs as expected, employees should accumulate a substantial capital holding over time, which can be reinvested to provide them with a retirement income and with the benefits of future capital appreciation from their investment. For an ESOP to have an impact upon the overall distribution of wealth, the beneficiaries of the plan must reinvest their capital holding which, if undertaken judiciously, could appreciate in value. If the recipients cash in their holdings, as employees with relatively low incomes might be inclined to do, ESOPs will not lead to a broader distribution of wealth. This limitation was recognized by Kelso and Adler: "So far as the creation of new capitalists is concerned, the usefulness of an equity-sharing plan is severely impaired if the arrangements are such that, when the employee obtains his portion of the trust, the equities are sold and the proceeds spent on consumer goods" (1958, 191).

It is not clear at this point to what extent beneficiaries of ESOPs remain capitalists once they receive their entitlement. It should also be noted that even if the beneficiaries of ESOPs retain their capital holding, the impact on the overall distribution of wealth is likely to be small, because stocks involve only about 10 percent of the net wealth owned by U.S. households. Other forms of wealth (for example, real estate, bonds, savings accounts) reflect the same forms of monopoly concentration as stocks (Rosen 1991).

Kelso touted the ESOP as "the Trojan Horse for democratizing American capitalism" (Kelso and Hetter Kelso 1986, 53). By "democratizing," Kelso was referring to economic democracy as reflected in a broader distribution of wealth, not workplace democracy, which he described disparagingly as "participation in management by amateur and unqualified people" (Kelso and Hetter Kelso 1986, 164). Like Spedan Lewis, Kelso's view on this issue was paternalistic. He lacked confidence in the ability of employees to participate effectively in workplace decision making, and instead, emphasized achieving a more equitable distribution of wealth. He differed from Lewis (as well as Ernest Bader), however, in that he wanted employees to become shareholders and to gain the benefits from the increased equity within their workplace and the dividends resulting from profits—both of which he felt were essential if wealth was to be distributed more broadly. Whereas both Lewis and Bader attempted to nullify the impact of capital by placing their shares in a trust and promoting that concept of ownership, Kelso by contrast magnified the importance of capital and made its attainment a basic right of every employee and its broader distribution a social priority. In the U.S., Kelso became the father of the employee share-ownership movement that he hoped would transform the capitalist system.

Participants in an ESOP, Kelso suggested, should have the same rights as shareholders in general. Not all ESOPs have achieved the standard that Kelso proposed. In publicly traded companies, the members of an ESOP are required to have the same rights as other shareholders; in closely held companies, it is estimated that only 15 to 20 percent enjoy full voting rights (McWhirter 1991). Unless an ESOP has full voting rights, the members are limited to voting their shares on major issues such as mergers, acquisitions, and the sale of corporate assets. There are also a small number of ESOPs in which the trustees are "instructed" in their votes by a side election of members of the plan, each with one vote (as opposed to the usual arrangement of members voting their shares). However, in general, ESOPs have been a mechanism for sharing a small amount of a company's equity and for extending either full or partial shareholder rights to employees, but not for changing the relationship between employees and management. Some ESOP advocates argue that a participatory culture is important to the success of an employee-owned company (Blasi and Kruse 1990; Brohawn 1994; National Center for Employee Ownership 1995). Only a small subset of ESOP companies, however, have introduced broad employee participation in decision making.

According to Corey Rosen, the executive director of the National Center for Employee Ownership, in 1996, there were about 9,500 ESOPs covering 10 million employees.[1] About half of the ESOPs have involved the sale of a family business to employees. Through a sale to an ESOP, it has been possible for the owners of family firms (usually lacking successors) to get their equity out of the business and for the business to retain its independence. Of the sales of family firms, about half are majority owned, and of that group about one-third provide full voting rights for such issues as election to the board of directors.[2] However, in only a small subset of firms (about 200 to 300) do employees elect nonmanagement people to the board.

ALLIED PLYWOOD

Allied Plywood is a wholesale distributor of building materials headquartered in Alexandria, Virginia, near Washington, D.C. Ed and Phyllis Sanders, a husband-and-wife team that served as the president and secretary/treasurer respectively, originally owned the company. At the end of 1995, 13 years after the Sanders completed the sale of the company to the employees, it had 189 people working from 13 warehouses and two sales facilities in metropolitan Washington D.C. (Maryland and Virginia), as well as in Georgia, North Carolina, and Tennessee, areas in which the company had more recently expanded. Allied has grown steadily, realizing a 10-year sales increase of 17.8 percent per year to $59 million at the end of 1995, and has been consistently profitable throughout its history.[3]

Allied was started in 1951 in Akron, Ohio, in an abandoned coal yard with an adjoining railroad track upon which a freight car could deliver plywood from a nearby mill. The Sanders arranged orders from a small office with an old potbelly stove that they had removed upon moving in, and a neighbor made the deliveries to manufacturers in a truck. The 1952 financial statement (a year after they started) showed a small profit of $3,000 on sales of only $136, 299.

However, the Sanders, who shared a dream of having their own business, had the strength to tough out the lean start-up period. Originating from middle class families with a business background, they had the confidence and the determination to make Allied a success. Ed was an engineer, with a degree from MIT, and Phyllis was a graduate of North Dakota State, who started out teaching algebra and geometry but "couldn't stand it." After five years of operating Allied in Akron, they decided to move the business to the East Coast where the housing construction industry was booming. After a weekend trip to Washington, they fell in love with the city. They started the company again, selling its assets but maintaining the name, which was eventually registered in Virginia. "We came here cold turkey," Ed Sanders recalls, "just the two of us with $50,000, and started up. Then, it seemed like plenty; today, it would be ridiculous. But it seemed like a more peaceful time."

At first, Allied was strictly a wholesaler, selling only to companies needing plywood for business purposes—cabinet shops, builders, government agencies, lumber yards—that is, anyone who did not buy for personal use. (In recent years, the company has also engaged in a small amount of retailing.) The Washington-area market is highly competitive, and the price of plywood is volatile, with ups and downs that affect the performance of companies like Allied. However, the company grew steadily, and by the mid-70s it had achieved sales of about $6 million, while remaining consistently profitable. Nevertheless, it was a small operation, with only 19 employees and with work relations that were highly personal. Not having children of their own, the Sanders regarded their employees as an ersatz family. "You would see them every day," Phyllis remembers. "You became friends, and you didn't want anything bad to happen to them."

That thought was foremost for the Sanders when they began planning their exit from the company. Like other small business owners without heirs, they considered the available options of a cash sale to another company, trading for stock in a larger corporation that would take over Allied, or going public with the shares. None of these options appealed to them, largely because of concern for their employees to whom they felt great loyalty. "We had opportunities to sell," Ed Sanders states, "but we saw what happened to the employees in other companies that did this. We were so close to the employees." Phyllis adds: "We did not want to do that to them. We thought that because the employees really built up the company, then they deserved to own it."

The Sanders had heard of the ESOP, but their initial impressions were unfavorable. Then one of their employees died, and they were spurred into learning more because Allied lacked a retirement fund. The impetus came from a fortuitous event—a letter to the *Washington Post* by Norman Kurland, a local attorney and proponent of ESOPs. Seeing that letter proved to be a defining moment for the Sanders and their conversion to the ESOP. The Sanders met with Kurland, formed a friendship that has endured to this day, and introduced an ESOP through which they could sell their holding to the employees.

Prior to the introduction of the ESOP, the Sanders considered the direct sale of their stock to the employees. However, the employees lacked the cash, and raising it would have presented a financial hardship to them. Nevertheless, a small portion of the stock was sold in this way. The Sanders also looked into Allied Plywood buying their stock. However, the Internal Revenue Service ruled that such a sale would be a redemption and therefore subject to both income and capital gains tax amounting to 70 percent of the proceeds. The ESOP, which was introduced at Allied in 1977, overcame some of these problems. There was no direct cash outlay from the employees. Rather, the company contributed cash to the ESOP (about 25 percent of payroll per year) which, in turn, was used to purchase shares from the Sanders that were distributed to the employees. By arranging the purchase through the intermediary of the ESOP, both the company and the Sanders made substantial savings on their tax. The company's contributions to the ESOP could be deducted against its tax and the Sanders' proceeds were no longer subject to income tax (though they still had to pay capital gains).

However, the Sanders could have achieved even greater tax savings by selling to another company. In that event, the capital gains tax would not have been paid. Although this loss of income was insufficient for the Sanders to change their strategy of selling to the employees, they became involved in the ESOP movement and lobbied the federal government to change the tax provisions so that owners who sold to ESOPs would receive the same tax treatment as owners who sold to other companies. In a 1978 letter to the Senate Finance Committee, chaired by the Honorable Russell Long, Ed Sanders stated:

Think about our employees. Without an ESOP, few of them would acquire stock in our free enterprise system. Thousands of ESOPs surely are never formed because of taxes which must be paid when stock is sold to an ESOP trust. Why should not employees be able to have "a piece of the action" just as easily as another corporation via a merger? . . . I cannot close this letter without mentioning that ESOPs should be encouraged because they represent new capital in the hands of ordinary workers. There is a repressive maldistribution of capital ownership in our country at present, and I believe it is the duty of our legislators to try hard to give citizens at least the same rules of stock exchanges that corporations now enjoy (Sanders July 17, 1978).

The provision that the Sanders lobbied for—referred to as the tax-free rollover, and also by some as the Sanders' provision—has allowed the tax-deferred sale of stock to an ESOP, provided that the proceeds are reinvested in the securities of another business within one year and the sale involves at least 30 percent of the company. Unfortunately for Ed and Phyllis Sanders, this provision, which was enacted in 1984, came too late to be of benefit to them.

THE SALE

By 1982, the Sanders had sold nearly half of the company to the ESOP, and they had to make a decision about the remaining portion. Both were 61 years old and not yet ready to retire, but the company was poised to expand and the timing seemed right for the changeover. The Sanders appointed their successors. Bob Shaw (their former newspaper boy who started working with Allied doing odd jobs in the warehouse and office during high school and college vacations, and eventually worked his way up to vice president) took over from Ed Sanders as president; Gene Scales (who started with Allied driving trucks and eventually became warehouse manager) took over from Phyllis as the secretary/treasurer. The sale was completed using a leveraged ESOP whereby the company's assets became the collateral for a bank loan to the ESOP that was used to purchase the Sanders' remaining shares. Since Allied had a proven track record as a company with growing sales and consistent profitability, the procedure should have been relatively straightforward. However, in 1982, the ESOP was still not that well known to banks, and the sale of a profitable company to all of the employees (in contrast to a small management group) was unusual. Therefore, before the deal could proceed, Bob Shaw had to find a bank that would provide financing. The Sanders' remaining holding (just over 50 percent of the stock) was evaluated at $550,000, using the book value of the company.[4]

The leveraged ESOP permitted the Sanders to cash out their holding, and it also gave the company cheap financing, because both the principal and interest payments of the loan were tax deductible. However, Allied's cash was tied up until the loan was paid off. "We had to bet the farm to buy out the Sanders," Bob Shaw admits, "and use every bit of our line of credit because it was a cash deal." Had the ESOP not purchased stock from 1977 to 1982, Allied might have been burdened with an unmanageable debt. However, with nearly half of the stock already purchased, the loan was paid off in less than three years (half of the allotted time) and by 1985, the company was in a position to start the process of expansion that it has undertaken for the past ten years.

The straight cash purchase made it possible for the Sanders to make a clean break from the company. "If we were there, we would have been second-guessing everything," Ed Sanders believes. Bob Shaw agrees that he and the other employees purchased a company in a sound financial position without a cash outlay. Ed Sanders recalls with amusement one employee who would kid him that ESOP stood for "Ed Sanders Opportunity for Profit." In general, however, the employees supported the purchase: "There was no mistrust," Gene Scales states. "The company was sound and there was no employee investment. It was like a genie who has popped out of a bottle and has granted a wish. People were happy about it." To ease the transition, the Sanders worked with the new management for five months.

The Sanders' legacy included both the ESOP and a system of compensation that is weighted heavily by company performance. Since 1982, the company has contributed 10 percent of payroll each year to the ESOP as a benefit for the employees. This substantial contribution has permitted long-time employees to build up sizable holdings in their accounts. For employees who have been with Allied since 1980, all (including truck drivers and sales representatives) have at least $200,000 in the plan, and management has a higher stake. Therefore, the net financial worth of long-time employees is very much tied to the future of the company. During the period that Allied has had an ESOP, share values have risen from $200 to about $500.

For newer employees, although the company makes the same contributions of 10 percent of payroll, they have no entitlement to the money until they are vested in the plan. The vesting begins after the third year of employment and increases by equal steps of 20 percent until a 100 percent entitlement is reached after the seventh year. Therefore, there is an incentive for new employees to remain at Allied for at least seven years in order to access the company's contributions on their behalf. Sasha McMurrer, a customer service representative with four years of service, acknowledges that incentive: "It gives me a reason to stay with the company rather than bailing out and going elsewhere." Indeed, Allied has had a very low staff turnover throughout its history.

Having employees with sizable capital holdings ($9 million at the end of 1995) means that Allied also has large liabilities. At some point in the future, Allied will have to meet this obligation, and, consequently, is undertaking liquidity analyses of the estimated costs and setting aside sufficient cash to cover the projected payouts. These allocations, averaging about 25 percent of the ESOP contribution, are placed in a cash account and invested in a diversified set of securities outside of the company. Whereas the value of stock contributions to the ESOP depend upon the performance of the company, the cash account depends on the performance of external investments (which tend to be conservative). Therefore, in the event that Allied became insolvent, and assuming average success in outside investments, employees could expect to receive approximately 25 percent of their ESOP holding.

To meet its obligations to its employees, Allied has to continue to grow and generate increased cash flow, something that it has been successful in doing up to now. Nevertheless, this arrangement puts much pressure on the company and its employees. To a degree, the company (like other companies with ESOPs) is assisted by the tax deductibility of its contributions to the ESOP; thus, for every dollar that it contributes, Allied (based on its tax rate) is actually paying about 60 cents. However, ensuring that sufficient money is set aside to cover the repurchase liabilities is a constant concern. Moreover, this concern is exacerbated because an employee can leave unexpectedly for another job. For example, Allied is currently paying $50,000 per year to an employee with $250,000 in the ESOP when he left the company. In such circumstances, the company's policy is to pay former employees over a five-year period. However, it is also considering whether to delay the initial payout by five years when employees leave prior to retirement. Of concern, also, are unexpected deaths and the desire to pay the estate immediately. To protect itself, Allied has taken out insurance.

Bob Shaw and Gene Scales, as the largest stakeholders and at an age when their own retirements are not too far down the road, have an extra incentive in ensuring that the plan has sufficient cash to cover its obligations. Gene Scales, whose primary responsibility is employee compensation, notes that:

The ESOP can only work if the company increases its profits. If the profits don't increase, the company is likely to go public because that is the only way to raise enough money to pay people off. And in most cases, the top officials get fully compensated and the rank and file get virtually nothing—people with fewer than three years get nothing because they aren't vested and people with three to seven years receive only partial compensation.

Thus far, Allied has been able to grow at a sufficient rate to meet its obligations. But an increasingly competitive market now includes large retailers like Wal-Mart and Home Depot that deal directly with manufacturers who previously purchased exclusively from wholesalers like Allied. Thus, the company is under pressure to expand and to be available to manufacturers in many locations. This expansion, however, has come at a price, because the markets in some of the newer locations have not generated the same level of sales as the Washington market.

The ESOP at Allied may be seen as a major benefit for the employees. It is one piece in a complex compensation system originating with the Sanders—a system that links the employees' fortunes to that of the company. It goes beyond the typical profit-sharing scheme in that the earnings from Allied's program have averaged about 50 percent of total compensation and in good years have amounted to more than double the base pay (set at below-market rates for similar jobs in the industry). In addition to the base pay and ESOP, employees also receive fully paid health coverage (including dental), life insurance, and the use of vehicles by the outside sales staff.

These items may be viewed as the fixed compensation. The variable compensation comes in two forms: a monthly profit-sharing plan and a plan referred to as the year-end bonus. For the monthly profit sharing, which is the primary supplement to the base pay, the company uses the previous month's expenses to calculate a break-even for every work unit (for example, the warehouses). For every $500 over the break-even, 30 percent is shared equally among all of the employees. This procedure gives the employees an incentive to increase sales and to keep their numbers as low as possible (because the more people in the work unit, the smaller the share for each person). Monthly profit sharing also has a leveling effect upon the distribution of other forms of compensation in that everyone in a work unit, regardless of their salary, receives the same share of profits. Bob Shaw jokes that the monthly profit sharing is Allied's "form of socialism."

The year-end bonus is a conventional profit-sharing arrangement based upon evaluations of the employees (including management) by each other. The size of the bonus is determined by senior management, and it is discretionary, meaning payment depends upon the company's net income and the employees' evaluations. Not all employees receive one, and in general it is not as large a part of the employees' income as the monthly profit sharing. The current policy for the year-end bonus represents a change from the Sanders' tenure when all employees received a bonus just before Christmas each year.

Through the payment system at Allied, employees have been able to earn more than the industry norms for equivalent jobs. However, there is a stress factor built into the system that is widely acknowledged by both senior management and other employees. Priscilla Roberts, who states that she has done well by the compensation system, nevertheless expresses the concern of many employees that "it is hard to budget when you never know how much you will make." Gene Scales says: "Six months ago the profits were down and everyone was bellyaching. Now profits are up and everyone has a big smile." During the Sanders' tenure, employees were given a choice whether to participate in the profit sharing or to opt for a fixed salary. At this point, Allied requires that all employees participate in the profit sharing.

For Norm Kurland, who serves on Allied's board of directors, the profit-sharing plan at Allied is an important component of employee ownership: "If you are trying to transform the culture, you want the employees to identify with the bottom line. This is lifting them above the wage system; the sharing of profits comes close to ownership." Kurland feels that education is important to the success of the profit-sharing system. "The problem is that people have expectations because they haven't been educated about how the whole system hangs together. You are always wrestling with the balance between immediate gratification and sustaining the ESOP culture."

One of the arguments used in favor of the compensation system at Allied is that when there is a downturn in company fortunes, as is inevitable in a cyclical service that depends upon the price of plywood and the state of the building industry, the reduced fixed-labor costs make it easier for the company to avoid layoffs. Bob Shaw makes this argument, stating proudly that "we haven't had to lay people off because our base fixed wage is lower than the economy." Although there is some evidence from research to support that point of view (referred to as stability theory), recent findings (Kruse 1993) suggest that the effect is not that great. However, few of the companies in Kruse's research had as radical a system of variable compensation as Allied, and it would, therefore, be surprising if the lower fixed-labor costs did not provide some job protection when there was a business downturn.

DECISION MAKING

Allied started as a very small company in one location and the decision-making processes were relatively informal. After the Sanders sold the company, a five-person board of directors was established, with two places for nonmanagerial employees elected by their peers. However, there has never been a subsequent election, and the board is relatively inactive. Bob Shaw and Gene Scales have assumed the executive position held by the Sanders, and recently Ken Harris, the Chief Financial Officer, has assisted them. Given the expansion of the company to 189 employees, the management and related support structure are modest by corporate standards. Like the Sanders before them, Shaw and Scales have attempted to maintain a personalized style of decision making, but also one that is quite traditional given the expansion of the company to 15 locations in five states. There is no formal accountability mechanism at this point. They have a plan to renew the board of directors and have it represent three stakeholder groups—nonmanagement employees, executives, and outside experts. Under this plan, the employees in various locations would elect representatives. Unfortunately, Scales adds, "we've been expanding so fast that we don't have the time to implement the strategic plan. We don't have secretaries or assistants."

Although Louis Kelso did not want employees to participate in managerial decisions, he expected that employees would have full voting rights as shareholders. At Allied, as in most closely held companies, full voting rights have not been passed through to the employee shareholders; as specified by law, employees have the right to vote their shares only on such issues as mergers, acquisitions, and the sale of corporate assets. There are no shareholder meetings, and the members of the board of directors serve as the trustees of the ESOP. The employees accept this situation, in part because they respect the leadership of the company. Raymond Prozzillo, a seven-year employee, states: "Although we are employee owned, we are not employee managed." However, there is also some question as to whether it would be in the interests of the company for employees to have a more active shareholder role: "It would be very nice in the bigger decisions to have voting," says Priscilla Roberts. "It would make everybody feel part owner, motivate us a bit more, make us feel that we are a team and that we do indeed own the company."

Allied does provide financial information to its employees through both regular reports and the company newsletter. In part, this provision is necessitated by the profit-sharing arrangement, but it has also been part of the company's philosophy from the Sanders' era. Bob Shaw has made it known that any employee of the company can have full access to the books, but to date, only one person has taken him up on his offer. Generally speaking, Allied may be seen as falling into the genre of companies with open-book management (Case 1995; Stack 1992). However, its practices differ in that the goals for both the work units and the company are set by senior management, not by a participatory process involving the employees.

Employment issues such as pay, work conditions, and grievances are dealt with in a conventional manner. Senior management, to whom complaints are individually directed, sets pay. Employees who complain about their pay to each other are subject to dismissal. There is a formal grievance process, but senior management is the final judge. Although the ESOP provides a collective process for dealing with a limited set of ownership issues, there is no collective process for employment issues. These are matters between each individual and management.

CONCLUSION

Allied provides an excellent example of how an ESOP can be used in a small firm to transfer ownership to the employees. It also demonstrates the ESOP's use as a benefit plan. Employees of Allied since 1980, including those in sales and in driving jobs, have been able to accumulate stakes of over $200,000. With continued employment and company growth, their holdings will increase. Therefore, Allied may be seen as a good example of Kelso's philosophy on how new wealth can be shared more equitably. The company's growth represents new wealth that is owned by employees who, under conventional ownership arrangements, would not have access to this wealth. There are two distinct employee interests with respect to Allied's wealth. First, there is the interest of existing employees at any given point in time. Allied will remain converted from conventional ownership as long as the existing employees decide to maintain their ownership. For that to happen, the employees must not only have the will to continue to own the company, but the company must also be sufficiently successful to support employee ownership. If Allied comes under financial pressure, this would be problematic for the ESOP, since the company depends upon increased cash flow in order to meet its obligations to the employee shareholders.

Second, and distinct from the existing employees, is the interest of the retired employees and their heirs, who have withdrawn their capital from the company. Once the employees receive their capital holding, it remains to be seen whether it will be reinvested and allowed to appreciate in value or the capital asset will gradually be depleted as it is liquidated for retirement income. Without other forms of retirement income, this depletion is likely to occur. Unless the employees maintain their capital holdings, the redistribution of wealth (that Kelso anticipated) from converting the company to employee ownership using an ESOP would be reduced.

The use of the ESOP as a retirement savings vehicle leads to the question of whether Allied's employees would have been better off having their retirement income through a company pension plan that, unlike an ESOP, was invested outside of the firm and therefore was not tied to its success. (As mentioned, there is a reserve for the ESOP that is invested in this manner, but not the ESOP itself.) Given the appreciation of Allied's stock by 2.5 times since the buyout, and the company's high level of contribution to the ESOP, it is unlikely that the employees would have come out ahead with a conventional pension plan. But until employees withdraw their holdings from the ESOP and convert them to a more diversified retirement arrangement, in comparison to a pension plan their investment is at greater risk and inextricably linked to the success of the company. This dependency upon company performance is accentuated by the pay system, about half of which is profit related. In theory, the strong tie between earnings and performance should enhance employee commitment and thereby improve the company, but for employees lacking in additional savings, the stakes are much higher than for the average businessperson.

Both the ESOP and the pay system at Allied are intended to emphasize the ownership role assumed by the employees. But that role also differs from that of typical shareholders because it lacks full voting rights. In other words, employee rights are restricted to equity participation and the legally mandated right to vote on major items such as the sale of the company. In addition to their ownership role, Allied's employees have a distinct employee role. Whereas the ownership role exemplifies what can be accomplished through an ESOP—namely, that without any direct cash outlay from employees Allied has become 100 percent employee owned with widely dispersed shareholding—the employee role, in most respects, is traditional. Senior management sets the company's direction with limited employee involvement in policy formation. Other than the bottom line, there isn't a formal accountability structure for senior management.

Given this decision-making arrangement, one might expect that the continuation of the company under employee ownership would depend upon the choice of the next senior management. It would also depend upon the company's ability to generate increased cash flow to cover the repurchase liabilities associated with the employee holdings in the company. Such concerns are not particular to Allied, but are reflective of ESOP ownership in general.

Ed and Phyllis Sanders are heartened to see Allied blossom as an employee-owned company. Now, except for occasional events such as Christmas parties, they view the company from a distance and occupy themselves with volunteer work, such as a lunch program through their church. "The employees have done a super job," Phyllis states proudly on behalf of Ed and herself. And the feeling seems to be reciprocal. Even among new employees such as Larry Testa, there is recognition of the Sanders' legacy and of Allied Plywood being different from other companies in which he has worked.

Allied Plywood illustrates the utility of the ESOP as a mechanism for transferring ownership of an existing business and also for generating employee benefits. Without an ESOP, it is unlikely that Allied and the many family firms like it could have been transferred to employee ownership.

The jury still is out as to whether the ESOP is contributing to economic democracy, as Louis Kelso and associates had hoped. Kelso was not simply interested in employee ownership as an end in itself, but also viewed it as a mechanism for creating a broader distribution of wealth. Having a society in which all members have access to capital credit and are able to share in the newly created wealth was the rationale behind the ESOP and the basis, in Kelso's view, of creating an economic democracy. As noted, he differentiated an economic democracy from a workplace democracy in which employees participate actively in the domain of management. In short, he was not a proponent of workplace democracy, but of a more equitable distribution of wealth. That ideal has been a defining feature of the U.S. ESOP movement, but not all companies with ESOPs live up to the standard that Allied has set. Some businesses use the ESOP to gain advantage of the related tax credits without any genuine effort at creating a benefit to which the company contributes in any significant way (Rosen 1986). In these cases, the ESOP is simply a form of cheap financing. However, about half of ESOPs are being set up in companies in which retiring owners without successors in their families desire to transfer the firm to their employees. It remains to be seen whether this phenomenon will become more commonplace.

Therefore, even though the ESOP movement has grown rapidly in the U.S., and has become a practical measure for creating employee share-ownership, it is not evident that the transformative vision of a broader distribution of wealth that Louis Kelso set out in *The Capitalist Manifesto* can be realized through this approach. Employee share-ownership is a reform movement that can easily be integrated within the capitalist system. Kelso's vision for using the ESOP to redistribute wealth represents a longer-term goal and a more fundamental challenge to the system.

ALLIED PLYWOOD

1921   Ed and Phyllis Sanders are born in the U.S. midwest.

1951   Allied Plywood is founded by the Sanders as a plywood wholesaler in Akron, Ohio.

1956   The Sanders move the firm to Washington, D.C.

1956   Louis Kelso develops the first ESOP in the U.S.

1958   Louis Kelso and Mortimer Adler publish *The Capitalist Manifesto,* the seminal work on the ESOP movement. It is the first of a series of books on the ESOP by Kelso (subsequent ones authored with his wife Patricia Hetter Kelso).

1974   Through the leadership of Senator Russell Long of Louisiana, the U.S. government approves tax changes to provide incentives for firms to create ESOPs. The legislation leads to a broader use of the ESOP.

1977   The Sanders introduce an ESOP at Allied Plywood.

1978   Ed Sanders lobbies the Senate Finance Committee for a capital gains rollover provision for the sale of company shares to an ESOP.

1982   The Sanders sell their remaining shares to the ESOP, thereby creating the basis for 100 percent employee ownership at Allied. The Sanders appoint two of Allied's management as their replacements—Bob Shaw as president and Gene Scales as secretary/treasurer.

1984   Congress enacts the tax-free rollover (also known as the Sanders provision) for sales of company stock to an ESOP.

1985   Allied pays off the bank loan needed to finance the purchase of the Sanders shares and starts to expand.

1995   Allied has 189 employees in 15 locations in Washington, D.C. and in the southeast U.S. Company sales total $59 million.

NOTES

Unless otherwise specified, quotes from the following employees and associates of Allied were taken from interviews conducted by the author in June 1996: Ken Harris, Norman Kurland, Sasha McMurrer, Raymond Prozzillo, Priscilla Roberts, Robert Saldana, Ed Sanders, Phyllis Sanders, Gene Scales, Bob Shaw, and Larry Testa.

1. Personal communication, March 1998.

2. Ibid.

3. Figures are taken from company documents.

4. At present, the shares in ESOPs are evaluated by independent consultants using a series of factors related both to the performance of the company and the industry within which the company operates.

6

The Baxi Partnership and the Tullis Russell Group

The employee share-ownership movement and the associated philosophy of broadening access to wealth have also been influential in the U.K. As will be seen from the two case studies in this chapter, however, there are significant differences reflecting both the Western European tradition for involving employees in workplace decision making as well as the influence of Spedan Lewis's philosophy that the obligations to the current employees must be balanced with those to future workers and to the surrounding community. Whereas the U.S. tradition for employee share-ownership has attempted to create an ownership outlook (often referred to as a "company of owners") by tying both retirement benefits and a substantial portion of pay to company performance, the British model (as shall be seen) values the employee role and accepts that it can coexist with the ownership role.

In this chapter, I shall discuss two firms: Baxi Heating (located just outside of Preston in northwestern England) and a Scottish firm, Tullis Russell, a manufacturer of high-quality paper products. Both are successful multigenerational family businesses that were converted to employee ownership through a combination of direct share-ownership and a trust. Like the John Lewis Partnership and the Scott Bader Commonwealth, Baxi was primarily an endowment (that is, the owners settled for a fraction of what a competitive bidding process would have yielded), whereas shares in Tullis Russell (like those of Allied Plywood) were sold at a fair market value and, in that respect, is a more realistic model for family firms converting to employee ownership.

THE BAXI PARTNERSHIP

Phil Baxendale was the third generation of his family to manage the firm that started in 1866 as Richard Baxendale & Sons and was originally a small iron foundry. After a stint in another of the family's businesses (a laundry near Blackpool), where—in Baxendale's words, "he learned to manage by managing"[1]—he joined Baxi, and in 1955 he replaced his father as the managing director. Under his leadership, Baxi became highly successful in the British market for heating products, its labor force increasing from 60 to nearly 800 by the mid-70s. About this time, Baxendale, then in his mid-50s, began to give serious consideration to the company's future leadership. Based upon his own relationship with his father, which he felt had been harmed after he became the managing director, and upon his observation of other family businesses, which he felt often suffered from depending upon family members for their leadership, he informed his four children that he did not want them to go into the business and would rather they developed their own careers. Baxendale's decision stemmed partly from a principled objection to large inheritances but was primarily pragmatic in that: "It wouldn't be the right thing for them; and the chances of them being just right for the business as it is were pretty small." At the same time, Baxendale ruled out the usual options for families seeking an exit from their business—either selling to a competitor or a public flotation on the stock market—largely because he felt that the likely purchaser would be a competitor acquiring market share rather than someone desiring to see the business continue. Baxendale felt a loyalty to the company's employees, many of whom had worked their entire careers with the firm.

"If the company were bought by a competitor," he argued, "the jobs of our present employees would be at risk and that unique company which is Baxi would disappear. I feel very strongly that I could not sell my share in Baxi to the highest bidder and not care what happened to the company or the people in it. I also believe that the company is not mine to sell, certainly not in the sense I would sell a car or a house" (Baxendale 1984, 4–5).

Immortality, or "continuing forever as an employee-owned business" (Baxendale 1994, 1), was the central objective of Baxendale's vision.

As a result of these convictions, Baxendale, who by 1974 had became the nonexecutive chairman of Baxi (a part-time role in contrast to the demanding managing director's position that he had held for the previous 20 years), began exploring alternatives that brought him into contact with various proponents of employee ownership. Baxendale had neither political nor religious convictions that motivated him. But his experience in the Royal Navy at the end of the Second World War had brought him, for the first time, into a close personal relationship with people from the working class and had helped him to realize that "They're great guys and they're capable of contributing."

Although Baxendale desired a sale to the employees, he was held back by a stereotype that equated employee ownership with "sloppy whole foods and sandals" rather than a professionally managed business. Once he actively began exploring alternatives for his firm, he overcame this stereotype through information that he received from key contacts. One of them was with Robert Oakeshott, author of the influential book *The Case for Workers' Co-ops* and the executive director of Job Ownership Ltd., a nonprofit organization that he set up in 1978 to promote employee ownership. Baxendale's stereotype was also challenged when in 1980 he went on a study tour to the Mondragon Group, the highly successful industrial worker cooperatives in the Basque region of Spain, and, subsequently, when he met the then chairman of the John Lewis Partnership, Peter Lewis (Spedan Lewis's nephew) at a conference. He recalls coming to understand that Baxi "could be a professionally managed, commercially viable company, but owned ultimately for the employees. That impressed me as a good idea."

Even though Baxi was a family-owned firm, Baxendale was in the enviable position of being the principal owner and having to deal with only one other family member with a large holding, his cousin Joan Caselton who was eager to liquidate her interests. (A small portion of shares was also held through family and charitable trusts.) Baxendale's controlling interest in the company and the willingness of his cousin to support employee ownership were critical to his proceeding expeditiously with the conversion. Another important factor was the company's strong financial position. In the year prior to the conversion, Baxi realized a profit of £5.8 million on sales of £30.6 million. Its profits represented a 35 percent return on capital. Sales, profits, and numbers of employees had climbed steadily over the decade.

Baxi's success as a firm has resulted from developing heating products at the forefront of the British market. The first of these, the coal-burning Baxi Burnall, was invented in 1935 by Baxendale's father John, its key component being an underfloor draught fire with an easily removable ash pit below the grate. By the 1960s, the company had moved into gas-heating products with the Baxi Bermuda, a gas-back boiler that was designed for British homes, typically with small kitchens and fireplaces in each room. The Bermuda, which came to dominate the market, resulted in the boiler coming out of the kitchen and being put into the fireplace, where it was covered by an attractive firefront designed to fit the surrounding decor. In spite of attempts by Baxi to limit distribution to specific parts of the country, the demand for the Bermuda was so great that by 1973 the product represented 40 percent of Britain's boiler market. Although Baxi had a full array of heating products, its own network of dealers, and a profitable service business, the success of the Bermuda accounted for the company's strong financial position (even during the recession of the early 1980s) when the conversion to employee ownership occurred.

THE SALE

Baxendale and his cousin agreed to sell the company for £5.2 million, a fraction of its estimated worth at eight to ten times that amount. Although the sale was not a total endowment, the price of less than the 1982 pre-tax profits of £5.8 million, and significantly less than the following year's profits of £8.4 million, left the company in a strong position to move forward. Moreover, because Baxi already had a history of retaining a large proportion of profits and paying only small amounts of dividends to shareholders (£77,000 of the 1982 profits), it was already cash rich and operating without any debts.

In spite of his generosity, Baxendale had to worry about potential tax liabilities that, in his words, would have made him a "negative multimillionaire." Although his share of the sale proceeds of £2.5 million was subject to a capital gains tax of 30 percent (leaving £1.75 million net), he was concerned that the Share Valuation Division of the government would rule that Capital Transfer Tax would have to be paid on the higher value of the company (that is, based upon the estimated value not the sales price). This would have created a tax liability of more than three times the £1.75 net that he had received. About one year after the sale, Baxendale received assurance that there was no liability to Capital Transfer Tax. In addition, Baxendale was concerned that if Baxi bought out his family's holdings using its cash reserves, the payment to the family would have been regarded as a distribution of retained earnings and, as such, subject to income tax. With the assistance of Jo Grimond, the former leader of the British Liberal Party and the first chairman of Job Ownership Ltd., Baxendale met with Nicholas Ridley, the Financial Secretary to the Treasury, and was advised on how to avoid the taxation problem.

Accordingly, the Baxi Partnership Employee Trust was established and given £15,000 by the company to purchase two percent of each shareholder's stock. The company then purchased the remainder of the shares and cancelled them, leaving in existence only the shares owned by the trust. The trust, therefore, owned the entire company in an arrangement analogous to that of the John Lewis Partnership. However, even though Baxendale wanted the trust always to hold a majority of the shares (a 51 percent minimum is specified in the trust deed), and, therefore, be able to protect the company against a sale to an external buyer, he also wanted the employees to hold shares directly which, in his words, would "provide for a long-term reward related to long-term success." Therefore, each year, 7.5 percent of company profits are used to distribute to the employees shares which, under the Finance Act of 1978, are treated as an employee benefit that is tax-exempt after five years. (The required period to qualify for tax exemption has just been reduced to three years.)

The Baxi model therefore differs from Allied Plywood and the U.S. ESOP in two important respects. First, in order to satisfy Phil Baxendale's concern about the immortality of the firm, the controlling interest in the company is held in the trust. Whereas the employees at Allied can sell the company if they desire to do so, the trust at Baxi can prevent that from occurring. Second, in comparison to Allied and the U.S. model that treat shares in an ESOP as a benefit to be realized at retirement, the British model allows the employees to liquidate their shares without penalty after three years (although normally the sale must be to the company).

Baxendale originally hoped that the employees would hold 49 percent of the stock directly, but he now doubts whether that goal will ever be achieved because, to obtain cash, many employees sell their shares back to the trust.

Baxendale attributes this tendency to the slow increase of share values from £2 in 1983, when the Partnership was formed, to just over £3 in 1995. "You could say, these bloody workers, all they want is cash. On the other hand, a sensible man who understands anything about finance would also sell them. You could do better putting your money in a building society."

In 1995, the employees owned about 20 percent of the shares directly; the other 80 percent were held by the trust, which serves as the warehouse for the shares. Each year, the shares are distributed equally to employees, the lowest-paid receiving the same number as the highest. Although the shares carry the entitlement of full voting rights (another difference from Allied), dividends are not paid to their holders; this is because, since 1965, the company has had a cash profit-sharing plan that, in the current context, is viewed as a substitute for dividends. The cash profit sharing, distributed according to salary, has averaged about 10 percent of salaries over the years. To maximize their tax exemption, employees tend to take their cash profit sharing in stock (under a stock option arrangement that the company makes available), hold the stock until it is exempt from tax, and then cash it in.

For employees wanting to sell shares, the company serves as the stock exchange, buying shares and selling to employees wanting to buy. To protect against external influence, only employees of the company are permitted to hold shares. The shares are appraised annually by the share-evaluation division of Inland Revenue through a complex formula that takes account of the historical performance of the company on such factors as net assets, capitalization, and profits. This formula has resulted in a low appraisal of stock but, given its consistency, the low evaluation does not affect the capital gains when employees want to sell. The distribution mechanism for shares is referred to as a Profit-Sharing Share Scheme, a statutory mechanism prescribed by law. Before the annual distribution, the Profit-Sharing Share Scheme buys all of the shares from employees wanting to sell, and if the Scheme requires more for the annual distribution, these can be purchased from the Baxi Partnership Employee Trust. Therefore, to finance employee share-ownership and the related cash profit sharing, Baxi absorbs the following costs against its pre-tax profits: 7.5 percent for the annual distribution of shares; the cost of purchasing shares from employees wanting to sell; and the cash profit sharing, averaging about 10 percent of the annual payroll.

GOVERNANCE

Baxi had a tradition for democratic decision making that preceded the conversion to employee ownership. As early as 1961, Ian Smith, the general manager who succeeded Phil Baxendale as managing director in 1974 and who remained in that office until 1989, set up a works council to which employees elected representatives and that attempted to make all of its decisions by consensus. Following the establishment of the Baxi Partnership in 1983, the governance was transformed into a two-tier structure modeled on the German system. The board at that time, consisting of the managing director and the other executives (five members in total), became known as the executive board; a new council (called the partnership council) was formed as the supervisory board consisting of three trustees (who also had responsibility for overseeing the trust fund) and 12 elected representatives of the employees. As the name supervisory board implies, the executive board was supposed to be governed by it. However, in practice, it did not work out that way. Although the managing director reported to the supervisory board on sales and other basic aspects of company performance, his reports were treated very superficially, and signs of weakening company performance such as increasing overheads were ignored.

Therefore, like Scott Bader and others firms in this book, the Baxi experience illustrates the difficulty that employee representatives on governing bodies have in holding senior management accountable. In this case, it seemed contradictory because the managing director had a past history of working democratically with employee representatives. Yet, according to Phil Baxendale, the attitude was: "We've set up this partnership thing but we don't want to interfere too much commercially." Baxendale blames himself that the partnership council was not more successful than it was. Although he expected that the executive board would be accountable to the partnership council, in practice, the company's managing director decided what he would account for. In retrospect, Baxendale believes that if he had taken the lead in getting the partnership council to monitor the executive board this problem could have been avoided.

As Baxi evolved from a company that operated exclusively from Preston to a multinational group of companies with a cluster of 10 subsidiaries in the U.K. (including the heating company, foundry, and the sheet metal and paint plant that were part of the original company in Preston) and mainland Europe (Denmark, France, and Sweden), the existing governance was transformed again in 1993 so as to give greater autonomy to the individual companies and to create opportunities for direct participation within the subsidiaries. With about half of Baxi's 1,400 employees working in its subsidiaries, the governance that was developed for the Preston plant had become outdated. In addition, the old works council (started in 1961) was still operating alongside the partnership council, a situation that created confusion because the employees were represented by two different bodies. Therefore, to overcome these problems, within each individual company a two-tiered structure was created: a company board consisting of the managing director, the executives of each company, and one elected employee director; and a company council comprised of the members of the executive board plus representatives of the employees elected for a three-year term by geographically based constituencies. The company council had to be presented with any major changes in the business, but its role was changed from supervisory to consultative. The intent was to make decision making more effective.

At the group level, the company structure was replicated, with the main board consisting of the managing director, two other executive directors, three trustees (nonexecutive directors, including Phil Baxendale), and two elected employee representatives. Within this arrangement, the trustees formed the audit committee and served as an independent check on Baxi's executives. Although the group board gave the employees a window into the group's operations, primary employee representation at the group level was the group council, consisting of one employee representative (normally the employee director) of each company.

Essentially, power at the group level is vested with the managing director and the company board, with the employee council in a consultative role. While this consultative role represents an important voice for the employees in company affairs, and embraces a broader range of issues than a union would typically deal with, the employee councils (both at the group and company levels) have largely supplanted the role of the unions (primarily the Sheet Metal Workers and Amalgamated Engineers) rather than added to it. There are collective agreements but their contents are worked through in the employee council rather than in a typical collective bargaining process.

In other words, both at the group level and within each company in the group, the governance consists of one body that is predominantly senior management and another that is predominantly nonmanagement employees, with official authority vested in the senior management body. The employee council attempts to reach agreement with the senior management board (i.e., the legally constituted, official board) not only on such employment issues as pay and work conditions but also on issues more typical of the shareholders' interests such as company performance and business plans. Given that Baxi's employees are in the upper quartile of British norms for pay and well in excess of the norm for U.K. manufacturers of cooking and heating appliances (Oakeshott 1994), it is difficult to argue that they would have done better if there were a traditional approach to collective bargaining. Nevertheless, viewed historically, it would appear that the official status of employees in the governance has diminished from the period of idealistic fervor following the conversion when the employee body was defined as the supervisory board and decisions were taken by consensus. This change at Baxi follows the pattern of the other case studies (that is, a loss of its innovative edge and a gradual shift in a more conservative direction).

There is no simple explanation for this change. In part, it is because the company's financial performance began to decline. Arguably, this decline, after many years of growth, could have occurred under any system of ownership. However, as mentioned, Phil Baxendale feels that part of the reason for this financial decline was the weakness of the original supervisory board vis-à-vis management. In addition, it should be noted that even though employees have accepted the conversion of Baxi to employee ownership, the changeover was not greeted with enthusiasm. Baxendale recalls, "I made the big mistake of thinking that it was self-evidently a good idea, that everybody would see it as such. That was a mistake; they don't see it in that way." Resistance to the conversion was led by union organizers who felt threatened and who had little experience with such a structure. Although the resistance has now evaporated, the employees' identification as owners is not strong, and they do not always take advantage of the opportunities for participation that are available to shareholders. For example, the annual general meeting is attended by only 20 percent of employees. Consequently, employees did not resist the increased centralization of managerial power that occurred when the Baxi Group was created in 1993.

ADDITIONAL OBSERVATIONS

In 1995, Baxi sustained its first loss in the post-war era—£2. 6 million before taxes against sales of £86.7 (Baxi Partnership 1995). The loss followed five years of relatively static sales and of profits that were declining as a percentage of sales. Essentially, the market for Baxi's signature product, the Baxi Bermuda, peaked in the late 1980s. Baxi was able to hold its share of the market (about 20 percent of all boiler sales) relative to its competitors, but the overall market for the product declined as older British houses already tended to have back boilers and newer houses had no need of them. In response to this situation, Baxi has undergone restructuring from a U.K. manufacturer of gas boilers to a European supplier of heating products, investing heavily both in a new product line and in European subsidiaries in Denmark, Sweden, and France that are developing and distributing heating products. As the market for the back boiler has continued to decline, Baxi has developed a cast iron wall-mounted gas heater (the Baxi Solo) and, together with its French manufacturer (Chaffoteaux et Maury SA), a combination boiler/heater designed specifically for the European market. Exports now comprise about 20 percent of Baxi's annual turnover, and the company is banking on a large increase in the export market in coming years.

In addition, since 1993, Baxi has attempted to diversify its production and services to include air management (that is, products for ventilation and ducting) and engineering, a group of companies that manufacture and supply components in support of the heating and air management firms. However, heating products still remain the company's bread-and-butter revenue source, accounting for 82 percent of annual turnover.

Even with its loss in 1995 and its heavy investment in new products, Baxi remains in a strong cash position (£39 million in 1995). Nevertheless, in 1995 there was no profit sharing, and since 1992, share values have fallen by more than £1, prompting a stern warning from the managing director Bryan Gray: "In recent years, profit growth has not kept up with the best companies, and therefore changes are necessary in order to justify above average pay and benefits" (Gray 1995, 5). It is not clear how these changes will affect employees' attitudes toward the Baxi Partnership. To date, the restructuring of the company, which involved difficult changes, has occurred without any industrial conflict. However, if there is a reduction in employee compensation, one might expect that the line between senior management and nonmanagerial employees would become more sharply drawn.

But in spite of Baxi's more hard-headed attitude toward business, and the apparent centralization of managerial authority relative to 1983, it would be inaccurate to argue that the company has suffered a loss of idealism. One of the four divisions that Baxi set up as part of its restructuring in 1993 was specifically to promote and assist employee ownership. Baxi has invested in Capital Strategies Ltd., a London-based firm of consultants who advise on all aspects of employee ownership. In addition, Baxi has launched an Employee Buyout Feasibility Fund to assist companies with an interest in employee ownership to prepare business plans. It has also put £3 million into an Employee Share Ownership Fund for investment in businesses converting a significant portion of their shares to employee ownership. Through these mechanisms, Baxi has already assisted an employee buyout of Barrhead, a ceramic sanitary-ware manufacturer near Glasgow. It has also invested in the Preston North End Football Club, a local professional club that was facing financial difficulties.

These initiatives are but some of Phil Baxendale's movement activities to promote employee ownership. From 1984 to 1995 he has served as the chairman of Job Ownership Ltd., lobbying for improved legislation for employee ownership, and organizing conferences and other events. Employee ownership is more than a passing interest; it is something he believes in passionately.

In 1996 at age 70, Baxendale (known affectionately at Baxi as "Mr. Phil") retired from the firm. Although the firm still carries the family name, he, in effect, severed the family connection that had existed since 1866. He has obvious pride about the Baxi Partnership but also mixed feelings. "I suppose that we are all disappointed," he states. "Spedan Lewis was terribly disappointed that nobody followed his example. I suppose that I am disappointed that nobody has rushed to follow our example, but the legislation in the U.K. was such that they couldn't." Nevertheless, Baxendale remains sanguine about the future of employee ownership in the U.K. and hopeful that other family firms will be influenced by the Baxi example. He takes heart from the conversion to employee ownership of Tullis Russell, the Scottish paper manufacturer, and is gratified that David Erdal, the chairman of Tullis Russell, has become the chairman of Baxi and has taken over from him as the chairman of Job Ownership Ltd., where he will continue Baxendale's work in lobbying for improved legislation and promoting employee ownership in the U.K. David Erdal first met Phil Baxendale in 1983, when he and his uncle (the chairman of Tullis Russell at that time) were actively exploring employee ownership as an option for their company. Although Tullis Russell developed from circumstances that were very different from those at Baxi, there are some striking similarities between the two conversions.

THE BAXI PARTNERSHIP

1866   Richard Baxendale starts a small foundry, Richard Baxendale & Sons, in Preston.
1926   Phil Baxendale is born.

1935   John Baxendale invents the Baxi Burnall and the company becomes a leader in the heating business.

1955   Phil Baxendale, the third generation of his family to be involved, becomes the managing director.

1960   The firm develops the Baxi Bermuda, a gas-back boiler that dominates the British market.

1974   Phil Baxendale becomes a nonexecutive chairman and appoints Ian Smith as the managing director.

circa 1980   Key contacts are made with Job Ownership Ltd., the Mondragon Group of cooperatives in the Basque Region of Spain, and Peter Lewis, the chairman of the John Lewis Partnership.

1983   Phil Baxendale creates the Baxi Partnership, a hybrid of the John Lewis Partnership that also includes employee share-ownership. He also introduces democratic decision-making structures.

1984   Phil Baxendale becomes the chairman of Job Ownership Ltd. and holds that position to 1995.

1995   The Baxi Partnership suffers the first loss in its history, £2.6 million against sales of £87 million. The company has a labor force of 1,400 in its Preston plant and in subsidiaries in the U.K., Denmark, France, and Sweden.

TULLIS RUSSELL[2]

A family who had a history of concern for their employees undertook the Tullis Russell conversion. But unlike John Lewis, Scott Bader, and the other British businesses discussed to this point, the conversion to employee ownership was not an endowment but a sale based on fair market value. The family ownership of the firm was also more complex in that there was not one principal owner who controlled the firm, but a widespread holding among a large number of family members. These factors, therefore, make Tullis Russell a more typical case than the others we have considered. Also, unlike John Lewis and Scott Bader, in which the employees were owners in name but without shares in the company, Tullis Russell (like Baxi) was designed to involve direct share ownership by the employees in combination with a trust.

The Tullis Russell Group is a manufacturer of high-quality paper, with its main plant in Markinch, just north of Edinburgh. Three subsidiaries (one near Glasgow and two others in the English midlands) produce paper for specialized use such as stamps, book coverings (for example, the British yellow pages), board games such as Trivial Pursuit, and the decoration of ceramics and china. Started in 1809 by a printer named Robert Tullis, the company was purchased by the Russell family in two equal stages (one in the 1870s and another in the 1920s and incorporated in 1906 as a limited private company). The Russell family sold the company to the employees in 1994. Tullis Russell employs about 1,250 people, two-thirds in the Markinch plant and the remainder in its three manufacturing subsidiaries and three international sales offices. The company has been consistently profitable, generating £5.3 million of pre-tax profits in 1996 on sales of £141 million, 40 percent of which are exports throughout the world (Tullis Russell 1996).

In the words of chairman David Erdal, the primary architect of the conversion, the philosophy of the Russell family (of which he was from the fourth generation to lead the company) was "enlightened paternalism" (Erdal 1995, 1). Tullis Russell has employed successive generations of families, whose entire work life has been at the paper mill, and has helped to support a local community with limited opportunities for other types of employment. With respect to its responsibilities to the community, Sir David Russell (the chairman in 1947) set up a charitable trust (the Russell Trust) from the 25 percent share of the company that would have gone to his son Patrick who was killed in the war. In addition to donations from the trust, Tullis Russell donates one percent of its pre-tax profits each year to causes within the community.

SUCCESSION

As with many family firms, succession and continued independence eventually became an issue, particularly as the size of the company increased. In the early 1970s when Dr. David Russell (Sir David's son) was the chairman, he explored the John Lewis Partnership model of ownership, but was against it because he felt that the unions representing the employees would be opposed (Erdal 1995). As a defensive measure, in 1975 Tullis Russell's shareholders gave the Russell Trust voting control of the company, its trustees (from family and management) selected because they were in agreement with the Trust's philosophy of maintaining the company's independence in a manner that would serve the interests of the employees. Therefore, the Russell family was open to employee ownership when David Erdal succeeded his uncle ten years later.

Although Erdal's succession represented an orderly process for the company, for him personally it symbolized a sharp turnaround in his attitude toward business. Judging by his rebellious youth, Erdal would not have been a likely candidate to lead Britain's largest independent paper maker. Antiestablishment in his views, in 1973 he became a full-time worker for the Trotskyists, travelling from strike to strike, selling the group's newspaper, and attempting to encourage a working-class revolution. The following year he went to China to learn about that country's revolution, but was disillusioned by the experience. Fortunately for him, Dr. David Russell was desperately searching for a successor from within the family. Although there were 17 family members (as well as a number of trusts) who held shares in Tullis Russell, including 14 from Erdal's generation, they lacked either the inclination or the skills to lead the company. Dr. David Russell, of whom Erdal had been very critical in the past, invited him to join the company, which he did in 1977. After a training stint designed for an heir-apparent and after earning an M.B.A. at Harvard, Erdal took the helm, but not without his idealism, which he channeled into the employee-ownership movement gaining strength in

Britain at that time. "All the time," he stated, "I was looking for ways of redressing the wrongs being done by the system to ordinary people. The revolution was the first idea. This [employee ownership] is trying to produce a very similar end effect, but in a way that works and is evolutionary rather than revolutionary."

Although three older members of the Russell family had to be persuaded of the wisdom of selling their shares, Erdal's advocacy of employee ownership was timely for most family members, some needing financing for their own businesses and others, at retirement age, wanting to liquidate their holding in the company. Yet they also wanted to see Tullis Russell continue its proud tradition of service to the community and to its employees.

Upon becoming chairman and managing director in 1985, Erdal took some initiatives that helped to allay employee concerns about becoming owners and also helped family members to recognize that their needs could be satisfied in this manner. A profit-sharing scheme was set up under the Finance Act of 1978 through which 7.5 percent of each year's profits were used to purchase shares from family members wanting to sell. These shares, amounting to about one percent of the company per year, were then allocated free of charge to employees. This approach, according to Erdal, "Stimulated the appetite in the family for selling their shares." Two years later, an Employee Benefit Trust was set up and was used as a market mechanism for buying and selling shares. The trust purchased £5 million of family shares, using borrowed funds guaranteed by the company. Therefore, when the idea of a conversion to employee ownership was presented, 7 percent of the shares were already owned directly by the employees and another 13 percent were held in the Employee Benefit Trust. More importantly, both the Russell family and the employees began to feel that employee ownership could be of mutual benefit. The other options available to the family—sale to a competitor, flotation on the stock exchange, or sale of family shares to a financial institution—either provided less security for the employees or threatened the continued independence of the company.

Nevertheless, the conversion to employee ownership was not without its problems. The remaining family holding of 55 percent (not including the 25 percent stake of the Russell Trust, which after 1975 was primarily under the control of management trustees) was evaluated at £19.3 million through negotiations between independent merchant bankers representing the family and the company. If the company had to finance such a large sum externally, the borrowing charges might prove too onerous, particularly with a downturn in the highly cyclical paper industry such as occurred in the early 1990s. In addition, the first merchant banker hired by the Russell family was hostile to employee ownership, attempted to persuade the family against the deal and, subsequently, encouraged a competitor to make a bid for the company at a price higher than that offered by the employee trust.

Even though the Russell family might have realized a higher price from competitive bids, that gain was offset by provisions in the 1994 Finance Act which permitted family members to avoid capital gains tax (the capital gains rollover) by selling their holdings to the employee trust (legislation similar to that enacted by the U.S. Congress in 1984). When the 1982 baseline for assessing capital gains in Britain was established, shares in Tullis Russell were only at four pence (an artificially low evaluation that was in the family's interest at the time). The 80-pence evaluation of the shares in 1994 meant that about £7 million (40 percent of the capital gains) would be paid in taxes if the sale were to an outside group. Therefore, the family gained a major tax benefit by selling to the employee trust, which, as David Erdal states, "was a key factor in persuading them that they were not losing out. The broadly favorable feeling amongst family shareholders that they were not only gaining their capital but were also helping to set up something that was of benefit to employees and to the community was a very important element in enabling us to achieve 100 percent agreement."

PROVISIONS OF THE SALE

The purchase arrangement for Tullis Russell was analogous to the sale of a family dwelling by a vendor who takes back a large mortgage to finance the purchase. The Russell family financed the buyout by agreeing to exchange their shares in Tullis Russell for convertible loan stock in the Tullis Russell Group, the corporate name of the company owned by the employees. The employee trust contracted to pay the Russell family members £19.3 million for their convertible loan stock and 7.5 percent interest on the outstanding balance. The convertible loan stock was to be paid off in three equal payments, the first occurring in 1996, and subsequent payments scheduled for 1999 and 2002, when the purchase would be completed. Tullis Russell also had the option to speed up the purchase, as it did in 1995 because of the company's strong financial performance that year.

This arrangement had major advantages for both the employees and the family. For the employees, it reduced some of the risk associated with the purchase, because the family was supportive of employee ownership and, in the event of financial difficulties, it would be easier on the company than an external lender. (A two percent interest-rate penalty for late payments was written into the agreement.) Also, the rate of interest that the company was paying to the family was less than for unsecured loan stock sold on the open market. For the family, their shares in the company were evaluated at a premium, estimated at 77 percent relative to the 1993 evaluation of the stock. The increased value of the shares was due primarily to the improved performance of the company following the recession. In addition, the 7.5 percent interest on the loan stock yielded a large increase in income (from 232 to 269 percent depending upon the type of share) relative to the dividends that were being earned.

As the loan stock held by the family is cashed in, it is converted to shares in the company, bought by the ESOT or Employee Share Ownership Trust (also known as the QUEST or Qualifying Employee Share Ownership Trust) and distributed over several years to the employees. The sale to the ESOT qualifies the Russell family for the aforementioned capital gains tax rollover, and it also makes the company eligible for a tax deduction on both the principal and interest of the money that the ESOT borrows to purchase the stock. (Normally, only the interest of a loan for such a purpose would be tax deductible.) Tullis Russell estimates that this tax benefit will represent a savings to the company of approximately £6 million over the period from 1994 to 2002 when the purchase is scheduled for completion.

Tullis Russell Group shares are distributed to the employees through a number of mechanisms. Each year the company sets aside 7.5 percent of its profits to purchase shares from the ESOT. The shares are purchased by the Profit-Sharing Share Scheme (the distribution mechanism) and then allocated to the employees as individuals—30 percent are allocated equally and 70 percent according to salary. All employees who have worked one year with the company and who have signed a certificate of participation are eligible (currently about 90 percent of the work force). According to the law, these shares (viewed as a company benefit) must be distributed to the employees within 20 years. The Tullis Russell plan calls for their distribution over a 10-to-15-year period, after which it is estimated that the average employee will hold £16,000 of stock, a figure that assumes there will be no change of performance in the company. In the first two years after distribution, the shares are held in trust within the company, but after that time, they belong to the individual employees, who can keep them or sell them. As an incentive for employees to hold their stock, they pay tax upon the proceeds of a sale (under current procedures) within three years of the original allocation; after that time, there is a tax exemption.

Given that more stock is being purchased from the Russell family than is being distributed to employees as a company benefit, Tullis Russell is using the Employee Benefit Trust as a warehouse for unallocated shares. Some of these shares will be distributed to employees who join the company after the current allocation of shares is completed, and others are being held in reserve for various plans to encourage additional share purchases by employees. These plans include: an Executive Share Option in which senior management is eligible to purchase about 5 percent of the ordinary shares at 85 percent of the price; a Save As You Earn plan in which employees commit themselves to save for five years and have the option to purchase shares at the price existing at the beginning of the contract; and a Buy One Get One Free plan.

As noted, the Employee Benefit Trust also serves as an internal marketplace, buying shares from employees wanting to sell and selling to prospective purchasers at a price established by a merchant bank and agreed to by Inland Revenue. Given the company's hefty investment in purchasing the loan stock from the Russell family and in allocating shares free of charge to employees, it has limited the amount for share purchases through the Employee Benefit Trust to £100,000 annually, and has restricted allowable purchases to estates of the deceased, retirees, and those who have left for other reasons. Once these other financial obligations are completed, there should be sufficient cash available for the Employee Benefit Trust to purchase the shares of all employees wanting to sell. It is anticipated that by the year 2004, the Tullis Russell Group's shares will be divided as follows: 45 percent in the Employee Benefit Trust; 30 percent in direct ownership by employees; and 25 percent in the Russell Trust. Although the Employee Benefit Trust and individual employees, including management, will own 75 percent of the stock, the division between the trust and individuals will depend upon the ratio of buyers to sellers and the speed at which shares are allocated through the Profit-Sharing Share Scheme.

SHARING EQUITY

In line with the widely held view on this matter, David Erdal argues that employee ownership "gives you that direct connection, a new relationship to the company." However, he recognizes that the subjective feeling of ownership does not automatically follow from having stock. Therefore, one of the objectives of the transfer of ownership is to make the employees feel that Tullis Russell is their company. Tullis Russell has invested heavily in an education campaign designed both to create a greater understanding of the ownership arrangement and to remind the employees that together they are now the majority owners. The company distributes two newsletters, one using the John Lewis Partnership practice of anonymous letters with replies from senior management, as well as a quarterly magazine and company reports, including the annual financial statements. In addition, there are briefing sessions, training days, and a hotline to answer questions.

The employee holding in Tullis Russell is administered by a share council consisting of 14 representatives elected according to the principle of one person/one vote through geographically based constituencies of no more than a hundred. To ensure that management views are represented, they are cast together into a constituency that also elects a representative. Meeting quarterly, the council attempts to develop policies that satisfy the concerns of the employee shareholders and communicates these to the board of directors with which it meets twice yearly. Both the share council and the group board select four trustees each to administer the employee trusts; the other trustees select a ninth, a legal expert. About 70 percent of employees participate in the elections to the share council, but only 10 percent attend the annual general meeting, an indication that they are still not at one with their ownership role.

Even though the employees at Tullis Russell are gradually becoming the shareholders and are participating more fully in the ownership role, unlike Allied Plywood and the U.S. ESOP movement more generally, the company accepts the legitimacy of the employee role. In other words, everyone in the company has two distinct but related roles: one as an employee and another as a share owner. At Tullis Russell, employee compensation is tied to company performance because it affects the value of the shares and the degree of profit sharing, but this link is not nearly as extreme as at Allied Plywood. At Tullis Russell, there is a clearly demarcated employee role as reflected in the close working relationship between management and the unions representing employees. In two subsidiaries without unions, company councils have been set up to ensure that employees are represented with respect to employment issues. A union/management team planned and organized a work redesign program that involved the company going to five shifts. When the company brought in voluntary redundancy programs to reduce numbers (most recently in the recession of the early 1990s), it was done through a collective agreement negotiated with the unions. Nevertheless, there was initial suspicion on the part of the unions about the distribution of shares to employees and even toward the company newsletters, which, editor Pam Landells recalls, "weren't very popular with the unions because they felt it took away something from them."

Essentially, Tullis Russell is attempting to produce a "change of culture" through a set of policies designed to give employees greater control over their work (for example, work teams) as well as to involve them as shareholders in the ownership of the company. But there are clear limits to this change. At present, the employee shareholders are not represented on the board of directors. The concept of employee directors has been studied by a committee of two board members and two share councilors and rejected in favor of having six meetings each year between the share council and the board. This arrangement, it was felt, would increase the employee involvement in decision making more than board representation.

Therefore, the share council is the primary body for representing the interests of employees as shareholders. Although its authority is subordinate to the board of directors, its views on issues carry weight. Douglas Hamilton, a representative of the engineering department on the council, states: "I think that we are getting stronger all of the time. In the early days, it was all very new, and a lot of people were just feeling the water. There's a lot more interest now." Recently, in response to feedback from members who were dissatisfied with the 70 percent share allocation in relation to salary, the share council challenged the planned distribution of shares. If the company exceeds its profit projections, the share council's proposal (accepted by the board) would lead to a more egalitarian distribution of shares.

ADDITIONAL COMMENTS

For David Erdal, the conversion of Tullis Russell to employee ownership was not simply a method of changing the culture of the company but was part of a broader social agenda to which he has devoted himself in his role as chairman of Job Ownership Ltd. He argues "that the current distribution of wealth produced by capital instruments and the capital markets is wrong." In words that are reminiscent of Louis Kelso, he states: "Employee ownership is a very little used mechanism for redistributing wealth, and part of what I want to explore is how far it can be used."

It remains to be determined whether employee ownership can serve the purpose that Erdal projects. Relative to conventionally owned firms, there is reason to believe that the employees of companies like Tullis Russell will come out ahead. First, any increase in the net worth of the company will be reflected in the value of the shares owned by the employees. Therefore, the employee shareholders become the beneficiaries of investments in technology and other improvements in the company that normally are realized by outside shareholders. Second, the 40 percent of profits normally distributed to shareholders would, because of employee ownership, be available for employees, either as a share dividend or as some other form of remuneration. Given that outside shareholders are demanding more attention to the bottom line, having employees as the recipients of shareholder gains (both dividends and equity) could be a significant financial advantage. Third, the tax advantages associated with ESOTs (for example, the tax exemption on shares held for three years) should lead to greater overall earnings for employee shareholders as well as their company. Therefore, relative to employees of conventionally owned companies, one would expect that the workers in employee-owned companies would be at a financial advantage.

However, if the unit of analysis is a specific company such as Tullis Russell (rather than the entire labor force), there is reason to doubt whether employee ownership would lead to a redistribution of wealth. The initial distribution of shares in companies adopting employee share-ownership plans tends to mirror the distribution of incomes, with higher-paid staff receiving more shares than lower-paid staff. Tullis Russell has made share distribution more egalitarian by allocating 30 percent of the shares equally and 70 percent according to salary. However, over time, there is a tendency for the initial share distribution to become more unequal because, in response to income needs, lower-paid workers tend to sell their shares more quickly than those on higher incomes. In companies where the market for shares is restricted to the employees, the purchasers tend to be the higher-paid shareholders (management and higher-paid professionals)—that is, the people with more available cash and the capacity to forestall liquidating their shares. Although there is some hope at Tullis Russell that this tendency will not occur, there are already indications that it might. For example, the executive share option, which has a 100 percent subscription, will place more than 5 percent of the shares with the senior management. The demand among employees to sell their shares is greater than the capacity of the Employee Benefit Trust to purchase them. Isabel James, who works in the company's finishing department and has been a share councillor for six years, laments the trend: "This is a problem we have every year. It is very hard for people who have bills to pay not to sell their shares rather than go to the bank."

Tullis Russell's policies will attenuate the tendency toward a share sell-off by the lower paid because, during the time that the company is purchasing the loan stock from the Russell family and distributing shares without direct charge to employees, it will not be in a position to finance the purchase of shares by the Employee Benefit Trust from current employees (the purchase, at this point, being limited to retirees and other leavers). However, eventually that constraint will disappear, and the company will be able to finance the Employee Benefit Trust sufficiently to purchase shares from all prospective vendors.

As noted in chapter 5, the U.S. ESOP forestalls this problem by locking in the employee investment until either retirement or earlier departure. This also occurs in some worker cooperatives, for example, the Mondragon Group of firms in the Basque region of Spain (Ellerman 1990; Oakeshott 1978). However, that type of solution—although it may enhance employees' capital accumulations—also creates a large liability for the company that has to be met when employees retire or leave. Furthermore, it is not clear whether having a share-ownership arrangement that leads to a larger capital stake at retirement reduces the tendency of those with lower incomes to liquidate their holdings. That would be an issue worth investigating.

While the impact of the Tullis Russell experiment on employee wealth is in need of research, there is another noteworthy feature of the ownership arrangement. By making Tullis Russell the stock market for the repurchase of employee shares, the likelihood that the company will remain independent is greatly enhanced. Also, the Russell Trust has a golden share that becomes activated if a bid is put forward to purchase the company and is accepted by the majority of the shareholders. Under such circumstances, the trust has the majority of the votes and can block the sale if it desires. The trustees are not legally obliged to block the sale; David Erdal allows that "there might be a circumstance in which the company should be sold." Therefore, even though the Russell Trust owns only a minority of the shares, it still serves (much like the trusts at the John Lewis Partnership, Scott Bader, Endenburg Electric, and Baxi) as the founder's overseer, seeking to maintain the company's independence and to provide continued service to its employees and the community. The Trust also embodies elements of paternalism that are a carryover from the past, in that it retains a veto over the election of directors to the company's board.

CONCLUSION

Both Tullis Russell and Baxi have succeeded in converting family firms to employee ownership through the use of an ESOT. By using a statutory trust, it has been possible for employees to assume the ownership of large companies that they would otherwise lack sufficient resources to purchase. The advantages of arranging employee ownership in this manner were illustrated by Louis Kelso, the pioneer of the ESOP in the United States (see chapter 5), and have been presented by subsequent proponents of that approach. Essentially, the assets of the company are levered to gain tax-assisted financing that permits the sale of shares to the employee trust and their subsequent allocation to the employees. The employees require no direct cash outlay. The approach is similar to management buyouts, the difference being that the beneficiaries in the case of Tullis Russell and Baxi are all of the employees, not just a small management group.

However, Tullis Russell and Baxi differ from the U.S. experience with ownership through statutory trusts in one important aspect. In both cases, the employee trust is subordinate to another trust designed to preserve the independence of the company. In neither case can the employees sell the company to make a quick gain. At Baxi, the trust must hold a majority of the stock; at Tullis Russell, the trust holds only a minority of the stock, but its golden share can be activated if survival is threatened. Although both companies have been relatively successful in satisfying their concerns about preservation, the goal of making the employees feel like owners has proven more difficult. In both companies, individual shareholding by employees has been much less than anticipated, because a portion of the shares are being sold back to the company as soon as they are held long enough to realize a tax exemption. In other words, some employees tend to treat the shares as a supplementary form of income rather than as a certificate of ownership that appreciates over the years.

The lack of feeling of ownership is a general problem in modern companies in which shares are widely held. Phil Baxendale acknowledges the difficulty: "The only people who feel like owners are the owners of a family business. Once the shares get spread, I don't know that anybody feels like an owner."

Although both Tullis Russell and Baxi are struggling with the issue of making the employees feel like owners, they have also had different experiences with this problem. Because the conversion of Tullis Russell occurred after nine years of employee shareholding, a period that included an education program and the development of a share council, the employees were prepared for ownership, and generally have been favorable to it. Whereas at Baxi, because of potential tax problems to the owners, the conversion was sudden, unexpected, and aroused initial suspicion among the employees even though, ironically, the shares were being sold at a fraction of their market value.

David Erdal is optimistic that the growing pains associated with employee ownership will be overcome with education and time. Although he remains involved in Tullis Russell as a nonexecutive board member, Erdal stepped down as chairman in 1996 to focus on helping other companies develop employee ownership. In that regard, he is building upon the work of Phil Baxendale when he served as chairman of Job Ownership Ltd. The dual-trust arrangement at Tullis Russell and the Baxi Partnership—one to purchase shares from the original owners and a second to preserve the independence of the company—is unique. The same is true of the hybrid arrangement of ownership through a trust and direct employee ownership. It will be interesting to follow these cases and observe whether the model pioneered by Baxendale and Erdal will be embraced elsewhere.

TULLIS RUSSELL

1809   Tullis Russell is started in Markinch, Scotland, by a printer named Robert Tullis.

1870   The firm is purchased in part by the Russell family. The purchase is completed in the 1920s.

1906   Tullis Russell is incorporated as a limited private company.

1944   David Erdal is born.

1947   Sir David Russell establishes the Russell Trust in the memory of his son Patrick, who was killed during the war. The trust owns 25 percent of the stock in Tullis Russell.

1975   The Russell Trust is given voting control of the company to protect against external takeover.

1977   David Erdal joins Tullis Russell.

1983   Erdal and his uncle meet with Phil Baxendale to consider options for the company.

1985   Erdal becomes the chairman and managing director. He starts a process of purchasing family shares using company profits and allocating them to employees.

1994   Tullis Russell is converted to employee ownership using an Employee Stock Ownership Trust to arrange the purchase.

1996   David Erdal steps down as chairman of Tullis Russell to focus on movement activities through his position as chairman of Job Ownership Ltd. At Tullis Russell he becomes a nonexecutive director and trustee. Tullis Russell has 1,250 employees in the main plant in Markinch and subsidiaries in the U.K., France, Germany, and the U.S. Sales are £141 million, of which 40 percent are from exports.

NOTES

The Baxi Partnership

In addition to an interview with Phil Baxendale, background information on Baxi was taken from the following sources: Annual Report & Accounts: 1994/95 (1995); Phil Baxendale, From Participation to Partnership (1984); Phil Baxendale, Baxi Partnership Founder's Vision (1994); and The Winding Road to X Efficiency: The First Ten Partnership Years at Baxi (1994) by Robert Oakeshott.

1. Unless otherwise specified, all quotes from Phil Baxendale as based upon an interview conducted by the author in April 1995.

The Tullis Russell Group

In addition to the interviews with David Erdal and the Tullis Russell employees specified in Note 2, background information on the firm was taken from company documents.

2. Unless otherwise specified, all quotes from David Erdal, Douglas Hamilton, Isabel James, and Pam Landells of Tullis Russell were based on interviews conducted in April 1995.

7

Harpell's Press

The case studies in chapters 2 through 6 involve innovations that focus on the quality of the workplace—in particular, the ownership arrangements and the decision-making processes. The case study in this chapter deals with that issue in part, but is also about the responsibility of a businessperson to improve the quality of the surrounding community. This is also the focus of the case studies in chapters 8 through 10.

In 1995, Harpell's Press, a printing and binding business in St. Anne-de-Bellevue, near Montreal, celebrated its 50th anniversary. On the surface, this business with about 140 employees and $13 million[1] in revenues does not stand out from any other medium-sized printing and binding firm. However, buried in its history is the fascinating story of its founder, James John Harpell, and his life's work as a successful entrepreneur, a pioneering adult educator, a muckraking journalist and publisher, and a philanthropic spirit whose acts included the sale at discounted prices to his employees of his highly successful business, the creation of a garden city where some of the employees and their families lived, and the establishment of a community center for the town of St. Anne-de-Bellevue.

SELF-STUDY

There is nothing in the Harpell family history that would suggest the direction taken by James John. He was born in 1874 on a farm near Kingston in south-eastern Ontario, a conservative area known for its concentration of United Empire Loyalists (people who stayed loyal to Britain during the American Revolution), of which the large Harpell family was one. Harpell quit school at age 12, intending to become a blacksmith. However, under the influence of the owner of the foundry where he apprenticed and an older employee, he came to recognize the importance of education and began studying at home, a practice that he called "self-study" (Harpell 1926, 1). He had shown no previous interest in schooling, even having to learn how to read again. The experience of self-study, however, led to a transformation: "This aroused such an intense desire for knowledge that at times I would study all night and work ten hours a day for six days a week in the foundry" (Harpell 1942, 29).

In 1898, at age 24, Harpell completed his high school and registered at Queen's University in Kingston, where he supported himself by teaching part-time, writing, and selling life insurance, until he had completed his B.A. At this time, he left formal education and concentrated upon his career as an agent for North American Life, marrying Annie Turbett, and beginning a family that would eventually include seven children. The relationship of Harpell and his wife, while close and loving, was also traditional; she assumed responsibility for the household and he was the family breadwinner.

An outward-looking man who was always searching for answers to questions by studying the experiences of other societies, Harpell embarked with his family in mid-1909 on a one-year tour of Western Europe, where they visited the major industrial centers. This experience left him with the conviction that the emphasis upon technical education in Europe was central to that continent's industrial success. That idea, together with his own convictions about the value of combining work and study (self-study), formed the foundation for his approach to business.

Shortly after his return from Europe, Harpell and Alexander Longwell, a fellow alumnus from Queen's University, entered into the publishing business, forming the Industrial and Educational Press (later renamed the Industrial and Educational Publishing Co.). Their aim was to become the leading publisher of industrial and trade periodicals in Canada, a goal that they accomplished rapidly through selective acquisitions (for example, the *Canadian Mining Journal* and the *Pulp and Paper Magazine of Canada*). Harpell, who was a staunch advocate of "thrift," attributed his ability to acquire the necessary financing for these purchases to the way in which he was educated—namely, "inexpensive and occasioning little or no interruption in my earnings" (Harpell 1926, 2). In short, he did not view self-study for adults as a last resort, but rather as a preferred strategy for acquiring an education. In that respect, Harpell's thinking might be viewed as a forerunner of one of the dominant themes in adult education—self-directed learning.

Harpell and Longwell proved to be skillful at business, quickly expanding their operation in downtown Toronto (which Longwell managed) to a second plant in Montreal. Although Harpell's business decisions were designed to earn a profit and to encourage growth, his objectives were guided by his social ideals. He wrote: "The business of the Industrial and Educational Publishing Company was not begun in 1911 as an ordinary commercial undertaking conceived in a desire to make a business and earn profits. Of course, it has to earn a fair return on the capital invested, if it is to continue" (Harpell 1926, 3). Rather Harpell's goals were to build a broad movement for educating tradespeople through self-study.

Shortly afterwards, the company sought more space and moved in 1918 from Montreal to the nearby town of St. Anne-de-Bellevue. Harpell fell in love with the community, authoring in 1926 a history in which he referred to it rather effusively as the "Gateway to Canada" because of its location at the junction of the St. Lawrence and Ottawa Rivers and because both of Canada's major railways had a station in the community. Although maintaining his hardheaded attitude toward the business, Harpell was a romantic visionary in his attitude to St. Anne-de-Bellevue. Drawing on experience from his trip to Europe, this unilingual English Canadian set out to transform St. Anne, a tiny francophone community, into a garden city—that is, a rural community, free from urban congestion, where there would be residences for employees within easy access of their workplace. Harpell's garden city, which he named Gardenvale, drew its inspiration from the English town planning movement of Sir Ebenezer Howard. Gardenvale had water gardens with red fish and water lilies, rock gardens with exotic plants, a huge greenhouse, tennis courts, skating rinks, and comfortable homes adorned with flower banks. The houses adjoining the press were located on Avenue Garden City, a wide boulevard with a flowered embankment in the middle, brightly lit by globe-shaped English-style light standards running along the side. As Harpell was to write, the objective was "to give the editors, educationalists, typesetters, pressmen, bookbinders, clerks and other occupants, healthy, cheerful and comfortable working conditions. It [the press] is well lighted, has high ceilings and a perpetually running fountain of spring water on each floor" (Harpell 1926, 51–52). The press building that Harpell constructed had a remarkable resemblance to the public schools of that period.

Although the publications bore the imprint of the Industrial and Educational Publishing Co., Ltd., the press became known as Garden City Press to reflect the image that Harpell intended for the community. In order to construct houses for the employees, a development company was established (Garden City Development Co.). Thirty-five houses were eventually built upon Avenue Garden City.

Within Garden City Press, Harpell established the Institute of Industrial Arts in 1922, "the main purpose of which is to encourage the industrial worker to 'study his job' and provide courses of instruction and study best calculated to assist the young industrial worker to make the transition from the classroom of the school, where he has been in the habit of being taught through lectures, to industry, where he must learn to improve himself through self-study" (Harpell 1926, 2–3). Harpell targeted the "many people who have either never had or who have missed the opportunity of getting an education." The Institute started producing correspondence courses (believed to be the first in Canada) for tradespeople in the various industries for which it published periodicals (for example, pulp and paper). Essentially Harpell, through connections that he made, was able to sell the business community upon the importance of education for its workers. Upon completion of a course, students received a diploma, printed on heavy plate paper suitable for framing, the intention being that it would lead to more pay. Therefore, the motto on the cover of each course was: "Learn More, Earn More."

Harpell also arranged night courses for his own employees, covering the costs himself. He did not require his employees to attend, but he made it clear that these courses were a means for advancement. At Garden City Press, he had the manner of a strict but kindly patriarch who took responsibility for his employees, much like a father in the family. Simone Crévier, who started working at Garden City in 1930 and eventually became the accountant, recalls that Harpell "didn't like the employees who did not want to take the courses." When students completed a course, they took an exam, and successful completion typically resulted in a pay increase of 10 to 15 cents per hour.

Harpell's involvement in education extended to the community as well where, as early as 1922, he helped to organize the Study Club of St. Anne-de-Bellevue (Harpell n.d.a.). At first, the St. Anne's Study Club had an uphill struggle enlisting members, who were expected to study such subjects as Everyday Science, to attend a schedule of lectures, and to take an examination. But by the winter of 1934, the Study Club was in big demand, its French section filling the Town Hall to capacity and its English section occupying the boardroom of Garden City Press.

Until his involvement in the St. Anne's Study Club, Harpell divorced critical social analysis from his educational agenda. Although his adult education programs had social objectives, these were relatively conventional: to help workers improve their education so they could advance in their workplace and to help Canadian industry become more productive through a better-educated work force. However, by the mid-1930s, the St. Anne's Study Club had adopted a more political posture, tackling such issues as the monopoly control of electric power and unemployment. Harpell was critical of the "huge fortunes" that were being made through private ownership of electrical utilities and "the impoverishing of the municipalities and their citizens" (Harpell n.d.b., 9). He wrote educational materials about economics ("Letters from a Business Man to a Student of Economics") for use by students of the St. Anne's Study Club and of other clubs. Primary reasons for this more political view of education were Harpell's frustration with the lack of progress in overcoming the Depression and the need he felt to mobilize people in response to the hardships that were being caused. In that respect, he appeared to be influenced by the Antigonish Movement in Nova Scotia that was also utilizing adult study groups as a mechanism for critical social analysis as well as for organizing credit unions and other types of cooperatives. Garden City Press published the Antigonish Movement's *Masters of Their Own Destiny,* in French, as well as promoting the English edition. In his 1937 book, Harpell also wrote about Robert Owen, whose experiments at New Lanark,

Scotland, in the early nineteenth century, were not dissimilar to his own at Gardenvale.

THE SOCIAL CRITIC

It was not until the 1930s that Harpell introduced critical social analysis into his adult education programs; but prior to his entry into business in 1911, his writings incorporated a trenchant critique of the insurance and banking industries as well as the advocacy of cooperatives as an alternative form of organization. Throughout these critiques, he maintained a populist orientation, his primary concern being the exploitation of the "average Canadian," an expression that he used repeatedly. His negative impressions of the insurance industry started when, as an agent of North American Life Insurance, he was asked to participate in an illegal kickback scheme. Life insurance, he argued, was "the most sacred of all trust funds" (Harpell 1906a, 1). "The so-called profits are nothing more than the over-charges made in the premiums above the amount required to meet the mortuary and endowment elements of the policy and to provide for the expenses. Life insurance reaches its ideal condition when it furnishes absolutely perfect protection, and at the lowest possible cost" (Harpell 1906b, 15–16). After studying the insurance systems of other countries, Harpell advocated two approaches. The first was fraternal or mutual insurance (that is, companies owned by the policyholders), which he argued (in a paraphrase of Abraham Lincoln) was "insurance by the people, for the people" (Harpell 1906b, 21). The second was "strict government regulation of the business of life insurance." The regulation in Canada, he felt, was "weak and inefficient" (Harpell 1906b, 89).

Harpell's critique of Canada's banks was no less forceful. In a 1908 monograph titled "Canadian Banking and Insurance Under Hon. W. S. Fielding, Finance Minister," he undertook a detailed analysis of their shortcomings, particularly their exorbitant interest charges and unwillingness to invest in small communities (Harpell 1908). Fielding must have been impressed with Harpell's critique, because he solicited his assistance in framing the Dominion Life Insurance Act of 1910, and three years after that he became Harpell's business partner, helping him to sell leading industrialists on the adult education courses of the Institute of Industrial Arts at Garden City Press.

Harpell also turned to cooperatives as an alternative to banks. He was familiar with the credit union/caisses populaires system started in Quebec in 1900 by Alphonse Desjardins, initially around church parishes, and also studied cooperative banking in Germany. He wrote:

The whole of the Canadian banking business is controlled by about one-half a dozen people, really by about two. By the existing system, the savings of the whole country are drawn to two or three centres, where they are too frequently used for stock gambling purposes, or from where they are shipped out of the country to be loaned on foreign stock exchanges. A system of co-operative banks would keep within each community the savings of its people to be used in increasing production and for the general upbuilding of the community. Furthermore, a system of co-operative banks would bring to each community its fair share of outside credit, which would be used to greater advantage for productive purposes than it is at present (Harpell 1911, 151–52).

From 1911 to the start of the Great Depression, Harpell toned down his social criticism and concentrated upon building Garden City Press into one of the most successful presses in Canada. He behaved pragmatically during this period, since the sales of Garden City Press's trade publications and adult education courses depended upon the willingness of business leaders to purchase them. However, it was not Harpell's mission just to be a successful businessperson. Once the Depression started, he launched a vitriolic campaign against the insurance industry, and particularly Sun Life Insurance, using as his voice the *Journal of Commerce* published by Garden City Press (Harpell 1932). Sun Life was no ordinary insurance company; at that time, it was the largest in Canada, with assets representing 37 percent of the entire Canadian industry. The directors of Sun Life were from the elite of Quebec business and politics and included the premier of the province, L. A. Taschereau. T. B. Macaulay, the president of the company and the object of Harpell's venom, was the son of the founder and one of the wealthiest men in the country.

Harpell argued that Sun Life had invested in speculative stocks with policyholders' monies and lacked the cash to cover its financial obligations. Sun Life obtained an injunction forcing the *Journal of Commerce* to cease publication and also charged Harpell with defamatory libel. Harpell was convicted of the charge and sentenced to three months in Montreal's Bordeaux Jail, a term that he served in the summer of 1933 after losing an appeal of his conviction. While in prison, true to his love for adult education, Harpell started a library for the inmates. He also wrote letters to the governor on behalf of prisoners, arguing that "there are many young men in this prison as first offenders who should not be here, if the object desired is correction" (Harpell 1937, 88).

POST-SUN LIFE

Notwithstanding the setback in Harpell's battle against Sun Life, Garden City Press continued to prosper, introducing equipment that permitted it to produce large print runs. Harpell was proud that in spite of the harsh economic conditions, Garden City Press did not "consign a single worthy worker to the ranks of the unemployed" (Harpell 1935, 15). As evidence of his view that employers had a moral obligation to help their employees retain their jobs, in April of 1933, he wrote a series of letters to the president of the Banque Canadienne Nationale in Montreal criticizing its dismissal of the son of a typesetter at Garden City Press: "An institution such as the Banque Canadienne Nationale has no valid reason for a policy calculated to enlarge the number of unemployed while it continues to pay dividends to its stockholders," he stated (cited in Harpell 1935, 155). In one of his many follow-up letters to the bank president, he asked: "Who is to feed, clothe and house this man Gauthier you dismissed a few days ago? How much will you contribute to his keep? He has been in your employ for many years at wages so small that he was unable to lay anything by for an emergency such as you now visit upon him" (cited in Harpell 1935, 157). The bank manager, who probably was not used to such correspondence, neither replied to Harpell nor rehired the bank's former employee.

Despite his disappointment about the inaction of the Canadian government in fighting unemployment, Harpell maintained a buoyant outlook, pinning his hopes on American President Franklin D. Roosevelt, for whom he had a great admiration. In Harpell's book, The *New Deal vs the Old System of Exploitation*, he argued that "Our forces are intact and more fit than ever for the day of prosperity which, we feel, will begin to dawn on this continent within a few months, largely as a result of the New Deal inaugurated by our great neighbour to the south" (Harpell 1935, 15). Harpell's repeated forecasts that the Depression was about to end reflected his optimistic and, at times, romantic outlook.

By the mid-1930s, Harpell, who was in his sixties, ceased to have a dual existence as businessman and social critic. These two dimensions of his being became integrated, and he increasingly turned his business acumen to organizing cooperatives that could serve as alternatives to conventional institutions and improve the quality of life in the community. In 1936, he organized an Arts and Crafts Cooperative (also referred to as a "Co-operative Community of Student Workers") to help young men and women work. He stated that the cooperative "will show the rising generation how to make use of the knowledge and the keys to greater knowledge which the schools give them. Such an institution . . . should stand as a bridge over which the rising generation passes from school life into a life of industry" (Harpell 1936, 4). The plan for the cooperative included a community center where the members would display and market their products, as well as a restaurant and hall where young people could congregate. However, the plan was shelved because of differences with St. Anne-de-Bellevue.

Harpell also organized two credit unions—the Caisse populaire de Gardenvale and the Caisse populaire de Ste.-Anne-de-Bellevue. The former, which is still in operation, was for Garden City Press's employees and their families. To encourage savings, Harpell paid the membership fee and also deposited 25 cents a week into each employee's account.

Other cooperatives organized by Harpell during this period were: the St. Anne's Home-Builders, a second-tier cooperative for other home-building societies designed for "assisting in the financing of homes, shops, libraries, gardens, schools, recreation grounds" (Harpell n.d.c., 4); and the Catholic Press of the Americas, for publishing and distributing religious materials. (Garden City Press would later be given exclusive manufacturing, distributing, and printing rights in Canada for all liturgical works of the Catholic Church.) Even as he prepared himself for retirement, Harpell did it in a manner that reflected his idealism and commitment both to his employees and the community of St. Anne.

THE TRANSFER

When his lifelong business partner Alexander Longwell died in 1940, the future of their business became of paramount concern for Harpell. At age 65 he was still in good health and able to work a full day, but he recognized that unless a plan were put in place, the continuation of the business would be in jeopardy. "My life work is nearing completion and with a view to its perpetuation, I wish to strengthen the foundation upon which it rests or, if necessary, to build a new foundation upon which it may be securely placed before I relinquish control" (Harpell 1942, 12).

The first transfer of Harpell's assets occurred in 1929 when he sold his major trade publications to six of his employees associated with the Institute of Industrial Arts (the educational wing of the business). The purchase by National Business Publications Ltd., to be paid in installments from the company's revenues, was negotiated before the onset of the Great Depression. In an act of generosity, Harpell reduced the price by $161,881 in 1933 to take account of the downturn in the economy (Harpell 1937). National Business Publications carried on for 50 years as a publisher of newspapers and annuals before it was sold to Southam Press in 1979.

Next, Harpell transferred ownership of the houses built by the Gardenvale Development Co. to his employees. In 1940, the Development Co. sold the houses to the employees for $40 per month over 10 years (Harpell n.d.c.). In addition to settling with his employees, Harpell was also very generous with the town of St. Anne, donating land for a community center (the Harpell Community Centre), and then, after the Second World War, donating money for the construction of the building. The Centre serves as a meeting place for youth; there is an outdoor pool and day camp in the summer. Upstairs in the Centre is Harpell's most cherished institution—the local library.

With respect to Garden City Press, Harpell first expressed his intentions in 1935 when he wrote "An industry belongs essentially to the community in which it is situated, and there the ownership and control of that industry should always reside. The contract we are working upon, by which the ownership and control of the Garden City Press will pass in perpetuity from the stockholders to those who have been employed in the Garden City Press for a period of at least ten years, is calculated to give permanency and stability to that business" (Harpell 1935, 25–26). Although Harpell's goal was to pass on the firm to his employees, like many of the other businesspeople in this book, he sought to balance two objectives: he wanted to increase the likelihood that the business would survive in the community, and, in addition, he wanted the employees to become the beneficiaries of the business. This became evident when he subsequently elaborated upon his intentions. "Labour," he stated, "is the only factor that creates goods and services as well as the tools and machinery and other facilities necessary to their creation and distribution" (Harpell 1942, 19). He lamented that over the past 23 years, his company had paid over $750,000 in dividends and interest for the loan of capital. What a magnificent job could have been done, had this been ploughed back into the business for the creation of additional opportunities for employment and additional facilities for the training of the rising generation, as well as for the creation of homes and social security of the workers. In the future, all those on the payroll of the Industrial & Educational Publishing Company, Limited, acting as a unit, will be their own employer and each will partake of the entire fruits of the joint efforts proportionate to the quantity and quality of his or her production" (Harpell 1942, 20).

After acquiring Alexander Longwell's shares from his estate, and thereby becoming the sole owner, Harpell organized the sale of his business to his employees in two separate worker cooperatives, one in Toronto and the other in St. Anne. The Toronto operation became Garden City Press Co-operative in May of 1945; initially, 38 of its 120 employees were members. Members held one $100 common share that permitted them to cast one vote at general meetings of the company. At the beginning of the application for incorporation, which Harpell signed, it stated that the purpose of the sale was "largely to convey to our employees benefits of their long and faithful services to the organization."[2] Not trusting the whims of the members, Harpell specifically designated that Percy Bell continue his management role as well as becoming president of the cooperative. Garden City Press continued as a cooperative until 1975 when it was purchased by Canada Law Books, Inc. and converted to a corporation under the Business Corporations Act. The company continued with about 40 employees and closed in 1994.

Although the Toronto operation was important to Harpell, the jewel in his crown was at St. Anne. It was converted to a worker cooperative in September of 1945, under the name Harpell's Press Co-operative (the name changed to Imprimerie coopérative Harpell in 1977). Harpell had written on several occasions about his intentions, but when he made them official, his employees were astonished. Georgette Prud'homme, who worked in the office and was a member of the first board of directors, recalls that: "We couldn't believe it!" A similar sentiment was expressed by Laurent Legault, who started in the company as a typesetter in 1922 at age 16 and who worked his way up to become the president and general manager from 1949 to 1974: "Everybody was surprised he gave us that."

Harpell sold the company for $500,000, to be paid out of revenues in monthly installments over 10 years (Vincent 1984). Of the total amount, $300,000 was to be paid directly to Harpell and the remainder into the cooperative's Educational and Welfare Fund. This fund was intended to promote the principles and practices of cooperation both among the members and more generally. In 1953, prior to departing for New Zealand on a holiday with his daughter Jean, Harpell (by then a widower stricken with cancer, which would result in his death six years later) settled with the cooperative for $412,000 and forgave the remaining amount. It is generally acknowledged that the price paid by the employees was much less than the value of the company.

The transfer of ownership to the cooperative was not, strictly speaking, an endowment, since Harpell was substantially compensated for his holding. However, like many of the other innovators in these case studies, he was the sole author of the conversion, arranging it for his employees who were initially only passive recipients. In the beginning, the employees made neither a direct cash outlay nor held any shares to reflect their new status as owners. The tangible indication of their ownership role was their right as members to receive dividends from any year-end profits (or surplus) based upon their labor contribution to the company (that is, labor dividends) and their right to cast one vote at the annual general meeting with respect to the business of the cooperative and thereby elect a board from their group. By those criteria, the rights accorded the employees through the conversion were similar to the John Lewis Partnership, the Scott Bader Commonwealth, and Endenburg Electric.

In transferring the company to his employees, Harpell maintained the same paternalistic style of management that had been his trademark; in the words of Georgette Prud'homme, "He was the boss!" A tall angular man whose sharp features looked as if they had been carved from granite, Harpell was strict, quick-tempered when he thought workers were slacking, and not above firing those whom he felt weren't doing their jobs properly. As a hands-on manager, he was involved in the day-to-day operations, keeping the same time schedule as his employees and working on the shop floor as well as in his office. After work, he would sometimes take a group of employees to Montreal and treat them to dinner at a restaurant. Although demanding, he was also warm and caring, finding time to inquire about their well-being and joking with them. In other words, his relationship with his staff was not simply that of an employer but also personal. For Harpell, his employees were an extension of his family, with himself as the strict and caring father who decided what was best for the household.

When there were disputes between employees, these were settled in his office, where he was the judge, jury, and court of last appeal. He was perceived as fair, but, ultimately, the decision was his. There was no collective mechanism for the employees to oppose decisions that they found objectionable; nor was there due process typical of grievance procedures. Although Harpell wrote sympathetically about unions and had an advisory committee of printers, from 1922 onward (after some members of the Montreal Typographical Union quit their jobs at Garden City in a dispute with him) he ran a nonunionized shop (Harpell 1937). He would proudly state that Garden City paid more than the standard of the Typographical Union and observed the union standard for hours of work. Harpell, however, liked to keep his own counsel. If he was to be generous, it was because he wanted to be, not because he was required to be by a contract with a union. What he shared with his employees, including the sale of his business, was on his terms, not because of a negotiated process.

Consequently, the transition from a structure of benign paternalism to a worker cooperative, based on a philosophy of workers' democratic control, was not an easy one. In the transition period following the sale, Harpell retained a leading role in the decision-making process. The cooperative's first president and general manager, Paul Desmarchais, was designated by him; Harpell's son John, who was vice president on the first board, became the president and general manager for a brief period; and Harpell sat as president on a three-person supervisory committee that included his daughter Jean. Throughout the transition period following the sale, Harpell maintained an office at the end of the hall on the second floor. Simone Crévier recalls that his presence made the transition "easy because he was here all of the time as a counsellor. . . . When he returned from the greenhouse and caught people talking on the job, he would rap his cane and say 'What's wrong, do you not have work to do!'"

Even though the employees of the company were ill-prepared for the new structure, the cooperative started with an excellent reputation for the quality of its work and with a large financial reserve. To prepare employees for the new structure, courses on the functioning of a worker cooperative were held two nights a week. "It was helpful," recalls Laurent Legault (the incoming general manager), "because many of us didn't know what a cooperative was." However, attendance at the workshops never surpassed 20 percent, and attendance at the cooperative's meetings was also low. According to Paul Vincent (a Quebec author with a special interest in Harpell): "Part of the reason for the low attendance at meetings was that the workers were not prepared to function as a co-op" (Vincent 1984, 23). For most employees, their primary identification with the firm was through their employment relationship, of which they had a long history, rather than as members of a worker cooperative, a role that was recent, unfamiliar, and largely the whim of their former boss. Many employees of the company simply did not understand what was happening. They were doing their jobs, in much the same way as before, but their boss was doing something that was a mystery to them.

But gradually, Harpell faded out of the picture. When Laurent Legault took over the dual role of president and general manager in 1949, Harpell continued to advise him. "He used to come with me down to the press room and the bindery." But shortly after that when the purchase was completed, the cooperative was on its own. Legault, who was general manager and president until 1974, used Harpell as a role model. Although more of the employees became members of the cooperative, the decision-making structure remained hierarchical. Like Harpell, Legault was opposed to having a union in the company: "They tried, but I never accepted that. It was only two guys making trouble; I almost fired them."

Nevertheless, the gradual transition to a democratic workplace continued. In 1974, after Legault's retirement, the cooperative decided that the positions of president and general manager could no longer be held by the same person, thereby reducing the centralization of control. In 1977, the method of paying dividends to members when the company had a year-end surplus was changed from one based on salary that favored the higher paid, particularly management and long-time skilled tradespeople, to one that was equal. In 1982, the probation period for membership was also reduced from five years to three, and subsequently to one year, as required by Quebec law. The one-year maximum specified in the legislation was largely to avoid the lengthy probation period that had existed at Harpell.

Therefore, over time, the membership role became more clearly identified, with all full-time workers becoming members of the cooperative after the one-year probation. About 60 percent attended general meetings and participated in electing the nine-person board of directors from among their group. Over the years, members also became investors in the cooperative through the retention of their labor dividends until retirement. (They were recorded in an account for each employee and the balance received an annual interest adjustment.) This trend to have members invest was precipitated by the financial pressures on the business. In 1994, in order to deal with the company's need for capital, the member investment was increased from $500 to $4,000. (Under Quebec tax law, workers' investment in their place of work is eligible for a tax deduction against income of up to 150 percent of the investment.) These practices resulted in Harpell workers having a substantial stake in the company, typically about $15,000 for those with 20 years of service.

In spite of these changes, however, the employment relationship remained dominant, as reflected in the ongoing efforts at organizing a union. The first such effort that led to certification was in 1981, when the tradespeople organized Local 145 of the Syndicat québécois de l'imprimerie et des communications; a similar attempt to organize the office staff failed. According to Bernard Lecuyer, president of the union local at Harpell: "The union started because the general manager (Maurice Desmarchais) was too strong and he wanted to run everything." Management contested the certification, arguing that a union interfered with the functioning of the worker cooperative, but the Labour Relations Board rejected the appeal, noting that "The management of the enterprise . . . is effectively the employer of the business. The members are under the control of this authority, as are the non-members. . . . The co-operative arrangement does not prevent the workers from arranging their collective products of work with management of the co-operative within a framework of unionization, as outlined by the Labour Code" (Tribunal du travail 1982, 145). The Harpell ruling is widely cited in Canada as evidence that even in a business where the workers have an ownership role, there is still an employment relationship.

After that, the union and the cooperative attempted to negotiate a first contract. But in 1984, when lengthy negotiations were unsuccessful in achieving an agreement and with members of the union under continuing pressure from management, the Ministry of Labour was asked to decertify the union. This time the request was upheld. Bernard Lecuyer believes that "the employees were afraid" and were coerced into decertification. As a substitute, management agreed to a liaison committee to facilitate communication with the employees.

However, the problems persisted, and in 1989, the tradespeople at Harpell again unionized. This time management accepted the bargaining unit—Local 145 of the Communications, Energy and Paperworkers. Pierre Laberge, the cooperative's director of finance, said: "Management accepts the usefulness of the union. It is easier for the company to deal with work-rule matters through the union." Reflecting upon the need for the union, Laberge said of the company's employees: "They were not able to express themselves on the problems that they had to deal with. They were always searching for some third party who would resolve their problems."

Laberge laments this situation and attributes it in part to Harpell's legacy: "They [the employees] saw the general manager as the father of the family—that is, the person who resolved all of the problems. The board of directors," Laberge feels, "did not play its role. Management was too strong. Workers expressed themselves more through their union. If we had operated without a union, we would have had to set up some equivalent."

It is not clear whether Harpell ever intended that the worker cooperative he created would involve broad employee participation in decision making. His goals, it would seem, were to transfer ownership to his employees and to have a strong and effective general manager who, as he had done, would run the company. In the 50 years since the cooperative was formed, those goals were largely achieved. Although employees were co-owners of the business and had related responsibilities, ownership rights had been exercised on their behalf over the years by senior management and, in particular, by the general manager. Through the union, the employees handled their concerns related to employment—salaries, benefits, and work rules.

Yet the union at Harpell did not function like one in a conventional company. Employees had complete access to all financial information both at union meetings and at the cooperative's board and general meetings. As union local president Bernard Lecuyer stated: "I know everything that happens here; I know every penny." And in their co-ownership role, the members of the union had willy-nilly to adopt a perspective that ensured the continued viability of the company and preserved their investment in it. For example, the members agreed in 1993 (the year following a large loss by the company) to accept an 11.5 percent reduction in salary as well as the elimination of overtime pay. This pay cut made it possible for the cooperative to invest $3.35 million in new equipment in order to compete in an industry that was undergoing rapid technological change.

But despite these sacrifices, the company's financial position remained precarious and it continued to lose money. In the spring of 1996, in order to attract outside investors, the members agreed to sell the company to a Montreal firm, Ultimate Electronics, that produces software for printing companies such as Harpell. Through this arrangement, Ultimate has taken over Harpell's assets and has assumed the liabilities. The worker cooperative still exists in name, but only for the employees' investment of about $2 million of nonvoting preferred shares in Harpell Printing Inc. The takeover agreement specifies that Ultimate will gradually purchase the employees' shares from the profits that Harpell earns. However, unless there is a sharp turnaround in the company's performance, it is unlikely that the members of the cooperative will realize much for their invest-ment. It is also anticipated that Harpell's work force will be sharply reduced from its current level.

Therefore, the status of the employees within Harpell has now returned, in large part, to what it was prior to 1945. Unlike that period, however, the company is no longer a family firm led by a father figure who was determined to ensure the jobs of his employees; rather, it is controlled by a parent corporation with a conditional relationship to its subsidiary based upon its profits.

CONCLUSION

The plight of the cooperatives started by Harpell is further evidence of the dif-ficulty in sustaining innovation within a firm that differs substantially from the predominant norms. Nevertheless, Imprimerie coopérative Harpell has had an important role in furthering the worker cooperative movement in the province of Quebec. In 1977, the cooperative began to participate in an advisory committee put in place by the Quebec Minister of Labour, which subsequently became the provincial committee of worker cooperatives. For several years, the president of Harpell was the head of that committee. Moreover, representatives of the coop-erative participated on the executive of both the Quebec Federation of Worker Co-operatives and the Canadian Worker Co-operative Federation. As one of the oldest worker cooperatives in Canada, Imprimerie coopérative Harpell con-stantly received delegations interested in learning from their experience.

In addition to innovations within the firm, Harpell created a business ethic transcending the conventional norm that highlights financial return to the share-holders and was a forerunner of a movement for corporate responsibility that was popularized in the 1980s by such firms as The Body Shop. His objective was to use the firm to improve the quality of the community—through developing pro-grams for adult learners, through building quality housing for his employees, through criticizing the monopoly control of banks and insurance companies, and through organizing credit unions and other forms of cooperatives as alternatives.

Today, most of the people at Harpell know little of the person who founded the company. Among those who had a personal relationship with him—men and women in their mid- to late-80s—there is great admiration for this unusual anglophone from eastern Ontario, who descended upon a tiny francophone com-munity determined, in the best romantic tradition, to transform it into a model of rural and industrial harmony. "If we had more men like him, the world would be better," says Simone Crévier. Georgette Prud'homme, her workmate for many years as well as her neighbor on Avenue Garden City, agreed: "I appreciated him; I wouldn't have changed him for any other boss in the world." Laurent Legault, at age 89, spoke of Harpell almost as if he were a father: "He was strict; that's why he made some good men out of the employees he had in those days. He helped me a lot."

Harpell was not a man who looked back. He did what he thought was best, often acting with great foresight, and then passed on quietly, leaving his legacy for others to manage, and also to transform.

HARPELL'S PRESS

1874 James John Harpell is born on a farm near Kingston, Ontario.

1911 Harpell and Alexander Longwell start the Industrial and Educational Publishing Co. in Toronto.

1918 A second outlet is opened in St. Anne-de-Bellevue near Montreal. Harpell decides to build a garden city where his employees can live. The press becomes known as Garden City Press.

1922 Harpell creates the Institute of Industrial Arts to promote adult education and self-study for industrial workers, particularly in the pulp and paper industry. Harpell also organizes courses for his employees at Garden City Press and starts the St. Anne-de-Bellevue study club for adult learners.

1929 Harpell sells the Institute for Industrial Arts to a group of his employees at a discounted price.

1933 Harpell is convicted of defamatory libel and sentenced to three months in jail for his criticism of the insurance industry and of the president of Sun Life.

1935 Harpell starts organizing credit unions and other cooperatives and uses Garden City Press to promote the publications of the Antigonish Movement.

1940 Harpell gives the houses built by the Gardenvale Development Co. to the employees at a nominal price.

1940 He donates land and subsequently pays for the cost of building a community center in St. Anne-de-Bellevue.

1945 He converts his business into two worker cooperatives—Garden City Press Co-operative in Toronto and Harpell's Press Co-operative in St. Anne-de-Bellevue. The price was to be paid from company revenues over 10 years.

1953 Harpell finalizes the sale and settles with the cooperatives for less than the agreed-upon price, six years before his death at age 75.

1977 Garden City Press is sold into private hands and operates as such until 1994, when it closes.

1996 Harpell Press Co-operative is sold and ceases to be a worker cooperative.

NOTES

I am particularly indebted to Paul Vincent, who made available his extensive collection of documents on Harpell for this research. Vincent's historical summary of the topic, l'Historique de l'Imprimerie coopérative Harpell," completed in 1984, served as a valuable background source. I am also grateful to Pierre Laberge, the director of finance at Imprimerie coopérative Harpell, and his replacement Jean Guy Champagne, for being so helpful in sharing information about the company and making its facilities available for me to do the research. During June 1995, I interviewed the following persons associated with Harpell: Simone Crévier, Jean Harpell, Pierre Laberge, Bernard Lecuyer, Laurent Legault, Georgette Prud'homme, and Paul Vincent. Follow-up interviews were done with Pierre Laberge and Jean Guy Champagne. Any quotes in this chapter associated with those persons are derived from these interviews, unless otherwise specified. I would also like to thank Alison Davidson and B. J. Richmond for helping with the library research related to this chapter.

1. In May 2000, Can.$1 purchased about U.S.$.67.

2. Application for Incorporation. May 18, 1945. County of York, Province of Ontario, p. 1.

8

The Body Shop

The founders of The Body Shop fall into the same broad classification as James John Harpell (chapter 7) and those that follow in chapters 9 and 10. In contrast to most of the case studies in this book, the primary agenda of The Body Shop has been to change the relationship between the corporation and the community (both locally and globally) rather than the ownership and decision-making processes within a corporation. The Body Shop is a leader in the movement for creating an ethic of social responsibility among corporations and is, arguably, one of the most controversial players within that movement. The Body Shop also stands out in another respect: in a business world dominated by men, its chief executive (until recently)[1] and driving force has been a dynamic middle-aged woman who has deliberately and provocatively challenged the most fundamental precepts of corporate behavior. In building The Body Shop into a corporate force, Anita Roddick has worked as a team with her husband Gordon (the chairman of the company). Anita has been the public figure, whereas Gordon has worked quietly behind the scenes. Therefore, The Body Shop provides the opportunity to focus on a woman entrepreneur who has presented a refreshing vision of how a modern corporation can combine skilled business acumen with social activism.

Anita Roddick is not the only businessperson with a passionate interest in social issues. What makes her unique is that she has demonstrated how social activism can be used to enhance the quality of a business. For example, The Body Shop has grown in less than 20 years to an international corporation with almost 1,500 stores in 46 countries,[2] with total employment of approximately 8,500, and in 1995, worldwide retail sales of approximately £600 million (The Body Shop 1995a). The Body Shop International is the parent corporation for this network of franchises. It operates its own shops either directly or through subsidiary companies in the U.K., the U.S., and Singapore, as well as the major production outlets in Littlehampton (England), Glasgow (Scotland), and Wake Forest (North Carolina). In the other countries, The Body Shop International deals with head franchisers who are licensed to sub-franchise with the owners of the retail outlets and, in some cases, the head franchiser also assembles particular products under license from The Body Shop International. Each franchise carries an exclusive line of The Body Shop products and a relatively standardized store design and franchise agreement. In the 1996 financial year, The Body Shop International had a turnover of £256 million, more than double that of five years earlier. Since becoming a publicly listed company in 1984, The Body Shop International has sustained a compound growth of 39 percent in its annual turnover.

The headquarters of The Body Shop International is located on England's south coast, in the seaside town of Littlehampton where Anita Roddick grew up. In the past five years, the headquarters has grown from 400 to 1,500 staff and has become the focal point of the town. Each year about 80,000 visitors from all over the world tour the corporate headquarters (including the research and manufacturing operations), the pagoda-like design reflecting the Roddicks' inclination for the unusual.

Although it has become a multinational corporation, The Body Shop retains elements of the family firm that opened its first shop on the back streets of Brighton in 1976. In addition to its executive role, the Roddick family owns about 25 percent of the stock, slightly more than their longtime friend Ian McGlinn, who loaned Anita £4,000 for the second store in exchange for half of the business. McGlinn has watched his investment grow by leaps and bounds to about £100 million. About 80 percent of the remaining stock is owned by large institutions and a small amount is held by private individuals and by employees through stock options and share-savings schemes available to them. In spite of The Body Shop's radical image, its financial management has been very conservative, with growth financed primarily from the company's earnings and capital raised from shareholders rather than borrowings. In the 1996 financial year, for example, the company was completely free of debt and was actually in a net cash position. In early 1996, The Body Shop abandoned a plan to repurchase all outside shares and go private—a step that would have allowed the Roddicks to put the shares in trust (along the same lines as the John Lewis Partnership) and so ensure that The Body Shop's social agenda would be preserved beyond their tenure. The repurchase would have required borrowing in excess of £250 million and, if undertaken, would have limited the capital available for expansion. Of more significance, the Roddicks were concerned with that level of indebtedness to financial institutions. The Roddicks—who vividly recall being rebuffed by the bank when Anita applied for a £4,000 loan for the first branch of The Body Shop—were worried that the type of company they had labored to create would be put in jeopardy. "The gap between success and failure was too narrow," Gordon states.

Nevertheless, as the Roddicks are aware, the current arrangement is not without its risks for the social agenda that they have labored to build. Although the Roddicks' share of ownership is substantial for a publicly traded company, they remain dependent upon their friend's support and must also be sensitive to the disposition of the large institutional investors who have a stake in the company. Their agenda is to change the norms for corporate behavior, but in pursuing that objective in a fiercely competitive industry, they are keenly attuned to feedback from their investors and clients—that is, market forces.

Even though there are risks involved, The Body Shop will continue as a publicly traded company. The Roddicks would be delighted if their daughters (Justine and Samantha) became involved and perhaps assumed a leadership role. However, they do not intend to use the wealth that they have accumulated to ensure that the company continues under the leadership of their family. Before they die, it is their intention to place their wealth in a charitable foundation. "We believe it would be obscene to die rich," Anita emphasizes, "and we intend to ensure we die poor by giving away all of our personal wealth through a foundation of some kind" (1991, 255). Their attitude, then, is just one of the many paradoxes surrounding the Roddicks: they are wealthy people who shun wealth!

THE FORMATIVE YEARS

Anita Roddick attributes her success to her mother, Gilda Perella, an Italian immigrant to Littlehampton where Anita was born in 1942.[3] From her early years, Anita had a sense of being different, an experience that was reinforced because the members of her family were the only Italian immigrants in a culturally homogenous community. Anita's mother emphasized being different as a positive attribute. "My mum told me 'You are different! You are different! You can do whatever you want.' She pushed me to bravery in everything I did. She rejected every sacred cow." From a young age, Anita developed antiestablishment attitudes, including opposition to the Church, because the local priest refused to give her father a Catholic burial. She also learned about work and entrepreneurship through helping in the family businesses, initially a small cafe, and subsequently, a Spanish-style night club called El Cubana that was an oddity in the staid town of Littlehampton. The night club, she felt, "was a lesson for me about the importance of creating a style" (1991, 47).

Anita's formal education was unremarkable—secondary school plus teacher's college. Her education, it seems, began in earnest after she started a journey around the world that took her to such diverse places as an Israeli kibbutz, Paris, Geneva, and Tahiti. She was very much a product of the social movements of the 60s—the hippie culture and the antiwar and other grassroots movements.

Gordon, like Anita, was travelling around the world when he stopped at El Cubana in Littlehampton. The couple fell in love and started living together. After the birth of their children (Justine in 1969 and Samantha two years later), they embarked upon some small business ventures—a picture-framing business, a small local hotel, and then a restaurant—from which they were able to eke out a living. It was in the restaurant that the Roddicks began the practice of combining social activism with business. On top of the blackboard with the daily menu, Gordon would write political messages attacking the local council. As Anita put it: "This was a foretaste of our belief that business should have a social conscience" (1991, 64). The pressures of running both a hotel and a restaurant proved too onerous and they sold the businesses. At that point, Gordon, who was very much an adventurer and romantic, took off to fulfill a dream of riding a horse from Buenos Aires to New York (a trip that he aborted in Peru), and during his absence, Anita opened the first branch of The Body Shop.

In formulating the plan for The Body Shop, Anita was driven by both a critique and a positive vision. The critique was of the cosmetics industry which, she argues, "hypes an outdated notion of glamour and sells false hopes and fantasy. With the muscle of multi-million dollar advertising budgets, the major cosmetics houses seek to persuade women that they can help them look younger and more beautiful. Yet they know that such claims are nonsense" (1991, 9).

Operating a business with "social responsibility" became the Roddick trademark. The positive vision was derived from Anita's travels to the Polynesian islands and her recollections of the organic potions that the women used for skin care. With only a shoestring budget, Anita found an herbalist who prepared 25 products that were put into recycled plastic containers. Unbeknown to her customers, the containers were the same as those used by hospitals to collect urine samples. Lacking the finances to produce an inventory that would fill the shelf space, she put the 25 products into containers of differing sizes. Brighton (near Littlehampton) was selected as the site for the first shop, because it had a strong student culture supporting alternative businesses.

The business struck the right chord and was an instant success. After Gordon returned from his horse-riding expedition, the Roddicks began franchising The Body Shop concept, at first (in 1978) through informal arrangements and subsequently, through formal agreements. The first U.S. shop opened in 1988, and almost instantly the company had 2,500 applications for franchises in that country. Yet, in spite of its rapid growth into a large corporation, Anita Roddick denies that The Body Shop is a big business, suggesting instead that it is a "multi-local business" often operated by families. "The constant tension for me," she says, "is to keep a small company style in a bloody big company. I want myself to find escape routes to areas where intimacy can be encouraged. I constantly try to challenge the staff; I bring out a magazine from my office [*Gobsmack*] that comes straight from my heart. This is a desperate attempt to keep intimacy; getting them to come back to talk to me."

That conception of The Body Shop as a small business with warm personal relationships is obviously important to Anita Roddick, and it also lays the groundwork for its anticorporate image—a theme that she reiterates in her public statements. In her trail of outspoken criticism of the corporate world, Roddick does not mince her words. For example, in *Body and Soul* she lashes out at top management and directors: "In the fifteen years I have been involved in the world of business it has taught me nothing. There is so much ignorance in top management and boards of directors: all the big companies seem to be led by accountants and lawyers and become moribund carbon-copy versions of each other. If there is excitement and adventure in their lives, it is contained in the figures on the profit-and-loss sheet. What an indictment!" (Roddick 1991, 19).

In one of her lectures titled "Spirituality and Service," she states: "It does not take a rocket scientist to know a basic truth, that business alienates humanity in every way. Businesses are tough places to nurture tender feelings" (1994a, 9). In another lecture titled "Corporate Responsibility," Roddick lashes out at free trade:

According to the theory some call free trade, but I call licentious trade, we should all be happy that the globe is rapidly becoming a playground for those who can move capital and projects quickly from place to place. . . . The new nomadic capital never sets down roots and never builds communities; it leaves behind toxic wastes and embittered workers. You may think this hyperbole. Please go out and check. Visit the cities capital flight has left behind in the U.S. and England. Go to the places I have been around the world where capital has newly—and temporarily—alighted. Hold the mutated babies, genetically handicapped by toxic wastes dumped in local streams. Meet the indigenous communities being driven out of existence" (1994b, 2–3).

In a statement, "Bringing Your Heart to Work with You," Roddick is equally outspoken: "Green marketing done duplicitously to cover a trail of slime is now one of corporate America's favourite pastimes" (Roddick n.d., 1).

Roddick, as these examples suggest, is passionate in her criticism of the corporate world—much like a social activist on the outside. Yet in spite of this image, she is not an outsider. To use her own descriptor: "I have established England's most effective and successful international retailing company" (1994b, 1). The Body Shop is very much a big business—not of the same scale as the multinational giants that dominate the world's economy but, nevertheless, large and growing larger. This, then, is another of the paradoxes surrounding The Body Shop: it is a big business with a chief executive who has espoused an anti-big-business point-of-view.

Another feature of The Body Shop is its reluctance to engage in conventional advertising. This policy is based largely on a feminist critique of the cosmetics industry's manipulation of women—a critique to which Roddick fiercely subscribes. In reference to the large cosmetics companies like Revlon and Estée Lauder, she states, "What they were selling and the way they were selling it was the antithesis of my own beliefs" (Roddick 1991, 95). Even though The Body Shop has avoided conventional advertising, it has promoted itself and its products vigorously, a matter that Roddick proudly notes: "We might not advertise, but we market our products brilliantly, whether it is through striking store-window promotions, by linking products to political and social messages, or by taking a high profile in the community" (1991, 217–18). This represents another paradox: a company that promotes itself vigorously without using conventional advertising.

Through the various types of initiatives in which The Body Shop is involved and through Anita Roddick's high profile and her willingness to say controversial things, The Body Shop is constantly in the news. Roddick estimates that the media coverage of The Body Shop might be worth as much as "£2 million" annually (1991, 218). Although this figure is pulled out of a hat, there is little question of the media coverage's value. Through various types of image-creating strategies, The Body Shop has been successful in promoting itself to consumers that identify with the issues that it raises. People who buy The Body Shop's products can also feel a sense of solidarity with its concerns about the environment, animal welfare, and human rights.

As The Body Shop invests more extensively in marketing within the U.S. market, there is speculation that it will modify its stand on formal advertising. Angela Bawtree, The Body Shop's head of investor relations, is quoted in *Advertising Age* as stating: "It would be wrong for people to think we have some kind of moral problem with using advertising. But using glamorized images or miracle cure claims—those kinds of things you won't see us doing" (Siler 1994, 4). Bawtree's comment seems to suggest a modification in The Body Shop's longtime position that would draw the firm closer to the norms of its competitors.

In spite of The Body Shop's ambivalence with respect to advertising, its public persona is very important. The Mission Statement begins by asserting that the company's reason for being is "to dedicate our business to the pursuit of social and environmental change" (The Body Shop, 1995b, 7). It goes on to affirm that the company will "passionately campaign for the protection of the environment, human and civil rights, and against animal testing within the cosmetics and toiletries industry." The tenor of the Mission Statement and the related Trading Charter, which proclaims that "The way we trade creates profits with principles" (The Body Shop, 1995b, 8), is more akin to what would be expected from a nonprofit advocacy organization than a profit-oriented business. In another of the paradoxes surrounding The Body Shop, these statements almost make the reader forget that they are coming from a business engaged in the retail trade of body products and, even more so, from a company that historically has realized large profits and rewarded its shareholders appropriately.

Therefore, even though it has the trappings of a conventional business—that is, shareholders, management, nonmanagement employees, suppliers, and customers—and has been highly successful in its business activities, The Body Shop has attempted to organize itself in such a way that its relationship to both the local communities served by its retail outlets and the broader global community is based upon a set of values different from those of conventional businesses. Although there may be some disagreement about the extent to which The Body Shop has been able to realize its ideals, the evidence suggests that the image it has projected through its promotions and campaigns has appealed to a large group of consumers and has helped the company's performance. For example, a 1993 survey found that 64 percent of British women had visited a branch of The Body Shop in the previous year and 55 percent had purchased a product (The Body Shop 1995b). In that same survey, nearly 80 percent claimed that their purchase was influenced by The Body Shop's ban on animal testing, and a high percentage claimed to be influenced by natural ingredients, the company's environmental aims, and no wasteful packaging. In The Body Shop's own social audit for 1995, its U.K. customers gave it similarly high marks for not testing its products on animals, trying to be environmentally responsible, and campaigning effectively on human rights, environmental protection, and animal welfare. The assessment of trading fairly with Third World countries is more mixed. Among U.S. customers, "environmentally conscious products" is the most frequently cited reason for making purchases.

It appears, therefore, that customers of The Body Shop are both conscious of its values and positively influenced by them in their purchases. That's not to say that the more standard criteria are not utilized; for example, in the U.K. survey, customers were influenced by the quality of the products, their value for money, and by their excitement and originality. The U.S. study noted similar factors as well as fragrance and nonallergic qualities. These data do not suggest that customers who support the company's values would pay more for products. Evidently, though, they are attracted by the company's image and, when asked, refer to the values associated with the image as a reason for their purchases.

THE SOCIAL AGENDA

The grist for The Body Shop's image is activities organized primarily through its department of Public Affairs. Most large companies have a Public Relations department, but in general, its purpose is to defend the business against complaints and criticisms and to lobby the government for favorable legislation. The Body Shop's Public Affairs department, like the PR departments of other companies, helps to create its public persona, but that is as far as the comparison goes. It is part of a unit (started in 1994) called Values and Vision, consisting of 39 people, many of whom were recruited from nonprofit agencies. Public Affairs organizes social campaigns for The Body Shop, often in conjunction with nonprofit agencies. Gavin Grant, the general manager of Public Affairs, previously served as the director of campaigns and public relations for the Royal Society for the Prevention of Cruelty to Animals in the U.K. His background of campaigning on social issues is typical of the members of the Public Affairs department, which has units that deal with human rights, animal protection, environmental issues, women's issues, and active citizenship. Grant reports directly to Anita Roddick, who also devotes much of her energy to the campaigns. Proposals for prospective campaigns are taken by Grant and his staff specializing in that particular area to the company's board for discussion and approval.

Sue Belgrave, who is general manager of Company Culture (and, indeed, might be the only general manager in the world of a corporate department with such a name), attempts to involve The Body Shop staff in either company projects or in community initiatives of their own choosing. Each employee of the company is granted one half-day of company time a month to participate in such projects. During 1995, about one-quarter of the more than 3,500 employees of The Body Shop International volunteered for community activities and, in so doing, contributed more than 19,000 hours of work. The rates of volunteering were somewhat higher at the head office in the U.K. than in the U.S., where they involved only 9 percent of employees. These figures do not include the volunteer efforts of franchises where the staff are not employed directly by The Body Shop International. Belgrave would like the rates of volunteering to be higher, but argues that it is not possible for the company to "look for activists when we are recruiting. But what we are hoping is that the staff will take the opportunities for participation that are available."

The Body Shop International's investment in its social agenda is considerable, but it is difficult to pin an exact financial value to it. In addition to its investment in the Public Affairs department and the Fair Trade unit, The Body Shop International made charitable donations in 1996 of over £800,000 and through The Body Shop Foundation additional contributions of more than £1 million. The Body Shop retail outlet in Harlem (New York) donates 50 percent of its profits to the local community, and 25 percent of profits are donated by the shop in Brixton (London) and the soapworks factory in Easterhouse, an economically depressed area of Glasgow. Then there are in-kind donations of products with slight flaws, such as The Body Shop massagers that are given to victims of torture, and in addition the volunteer time of staff. Anita Roddick asks: "How do you measure time? How do you measure standing outside Shell for four hours and picketing with 50 or 60 of your employees? Gordon has been over in Brazil for the past four weeks (working with one of The Body Shop community trade suppliers). How do you measure the time lost to the company? It's like breathing; it is so integrated."

The types of initiative taken on by The Body Shop fall into two broad categories: one-time campaigns on social issues, usually in association with other groups; and longer-term projects targeted at groups in need. It is the sociopolitical campaigns for which The Body Shop is best known and, arguably, the part of their social agenda that is most akin to marketing, because it contributes directly to the company's public image. The Body Shop began its campaigning in 1985, assisting Greenpeace in lobbying against the dumping of hazardous waste in the North Sea (Roddick 1991). A year later, it developed the prototype for many of its subsequent campaigns by using its retail outlets in the Save the Whale Campaign, also in conjunction with Greenpeace. This campaign also gave The Body Shop an opportunity to promote jojoba oil, one of its most popular products, which has properties similar to the oil from sperm whales. There was some resistance from franchise holders about being "too political," but Anita Roddick says "That was not an argument I was prepared to countenance" (1991, 112). Subsequently, The Body Shop conducted joint campaigns with Friends of the Earth on such issues as acid rain and ozone depletion. But as the company developed competence and experience with these activities and put in place its Environmental Projects Department, it started conducting its own campaigns. However, maintaining these external relationships was important to Roddick: "I felt a lot happier and a lot more excited mixing with environmentalists rather than financial analysts and stockbrokers. Whenever we had a franchiseholders' meeting, I always brought in an environmentalist to talk to the group, and I made sure that the tentacles of whatever campaign we were promoting spread right through the company" (1991, 116).

Since the mid-80s, when its campaigning practices started, The Body Shop has broadened the range of issues that it has addressed and strengthened its infrastructure for mounting campaigns. The campaigns involve animal welfare, environmental issues, and human rights. Some high-profile international campaigns are: CITES (Convention on International Trade in Endangered Species)—a petition campaign calling for stricter enforcement of rules to protect endangered species from illicit and harmful trade; No Time to Waste—promoting customer awareness of energy conservation and waste reduction; and Ken Saro-Wiwa and Ogoni Justice—a letter-writing and lobbying campaign to draw attention to the human rights and environmental abuses of the Ogoni tribe in southern Nigeria and the execution by the Nigerian government of political activist Ken Saro-Wiwa. In this campaign, The Body Shop has taken on Shell Oil, a megacorporation by comparison.

At any given point in time, dozens of The Body Shop campaigns are in operation. Many are initiated through the head office in the U.K., but some come from the franchises in other countries. For example, The Body Shop in Australia and New Zealand initiated a campaign against nuclear testing by the French government named: "Would They Do It in Paris?" The Body Shop International provided assistance. Such a campaign enjoyed broad support in Australia and New Zealand, but was much less popular in France where there are a similar number of branches of The Body Shop. The Body Shop in Canada has initiated campaigns denouncing violence against women, a theme that has been picked up by The Body Shop International for promotion in other countries.

The Body Shop also has become increasingly adept at lobbying governments. When The Body Shop in Australia and New Zealand mounted its campaign against nuclear testing by France, the head office used its political clout in Europe to open doors so that influential politicians could be lobbied. Gavin Grant says: "It confuses the hell out of people who think, 'You're a skin and hair corporation. What are you doing organizing people from the South Pacific against nuclear testing? What are you doing with these people from Nigeria?'" Quite often, The Body Shop provides logistical support for social organizations such as Amnesty International, Greenpeace, and some lesser-known groups. Grant states proudly: "What we have done is to provide a platform for social activism."

In addition to its issue campaigns, The Body Shop gets involved in longer-term projects that are of a lower profile. These are typically focused on groups in need both in the U.K. and internationally. In the U.K., projects have included *The Big Issue,* a newspaper for the homeless that provides jobs for members of that group. The Body Shop invested about £550 in the project, which is now self-sufficient. The company built its soap factory in Easterhouse, a slum area in Glasgow, and it currently provides 130 jobs. The Body Shop also provides its expertise to various charities in the U.K. on an ongoing basis.

Internationally, The Body Shop has developed a program called Community Trade (formerly called Trade Not Aid), which involves paying a fair price for raw materials and accessories purchased from communities in need. Some examples are: the purchase of Brazil nut oil from Kayapo villages in the Brazilian Amazon; products made from jute fibre from CORR The Jute Works, a trading organization of women's producer groups in Bangladesh; and the purchase of shea butter from a women's cooperative in the Tamale region of Ghana. Through Community Trade, The Body Shop purchases products from 23 suppliers in 13 countries, including the Phillipines, Zambia, Nepal, India, Mexico, Russia, and Nicaragua. In the financial year 1994/95, accessories and raw materials from these suppliers accounted for 17.8 percent (£2.1 million) and 2.2 percent (£183,521), respectively, of all those purchased by The Body Shop International (The Body Shop 1995b). Relative to the previous year, The Body Shop International's expenditure on Community Trade increased by one-third in 1994/95, and is projected to increase further.

One of The Body Shop's major projects is Children on the Edge (formerly known as the Eastern Europe Relief Drive), started in 1990 after the fall of the Ceaucescu regime in Romania, and extended more recently to Albania. The objective of the drive is to renovate orphanages where thousands of children have been abandoned. Hundreds of volunteers from The Body Shop in the U.K., Canada, U.S., and Japan have volunteered their time to assist in this work, which has been financed by The Body Shop Foundation. A similar-type project is the Brazilian Healthcare Project, which has led to immunization, hospitals, and healthcare education for Indians in 18 villages in the Funai region of the Amazon.

The various campaigns and projects that The Body Shop has undertaken are the basis for its public image as a socially responsible corporation. Whereas most cosmetics companies market their products with a promise of beauty and youth, The Body Shop is marketing social consciousness. People involved in organizing the campaigns recognize that the success of the business is the bottom line. John Grounds, the former head of public relations, is quite blunt about this point: "You only succeed in being a socially responsible business if you first succeed in being a business. You can't make change if you don't survive. So entrepreneurship and the ability to make money is very important." Steve McIvor, an animal welfare activist who heads up animal welfare policy and campaigns in the Public Affairs department of The Body Shop, indicates that "there is a point where we try to balance the commercial success of the company and the values. People like us are non-commercial people with strong ethical views. We are not brought in to say the right thing." Nevertheless, McIvor, who meets regularly with animal welfare groups in both the U.K. and internationally to search for common issues upon which they can mount campaigns, recognizes that there is a pragmatism of which he must be conscious and which might differ from that of other animal welfare activists. "In different markets," he states, "certain causes turn people on and turn people off. Animal testing is a big issue in the U.K. but not in Japan. I doubt whether there is one issue that crosses all markets. Nevertheless, The Body Shop still is campaigning actively against animal testing in countries like Japan where the issue is less popular."

Pragmatism enters into some issues (for example, animal welfare) more than others (for example, human rights). Richard Boele, the human rights coordinator in Public Affairs, who came to The Body Shop after three years with a little-known organization called Unrepresented Nations and Peoples, states that: "When I campaign on human rights issues, very rarely do I have commercial considerations in mind." When one dissects The Body Shop's campaigns, they are well organized, neatly packaged and, some might claim, quite slick. The campaigns do not promote particular products, but they do market the company that is selling those products. Yet, at the same time, it is impossible to dismiss the impact of these campaigns upon important social issues. In some respects, The Body Shop is in a stronger position to be effective on these issues because, on the surface, it has less of a vested interest in endangered species or the victims of torture than such organizations as Greenpeace and Amnesty International. Also, in a world in which multinational corporations have become a new plutocracy, a rising star within this elite (albeit one that would prefer to disassociate itself from the others) often carries greater clout than a nonprofit campaigning on a social issue.

THE NEW ICON

The success of The Body Shop in marketing itself as a socially responsible corporation also has had a downside. As The Body Shop has grown in stature, it has been subject to criticism that its practices do not measure up to the standards it advocates for others. The criticism started in 1992 with a program on British television (Channel 4) and was followed a couple of years later by a series of articles in the North American press by freelance journalist Jon Entine (Entine 1994; 1995a; 1995b). This criticism led to a spate of secondary commentaries in the media and dumping of The Body Shop stock, with the consequence that at one point the share value was halved. There is an irony to this criticism in that Anita Roddick, who achieved much publicity through being an anticorporate iconoclast, had essentially become an icon who was under attack for being the CEO of a corporation that was not living up to its ideals.

Although the criticism has ranged broadly, much of it has focused upon claims that The Body Shop's animal welfare practices—which have been central to the company's campaigns—are incongruent with what has been espoused. The Body Shop used to apply what was referred to as a Five Year Rolling Purchasing Rule, which meant that its suppliers must not have tested its ingredients on animals within the past five years. Although this allowed the use of ingredients that were tested prior to the five-year period, the vast majority of ingredients purchased by The Body Shop were free of animal testing by its suppliers. The Body Shop strengthened its policy in January, 1996, to state that no ingredient tested by suppliers for cosmetic purposes after the set date of December 31, 1990, would be used.

In an effort to protect its reputation, The Body Shop took Channel 4 to court and won a libel case for defamation. As part of the court's judgment, Channel 4 was restricted from publishing words or images indicating that The Body Shop's "policy on animal testing is no better than that of other major cosmetics companies" (Queen's Bench July 30, 1993, 4). Gordon Roddick also sent a detailed rebuttal of Jon Entine's criticisms to the subscribers of *Business Ethics,* one of the publications that picked up Entine's work (G. Roddick 1994). However, the public criticism signalled an end of innocence for the company and a process of internal re-evaluation. "After the Channel 4 libel case," Gordon Roddick states, "we ourselves began the process of producing a methodology for a definitive social audit of our company, following the lead of Ben & Jerry's (an ice cream franchise based in the U.S. that has been a leader in the corporate responsibility movement [Lager 1994]) and other companies. It is a mammoth undertaking, aimed at analyzing our social performance against the expectation created by ourselves and others" (G. Roddick 1994, 10). The Body Shop's auditing process has been prepared with the assistance of a British organization, the New Economics Foundation. The audits are extensive and include a detailed accounting of successes and shortcomings for social and environmental practices, including animal protection, as well as a study of employee-management relations. At the end of each section, there is a statement from the relevant senior management person, who indicates steps to be taken to remedy the problems.

The criticism of The Body Shop and the company's response with an open audit of its procedures reflects a stocktaking that is occurring throughout the movement for more responsible businesses. In recent years, there has been a tactical retreat from viewing social responsibility as an absolute to defining it as a relative position that looks for improvements over time. Relative to its formative period, the norms for this movement have converged with the standards for business in general. For example, Business for Social Responsibility, a U.S. organization with 800 corporate members, has opted for an all-inclusive membership policy rather than one that attempts to limit entry to companies that are meeting particular standards. In defense of this policy, Bob Dunn, the director of Business for Social Responsibility and a former vice president at Levi Strauss, is quoted in a recent issue of *Business Ethics* as saying: "It's too simplistic to say that there are some companies that are virtuous and others that are villainous.

We're listening, trying to strike the right balance, and hoping we can help all businesses become better in terms of responsibility" (cited in Scott 1995, 23).

There is an ambiguity, however, about using improvement as the standard: companies with relatively low standards might look better than those (like The Body Shop) that have maintained a high level of corporate responsibility in a broad range of its practices. Moreover, as a company that has been so critical of the social standards of the corporate world, and as a company that has indicated that it can do better, a tactical retreat to the standard of "improvement" is more problematic for The Body Shop than for corporations with more conventional social values. The horns of this dilemma are apparent in a presentation by Quig Tingley, the president of The Body Shop Canada, to a (November, 1996) conference sponsored by the Social Investment Organization: "The issue isn't about perfection; it's about improvement. Complete transparency about our record and our social issues is the goal. Through complete transparency, we can learn from others and from history. [But] given our public position, we feel that we are responsible for driving change, not merely responding to it. We must make the call to all companies to fight for the basic rights that all human beings should enjoy."[4]

In other words, although continuous improvement in achieving its social objectives is the goal, because of its tradition, The Body Shop must also have a high standard and push for the same in others. Improvement per se is insufficient. Moreover, it is evident from The Body Shop's practices (for example, its trade with communities in need, its high standard with respect to no animal testing, the recycling of its containers, minimal packaging, efforts at reducing energy consumption, its investment in wind energy, and, in particular, using forms of marketing that do not exploit women's anxieties about their appearance) that the company is making a sincere effort at justifying its claim to the moral high ground of social responsibility. However, the slope from such a position is slippery given that The Body Shop is manufacturing and retailing nonessential products for the better-off members of relatively affluent societies. In spite of the company's good intentions, it is also dependent upon the existing technologies for sourcing products, which means that a greater portion than it would like are tested on animals. The high-profile business publication *INC.* reminds The Body Shop of the standard by which it is being judged when it states: "the Roddicks' business has yet to transform the face of the earth" (Murphy 1994, 47). Even though *INC.*'s comments are cynical, The Body Shop is vulnerable to this type of criticism, because Anita Roddick is a leading critic of corporate behavior and has become the icon for corporate social responsibility.

CONCLUSION

Although there is some debate about whether the practices of The Body Shop live up to its ideals, the company has nevertheless proven itself to be an effective campaigner on an important array of social issues. To maintain its effectiveness, however, The Body Shop will have to defend itself against criticism. The company has taken the criticism seriously, as evidenced by both its own internal audit and external verification. However, the important lesson to be learned from The Body Shop is that a multinational corporation can take a stand on social issues, and the resulting publicity can benefit the marketing of its products as well as the social issues that it is addressing. There are other corporations that market idealism through their advertising. However, The Body Shop's marketing is based on concrete initiatives—campaigns, petitions, and projects related to an impressive array of social justice movements. Although cynics might argue that there is an element of gimmickry to some of these campaigns, there is undeniably substance as well.

As the Roddicks come to the end of their tenure at the helm of The Body Shop, one question that arises is whether the company will sustain its values once the couple departs. To date, The Body Shop has been successful in attracting franchisees who share the values of the founders. This selection is reinforced by the franchise agreements that (subject to provisions of local law) give the head franchiser for a territory the power to terminate agreements with sub-franchisees who don't work within the values framework of the company. This process, which might be seen as the business version of the litmus test, is used sparingly, but nevertheless, it is a factor in both who applies and who is selected. In spite of idealism that franchisees might display, it is likely that the current values will be maintained only as long as they are instrumental in the sale of soaps and shampoos—which, after all, is the basis of the business. The leadership of the Roddicks has been important in establishing these values and maintaining them. As noted, when Anita Roddick first involved The Body Shop in campaigns in the mid-80s, some of the franchise owners resisted. Given the critical role of the Roddicks' leadership, it must be asked whether those values will be maintained once new leaders have taken over.

In recognition of this concern, the Roddicks (as mentioned) seriously considered buying back the stock not owned by them and placing the entire stock in trust—along the same lines as The John Lewis Partnership. Having decided against that strategy, the company is now investing in a management school in London—The New Academy of Business—which will teach business managers about social responsibility. Through this approach, they are hoping to influence the culture of management. The Body Shop's values are crystallized in its Memorandum of Association and its Mission Statement, and the Roddicks remain hopeful that the ideals they have nurtured will be sustained. However, they accept that there will be changes. By 1998, the first signs were apparent, when Anita Roddick moved upstairs to co-chair the company with her husband Gordon, and was succeeded as CEO by French businessman Patrick Gournay. It is still premature to know whether this partial change of leadership will also signal a change in the company's philosophy. Gordon Roddick muses: "It will be very interesting to see what goes on into the next generation. The company will change and grow and develop, whether or not we are here."

THE BODY SHOP

1942   Anita Roddick is born in Littlehampton, England, the daughter of Italian immigrants.

1967   Anita and Gordon Roddick get together and start a series of small businesses including a restaurant. They write political messages on the blackboard with the daily menu.

1976   The first branch of The Body Shop opens in Brighton, England.

1977   The first franchise is issued and the first international franchise opens a year later in Brussels.

1984   The Body Shop is listed on the London Stock Exchange. Anita Roddick wins the Veuve Cliquot Businesswoman of the Year Award.

1985   The Body Shop assists Greenpeace in lobbying against dumping hazardous waste in the North Sea. A year later, the company launches the Save the Whale Campaign, also in conjunction with Greenpeace.

1987   The Body Shop is named the company of the year by the Confederation of British Industry.

1988   The Body Shop enters the U.S. market and also opens its Soapworks Factory in Easterhouse, Glasgow.

1989   The community trade initiatives begin with the General Paper Industries in Nepal.

1990   The first shop opens in Japan. Both the Eastern Europe Relief Drive and The Body Shop Foundation are launched that year.

1991   Anita Roddick's biography, *Body & Soul,* is published in 10 languages. The Body Shop launches *The Big Issue.*

1993   The Body Shop wins a defamation suit against Channel 4 TV for its unfair criticism of the firm a year earlier.

1995   The Body Shop has 1,500 stores in 46 countries, 8,500 employees, and £600 million of sales worldwide.

1996   The Body Shop publishes a comprehensive social audit of the company's performance with respect to social, environmental, and animal issues.

NOTES

Unless otherwise cited, the quotes in this chapter from the following employees of The Body Shop are from interviews conducted in March 1995: Nicky Amos, Angela Bawtree, Sue Belgrave, Richard Boele, John Grounds, Keith Croft, Gavin Grant, Clive James, Steve McIvor, Anita Roddick, Gordon Roddick.

1. Anita Roddick stepped down as CEO in 1998 and became the co-chair with her husband Gordon.

2. By mid-1998, there were 1,600 stores in 50 countries.

3. The family history is taken from interviews with the Roddicks and from Anita Roddick's book, *Body and Soul* (New York: Crown, 1991).

4. From Quig Tingley's presentation to the conference on Corporate Responsibility in a Global Economy (Sixth Annual Conference of the Social Investment Organization), Toronto: November 15, 1996.

9

Inmate Enterprises
and K. T. Footwear

The movement for increased corporate responsibility has focused on such issues as the environment, social marketing, and support for humanitarian organizations. The two businesses discussed in this chapter take corporate responsibility in a different direction. They have employed people who are on the margins of society, not because this particular labor force is optimal for a business, but because the owner's social objectives are oriented toward helping the members of these particular groups to improve themselves. The first part of the chapter deals with inmate businesses started by Fred Braun in Leavenworth, Kansas. Their purpose is to help prison inmates develop work skills and save money, thereby increasing their chances of adjusting to society after their release. The second part is about a shoe-manufacturing business in Auckland, New Zealand, started by a Maori businesswoman, Karroll Brent-Edmondson, who has achieved a high profile for her work. The employees are the hard-core unemployed, and are often people with disabilities (physical and emotional) and victims of racial discrimination.

INMATE ENTERPRISES

Henke is a small manufacturer of snow-removal equipment located in Leavenworth, Kansas. Although its 1995 sales were only $1.5 million, Henke has a significance that goes far beyond that figure: it is the third company taken over by Fred Braun, an unusual Kansas businessman, for the purpose of providing work for prison inmates. Between Henke and two other businesses (Zephyr, a sheet-metal-products manufacturer, and Heatron, a manufacturer of heating elements) about 100 inmates are employed at a given point in time. Since 1979 (when the program first started) and 1995, more than 500 inmates have been employed. These inmates are paid the minimum wage and also participate in the success of their employer through an ESOP. (In these cases, the ESOP is strictly as a benefit plan to allow the inmates to save for the future rather than a mechanism for transferring ownership to the inmates.) After paying taxes, restitution costs, and room and board at the prison, this system of remuneration has allowed longtime participants to accumulate benefits of up to $20,000 in the ESOP and to have savings in addition. More importantly, the work experience gives the inmates some dignity. Greg Mussleman, an inmate serving a life sentence for murder and one of the first to be employed under this program, speaks highly of the experience: "When I come here, I am in the real world of work. I have a full life, nine hours a day, even though I am incarcerated. That makes you a person." Brad Jones, another lifer, echoes Mussleman's sentiment: "I came to prison when I was 27; I am now 47. I didn't work and I didn't know how to. I didn't know if I could when I started here. I developed confidence, knowledge, and even a little wisdom along the way." Jones adds that he has saved $3,200 from his pay and has another $10,800 in his ESOP.

The inmates in the program are screened carefully for Braun by the state and by Jack Porter, a retired FBI agent who determines whether they will present a security risk. Many are in prison for serious offenses, but they are accepted if the screening process indicates that the risks at the time of their application are minimal. They are told that if they get themselves into trouble while in the program, they will not be given a second chance. Because of corrections' policies about integrating low-risk inmates into the community and monitoring them with electronic equipment, there is a shortage of employees for the program. The shortage also occurs because of a high turnover rate which, in addition to release from prison, comes about for such reasons as quitting or being fired, withdrawal by corrections officials for difficulties within the prison, or transfer to other institutions. The overall average length of employment is about 14 months, and for people who are paroled while working at one of the companies, the average is about 19 months.

Braun, who has made a commitment not to profit from these businesses, emphasizes that the inmates are involved in the "real world of work" through which they develop work habits and technical skills that help them to become gainfully employed upon completing their term. As a result of the publicity surrounding these enterprises, Braun has been able to build up a network of contacts that he uses to help his parolees (to whom he jokingly refers as his "successful alumni") to become employed. Not all of the parolees succeed on the outside; the recidivism rate is about 30 percent. But Braun is convinced that his alumni fare much better than the inmates who are paroled without savings and without the training to succeed in the labor market.

Fred Braun's entrée into rehabilitative work for inmates could not have been predicted from his early years. He was an ambitious person from a working-class family of German Mennonites who grew up in a small town near Philadelphia. After excelling at Lafayette College, he won a scholarship to the Harvard

Business School with the dream of becoming a vice president of sales for a large corporation. Following a series of business involvements, in which he honed his skills in turnarounds of failing companies, Braun hit the jackpot in the takeover of a money-losing division of a national corporation that produced coated bulk-storage containers. He made about $2 million from the sale of his investment, and then decided to go into politics. After losing narrowly in the 1974 Republican primary for Lieutenant Governor of Kansas, he had planned to run for Congress in a safe Republican seat in southeast Kansas. However, his life took an unexpected twist. His wife Marguerite, with whom he had four children, indicated that she was not prepared to move to Washington. Braun decided that he did not want to break up his family in order to pursue his political ambitions. But as a hard-driven man with a history of success in his many endeavors (including athletics, where he excelled at rowing and wrestling), he was thrown into a mid-life crisis: "What was I going to do with the rest of my life? I was miserable, because I am a goal-oriented person, sometimes tunnel focused. I was 42 years old, and everybody saw me as a tremendous success. But I looked into the mirror and said, 'Where am I going? What am I going to do?'"

Braun participated in a workshop at the Menninger Clinic and underwent a period of reflection. As a devoutly religious Episcopalian who taught Sunday school, he considered entering the ministry. He also thought about becoming a professor of business. However, continuing to focus his energies around making money was not something that he wanted to do: "$2 million was more than I ever dreamed I would have and, in some respects, I felt a little guilty about having it." Braun turned his business skills in another direction. The opportunity came through his work on a Governor's Task Force in Kansas, where he had the opportunity to visit the prisons. He observed that the inmates spent much of their day watching television and that they lacked a constructive work program. "That's how all this started," Braun recalls. "I had the money, the time, the ambition, and I wanted to change things. I had political interests, and prisons are highly political. I have strong religious convictions that my mother drummed into me. I feel an obligation to help other people. It is the obligation of people who do well to share what they have and to make good use of their abilities and talents."

Like his business decisions, Braun's taking on prison work was not an impulsive act. "I wasn't Saul on the road to Damascus," he emphasizes. He considered the options by asking where there was the greatest need and where could he make the greatest impact. "I still believe that one guy can change the system," he states optimistically, "if he goes about it the right way, busts his ass, and is lucky."

Although Braun was not unaware of the obstacles that he would encounter, the frustrations still proved immense. Prior to Braun, there were a few privately owned businesses using inmate labor (for example, the reservation center for Best Western motels in the Arizona Center for Women at Phoenix, Arizona). However, these involved service jobs inside of the prison. Braun's plan to have inmates work in outside manufacturing of hard goods presented security concerns for officials. Initially, he experimented with operating a business inside, but the incompatibility of business routines and the prison culture with a warden in charge proved too extreme; he therefore concluded that it would be better to operate outside.

Braun's mission was supported by several political initiatives. In 1979, Senator Charles Percy of Illinois introduced the Prison Industries Enhancement Act that set out guidelines for private-sector businesses involving inmates (Callison 1989). Percy was inspired in his initiative by Chief Justice Warren Burger, who had studied prison industries in Western Europe and who felt that they were useful in rehabilitating inmates. The Percy legislation attempted to ensure that the payment to inmates was not undercutting the prevailing wage rate, a concern of unions. This proved to be a contentious issue, since there were disincentives for employers to hire inmates at the prevailing wage rate. These disincentives included a high turnover, additional training costs (because of lack of work experience), and low productivity of some inmates. Braun initially started Zephyr using Kansas work-release legislation, thus justifying payment of the minimum rather than the prevailing wage. However, in 1981, after a complaint by one of Zephyr's competitors, the Kansas Department of Corrections commissioned an independent consultant to study the matter. The study concluded that: "Zephyr is not experiencing a positive competitive cost position through the use of inmate labor. Although having the advantage of being able to pay inmates at a substantially lower pay scale, the advantage is being offset primarily by the reduction in productivity" (Young 1981, 4).

The selling point in the Percy legislation was that gainfully employed prisoners would reduce the cost of incarceration through deductions for taxes, room and board, and restitution payments (Callison 1989). Within three years, 20 American states had passed legislation based upon the Percy framework. Kansas, which had its own legislation prior to Percy, broadened it in 1979 so that inmates could be hired by outside businesses such as those Braun wanted to set up.

STARTING OUT

In 1978, Fred Braun formed Creative Enterprises, Inc.; the statement of purpose described it as a "private, profit-oriented company, dedicated to rehabilitation of prisoners through private enterprise" (Callison 1989, 17). The plan was for Creative Enterprises to establish manufacturing companies inside or adjacent to prisons and "to provide realistic work opportunities for prisoners" (Callison 1989, 18). The initial stockholders (namely Braun, supplemented by a group of associates) were supported by an advisory board of politicians, correction officials, academics, and union representatives. About a year later, Braun arranged for the purchase of the first company, Zephyr Products, Inc., a sheet-metal fabricator, located in Kansas City, Missouri. The cost of $500,000 included notes of $450,000 of which Braun guaranteed $200,000 personally. Losses by the company between 1982 and 1984 increased Braun's investment by $500,000, but despite his investment and a heavy time commitment to the company, he did not draw any salary until 1986.

Braun's second acquisition was Heatron, a bankrupt company in Kansas City, Missouri, that manufactured heating elements. It was purchased for $50,000, but Braun and his wife had to invest another $400,000 when, in 1984 (three years after the purchase), the company was moved next to Zephyr in an industrial park in Leavenworth. The third acquisition—Henke—was a bankrupt Iowa manufacturer of snow-removal equipment that was moved to the Leavenworth industrial park in 1993. Braun and his family originally put $350,000 into Henke, but large initial losses and additional costs raised his total cash investment at one point to $1 million. (By 1995, his total investment in Henke was down to $400,000.) In other words, Braun took a lot of personal financial risk for businesses from which he had made a commitment not to profit personally. "When people ask 'Why did you do it?', I say it's my mission."

Braun's plan was to make these companies profitable, so that a return could be paid to investors, and then to transfer his portion of any increase in the equity to a public foundation (The Workman Fund) that would be used for investment in other businesses to provide training and employment for inmates. The fund's promotional literature refers to "Venture Capital for Real World Inmate Work Programs." The name, The Workman Fund, was intended to satisfy the public concern that real physical work was being undertaken in the businesses in which the fund invested. However, Braun expresses his disdain for the chain-gang programs, which he dismisses as punitive, and for prison-work programs that seldom teach useful skills and involve only nominal payments. Jesse Rodriguez, an employee of Henke who has served 17 years of a first-degree murder conviction, emphasizes the difference:

In prison, I make $21 per month; here I make $600 per month, plus it gives me a chance to show that I can work with people who are on the outside. I am learning about working with blueprints. I have saved $2,700 so far, not including the savings in the ESOP. We pay rent of $50 per week; we pay 10 percent of earnings to the crime victims' fund; the prison saves 5 percent to give to the inmates when they leave; and we can have money sent to our families and put into an account for us.

Starting with $250,000 transferred from Creative Enterprises, The Workman Fund has a target of $10 million to be achieved through profits from Braun's investments in the three inmate businesses, grants from other organizations, and outside donations that Braun and his assistant (Helen Flanner) solicit. Among the donors was Jesse Rodriguez, who gave $25 to the fund. Braun's vision is: "Factories either next to or inside prisons all over the country, with inmates with a much stronger orientation to real work so that, when they get out, they will be able to get jobs and stay out."

Realizing that vision has not been without its problems. Braun would have preferred to focus his energies on The Workman Fund and to have other people operate the companies that he has turned around. But, before it could be made profitable, each of the three businesses that he invested in has required more attention than originally anticipated. Two years after the purchase of Zephyr, Braun phased himself out of its daily activities and shifted his energies to Heatron. But Zephyr started losing money and, in 1983, Braun moved back into a full-time management role. After stabilizing the company and returning it to profitability, Braun sold it to a management and employees' group now led by Randy Reinhart, who previously handled Zephyr for a Kansas City bank. The sale was arranged through a leveraged ESOP, whereby Zephyr guaranteed a bank loan that was used to purchase Braun's holding in the company. The ESOP owns 65 percent of Zephyr, and a small management group led by Reinhart owns the remainder. The company makes annual contributions to the ESOP of about 10 percent of salary for all employees, including the inmates. This has meant that each inmate is getting on average about $1,200 in company stock per year. Given the relatively short tenure of inmate employment, the normal vesting period has been reduced to 50 percent after two years and 100 percent after three years. However, even with this reduced vesting period, only those inmates employed for longer than the average derive any benefit from the plan. Of the inmates who become vested, they can, upon departure, either transfer their savings in the ESOP to another retirement savings plan or, as is more likely, take the cash. In the latter case, after paying a 10 percent penalty for withdrawing their holdings prematurely from a retirement savings vehicle, and after paying tax on the income, they receive (if fully vested) about 70 percent. Therefore, the ESOP serves as a benefit plan through which long-term inmate-employees have been able to save substantial sums.

For Heatron (the second of the companies that he purchased), Braun was able to stabilize the finances more quickly. After two years of large losses, the company started making a profit in 1982 and has been profitable ever since, with steadily increasing sales that reached about $9 million in 1995. As with Zephyr, Braun sold the company to a management group using a leveraged ESOP. Mike Keenan and his partner, H. B. Turner, are the principal owners. The ESOP, which includes the inmate-employees, owns 43 percent, and the Braun family retains a 5 percent holding. Again, the ESOP serves as a benefit plan for the employees, providing for savings on top of those that are set aside from salaries. Because Heatron's stock has gone from 90 cents per share when the plan was first set up to over $5 in 1995, the shares in the ESOP have also increased in value.

MOVEMENT ACTIVITIES

Braun's objective is not simply to provide gainful employment to inmates within the three firms he has set up in Leavenworth, but mainly to use The Workman Fund to encourage private-sector employers across the U.S. to become involved in the employment and training of inmates. Once Henke, the third of the purchases, becomes profitable, Braun intends to sell it as well and to focus his energies on The Workman Fund. Although he is in excellent health, he is also at an age where people begin to think about their successors. Given the combination of business acumen and commitment to Braun's agenda that is required, finding an appropriate successor might be problematic. Gradually, Braun is transferring equity from Creative Enterprises, the holding company for his investments in the three enterprises, to The Workman Fund. Eventually, Creative Enterprises will be consolidated with The Workman Fund. One of the challenges in pursuing his vision of a network of inmate businesses across the U.S. is to find employers who share Braun's goals. In that respect, he has been fortunate that Randy Reinhart and Mike Keenan agreed readily, as one of the conditions of purchase, to continue the inmate program.

For the investments through The Workman Fund, which can be quite risky, Braun has also attempted to establish agreements with prospective employers of inmates around such issues as paying at least the minimum wage, training the inmates, and making available regular financial statements. However, the results of the initial investments have been mixed. In the first investment, an embroidery business, the company has been consistently slow in its loan repayments. The second business (owned by two hard-working Mormons) involves the sewing of clothing and has worked out well. The third business, involving native beading for clothing decoration, was closed down by the state after the inmates were not paid. Therefore, it seems that once the businesses are located outside the industrial park in Leavenworth where Braun is situated, there is a greater risk that the owners might not comply with the social objectives of the program. Once Braun retires, that risk might be increased many times.

However, Braun is not easily deterred from achieving his goals. "I am not only accomplishing things, but feeling good that it's helping people. It's very rare that anyone can do that. I have purpose in my life; I'm lucky to find that. I don't hold anything back. When my life is done, they'll say, 'he did his best! He shot all his bullets!'"

Braun maintains a relationship with the inmates that extends to the personal. In particular, he enjoys telling anecdotes about the successful alumni. Not all, he admits, make it outside of prison. Even if they are able to stay free from crime, the adjustment problems are immense. However, he takes pride in those who are able to function in society and in his contribution to their success. He also takes pride in the contributions of the inmates to society, noting that by 1995 those working at the three companies (Zephyr, Heatron, and Henke) had paid $ 2.6 million in taxes, in room and board, and in restitution costs.

INMATE ENTERPRISES

1925　Fred Braun is born in a religious Mennonite working-class family near Philadelphia.

1959　Braun graduates from Harvard with an MBA.

1971   He purchases Tec Tank, a financially troubled firm in Parsons, Kansas, and sells it six years later with a gain of about $2 million.

1976   Braun plans to run for Congress in a safe Republican seat in Kansas, but his wife balks at moving to Washington and this event precipitates a crisis for him.

1976   Braun is appointed to the Governor's Task Force reviewing the state penal system. He becomes interested in penal reform and, particularly, gainful employment for inmates.

1978   Braun forms Creative Enterprises to rehabilitate prisoners through private enterprise.

1979   Senator Charles Percy of Illinois introduces the Prison Industries Enhancement Act to ensure that payments to inmates do not undercut the prevailing wage market. The same year Braun opens Zephyr, the first of his businesses for inmates.

1985   Heatron becomes the second of Braun's inmate firms.

1990   The Workman Fund is started to invest in inmate enterprises. By 1993, the Fund had invested in three such businesses.

1993   Henke, the third of Braun's inmate firms, is purchased.

1995   The three inmate firms purchased by Braun have employed about 500 inmates who have paid $2.6 million for taxes, room and board, and restitution.

K. T. FOOTWEAR LTD.

Before visiting New Zealand, I received an e-mail message from a university contact in Auckland about a fascinating Maori woman who runs a shoe factory and has a lunch program for school children. He indicated that she had become widely known throughout New Zealand. In the brief period since 1990, when she returned from Australia after living there for 20 years, Karroll Brent-Edmondson has become a celebrity of sorts in her native New Zealand, which she had left at age 17 to get away from her unhappy past.

Upon her return home, New Zealand's economy was staggering under the pressures of an international recession and an austere restructuring program that, since the mid-80s, had resulted in economic stagnation (as reflected in no growth in its Gross Domestic Product over that period) (Kelsey 1995). Furthermore, the country's 100-year-old shoe industry was in decline due to competition with foreign imports. Karroll Brent-Edmondson started K. T. Footwear as a cottage industry making 20 pairs of shoes per week. In six years, K. T. (which is located in the Manurewa community of South Auckland) has grown to the fourth largest manufacturer in the country (and the largest manufacturer of school shoes) with an output of about 900 pairs a day and annual sales of more than $3 million.[1] Moreover, she had done this with a labor force consisting of the hard-core unemployed in the local community—people with physical and emotional disabilities, and with literacy and numeracy problems, most of them from marginalized cultures such as the Maoris and others of Pacific Island descent. Karroll, as she likes to be called, is fond of stating: "I am the only brown face in the shoe industry." Her reference is to the owners and not the employees.

"When K. T. shoes first started," recalls Arthur Bailey (the company's production manager in 1995 and a 30-year veteran of the shoe industry), "it was considered a bit of a joke in the trade; times were tough and factories were closing." However, five years later, the company can barely keep up with its orders, and Karroll has become a public celebrity, with speaking tours, TV appearances, and feature articles in some of the country's leading periodicals. She is in such demand for public appearances that she even has her own agent. Among the awards she and the company have received are: the Maori Business Woman of the Year; the Small Business of the Year; Pride in Disabilities Award; a 1996 scholarship to study business practices in the U.S.; and, most recently, membership in the New Zealand Order of Merit—an honor that allows her to put the letters MNZM after her name. After receiving this award, the self-effacing Karroll quipped: "See, you don't have to go to university to get letters after your name."

None of this would have been expected from Karroll's earlier years. She came from an abusive home and was taken under the protective wing of the Child Welfare department at age 10. Living with foster parents and struggling with life, she completed only ten grades of school before settling in Brisbane, Australia. "I wanted to disappear to Australia where I didn't have to tell anyone I was a ward of the state," Karroll remembers. Displaying the determination and resourcefulness that has helped her throughout her life, she embarked on a series of small business ventures, first doing industrial cleaning, and two years later, becoming the owner of a French restaurant, even though she knew nothing about French cuisine. "I even had to learn how to say Camembert," she jokes. However, she studied other French restaurants and began duplicating their practices. Her restaurant did well, and she became one of the caterers for the workers constructing Expo 88.

Although she and her family (her husband and three children) had achieved a comfortable lifestyle in Brisbane, returning to New Zealand was in the back of her mind: "New Zealand was always home, and I was always a Maori," she says with pride. She also wanted to see her brother and sister whom she had left behind, and she had something to prove to the people who felt that she would never achieve. "I was really young," she recalls, "when I heard people say that I would never be anything. This was my way of quietly saying to them, I told you so." Karroll had another motive as well: she felt some gratitude for the support that she had received from the state as a child, and "I wanted to come back to New Zealand to say thank you by putting something back into the community."

When Karroll returned to New Zealand, she did not have specific business plans. However, she had a keen sense of identification with young people growing up in circumstances similar to herself. In considering various business possibilities, she hit upon the idea of producing an affordable, quality shoe—in particular, for children of Polynesian background, who often had a wider foot than New Zealanders of other origins. Name imports were expensive, and she noticed that children coming from families in which the parents lacked money were wearing a cheap plastic sandal that was not good for the foot. Karroll knew nothing about manufacturing shoes, but as with her other business ventures, she learned quickly. The cash from the sale of her business in Brisbane was used to purchase equipment. She "pinched" patterns of existing shoes and copied them. Suppliers knew that she had cash and therefore were willing to deal with her. She naively thought that other manufacturers would welcome her into their industry and help her to learn the production process. However, their refusal to take her seriously only fueled her determination to show them that she could compete.

The first two years were difficult—some of the equipment was flawed and, like other small-scale start-ups, she had problems establishing markets. The stress surrounding the start-up period led to a break-up in her marriage and, as losses mounted, she also came perilously close to losing the business. However, Karroll had invested her life savings, and she was determined to succeed: "There was no way that I was going to watch my 20 years of hard work go down the drain."

The company got a break in 1993 when Karroll was able to strike an agreement with the country's second-largest retail chain, The Warehouse, to carry its shoes. The company's signature product became known as the Walkout, a wide, black-leather sports shoe ideally suited to the feet of children from the Pacific Islands. The Walkout was similar to the popular Doc Marten's shoe, but sold for about $30 less; it also matched well with school uniforms. For employees, Karroll turned to people with whom she identified strongly and who, like her as a child, were not being given a chance to develop themselves.

The fundamental changes occurring in New Zealand since the mid-80s were particularly difficult for the people Karroll sought to employ. As a result of policies to reduce public expenditure and to transfer to private ownership services previously provided through government, unemployment rose rapidly, particularly among the Maoris and other Pacific Islanders (Kelsey 1995). By 1992, the unemployment rate for the Maoris was 25.8 percent and that of other Pacific Islanders was 28.8 percent—about triple the rate for New Zealanders of European origin (the Pakeha) and about triple what it had been five years earlier. As the supports of the public sector were stripped away, the disparity between rich and poor increased, and it was estimated that about one in six were living below the poverty line. New Zealand's youth suicide rate rose sharply, and by 1992, it was the highest among the world's wealthiest countries (World Health Organization 1995).

The bulk of the labor force at K. T., numbering about 30, are people in their twenties and thirties who have never had full-time employment. They have lived on welfare and are disproportionately from the country's racial minorities. To integrate them, K. T. has established training programs (under contract to a government agency) to teach both the technical aspects of the job as well as basic literacy and numeracy. Many of the participants have never had a bank account and are helped to open one. After completion of formal training, usually from 12 to 24 weeks, the trainees stay with the company for another few months, where they receive on-the-job work experience. A few become part of the core staff with K. T., but most move on to other companies, something that they are helped to do by Karroll and Arthur Bailey, the production manager. Bailey states: "As far as the business is concerned, the training is more of a headache than a benefit because we are training people who, for the most part, are moving on. It is a social benefit, but not for the business."

The core employees have been with K. T. for an average of two-and-a-half years. Some of these will also move on to companies where they can earn more; others view K. T. as their employer for the long-term. Until recently, the pay at K. T. has been at the low end of market. Recently, however, the company has pushed for greater efficiency and higher salaries. As a result, the starting wage was bumped up to $8.50 per hour, and in the $10 to $12 range for those with experience. The employees also receive an annual bonus, are allocated stock in K. T. as part of a profit-sharing arrangement that has just started, and participate in a superannuation scheme. Although employees are expected to put out, the atmosphere remains relatively relaxed. Loud rock music blares over the factory floor so that it can be heard above the machines.

Karroll strongly dislikes the term "employee" and prefers to view the staff as a team, of which she is a part. (The initials K. T. refer to the Karroll team.) Though she also earns money from her public appearances, the salary that she draws from the company is similar to that of other staff. They meet every Monday morning to go over plans for the week and to discuss issues that they want to raise. Most tend to be shy and withdrawn. Karroll is like a mother figure to them, an image that is reinforced by invitations to her house for social gatherings, outings for dinner, or loans when they have some special need. It is also not uncommon for staff members to be living at her house because of difficulties that they are facing on their own. Lewis Tange, an employee of K. T. for four years who has worked his way up to foreman, and who lived at Karroll's, states: "Karroll can be tough, but she is a good employer. She is good-hearted."

One of the tasks undertaken by the staff at K. T. is their lunch program for children in need. Every day the business prepares hot meals for 50 children and delivers the meals to the local schools. When the business started five years earlier, 800 hot lunches were being prepared and, until recently, the number was 200. However, the amount of work proved unwieldy, and at Karroll's prodding, the city council has taken over responsibility for 150 of the lunches. Karroll's plan is for the company to expand its lunch program back to earlier levels as soon as this proves feasible.

The lunch program is just one of the initiatives undertaken by K. T. in the local community. Schools are given vouchers for children in need that can be used either as discounts for K. T. shoes or for school uniforms. The company sponsors 15 scholarships in the local schools as well as supporting sports teams, and Karroll and her partner (Nick) have established a trust fund for children in need. K. T. has also started a program for single parents with children in which all expenses are paid for a three-week summer vacation. In its purchases too, the company has demonstrated a loyalty to the community, buying its shoe soles locally at $2 in excess of what it would cost to import.

These initiatives have brought K. T. a lot of favorable publicity and, arguably, have helped to market its products—Karroll's primary job in the company. They have also been the main reason why Karroll has become a public figure in New Zealand and is so much in demand for interviews and speeches. Her high profile was one of the factors that led to the agreement with The Warehouse retail chain. Stephen Tindall, The Warehouse's principal owner and a philanthropist of some note, had a social vision similar to Karroll's. "He knew the type of people we were, and he knew what we were trying to do," Karroll states. Subsequently, K. T.'s products were picked up by the largest retail chain, Farmer's, and two other chains. Like Anita Roddick of The Body Shop, Karroll has been able to demonstrate that a responsible relationship to the community does more for marketing a company's products than formal advertising. Given that she is operating a small enterprise in a sparsely populated country, she has not received the international recognition accorded to Roddick. But within her native New Zealand, she has achieved a status that far exceeds the scale of her business. In part, this recognition might be due to her being a woman of color in a business community dominated by men of European origin; even more so, it might be because she has succeeded against all odds in a declining industry with a labor force of hard-core unemployed.

FUTURE PLANS

In spite of her social objectives, Karroll Brent-Edmondson is very much an entrepreneur with the dreams of an entrepreneur. Her vision is a chain of K. T.s that, like the first factory, would be set up in low-income communities throughout New Zealand to provide employment for the hard-core unemployed (thereby drawing into the labor market a group that would otherwise be on welfare) and to offer a giving relationship to the local community. Although the business is now turning a profit, it is not being run solely for that purpose. Whereas the typical mark-up for shoe manufacturing companies in New Zealand is about 30 percent, K. T.'s is only 5 to 7 percent. Arthur Bailey highlights the difference: "For most of the people that I've been employed by, the business is there to make money. If it doesn't make money, they are not interested. I've never worked before for someone who is working to keep people employed. It is a different way of approaching it."

As part of its push for greater efficiency, however, K. T. has paid greater attention to the bottom line. Therefore, like the other businesses in these case studies, the distinctiveness of the formative period has been reduced in response to market pressures. As the company has increased its volume, Karroll has been able to negotiate lower prices from suppliers. K. T. has also begun to diversify its products by introducing a sheepskin slipper and a sheepskin boot for men and women, as well as a pump (or court shoe) for working women, particularly those with large feet. K. T. now has a substantial presence in the New Zealand shoe industry and was recently written up in a book describing the country's 15 most successful businesses. Success, however, might be problematic for K. T., because the company's image is based, in part, upon its solidarity with the most vulnerable members of society. Therefore, even though K. T. has moved a long way from its beginnings as a cottage industry to a thriving small business, becoming too successful might harm its image. These concerns notwithstanding, K. T. is a remarkable example of how business efficiency can be combined with worthwhile social objectives. The company was forged from marginal members of society during a period when New Zealand's shoe industry (as well as many other types of industries) were experiencing great difficulty because of economic restructuring. Against all the odds, and largely due to the leadership of Karroll Brent-Edmondson, K. T. has become a major player in New Zealand's shoe industry. K. T. not only uplifted marginal members of New Zealand society to gainful employment by producing a valuable commodity, but has also proved of immense benefit to the community through its lunch and other give-back programs (remarkably, undertaken at a time when the company was struggling to survive). As an entrepreneur with a heartfelt identification with those who are the most marginalized members of society, Karroll is focused upon her mission. "My project," she says, "is 100 percent commitment to the factory. I live and breathe K. T. Footwear."

CONCLUSION

Both K. T. Footwear and the inmate enterprises started by Fred Braun are innovative examples of businesses employing the most marginalized members of society. Both entrepreneurs (Karroll Brent-Edmondson and Fred Braun) balance commercial objectives with social goals. Fred Braun is helping inmates develop the skills to become gainfully employed once they are released from prison; Karroll Brent-Edmondson is drawing into the labor force people who have been chronically unemployed and who have been discriminated against because of race and disability. Yet both their businesses have had to relate to the conditions in which they operate. Both have had to become profitable in order to survive; both have required external support in order to succeed. For the inmate enterprises, the support has come from the state in working out policies and administrative arrangements. It has also come from donors who contribute money to The Workman Fund and who therefore provide financing for other inmate businesses. For K. T. Footwear, the support has come from retailers who have been willing to carry the company's shoes when they might have been able to achieve higher profit margins from cheaper imports and from consumers who identify with the company's social objectives.

Both entrepreneurs have visions of extending the model: for Fred Braun, by using The Workman Fund to finance inmate businesses in other parts of the U.S.; for Karroll Brent-Edmondson, by creating a franchise of similar factories in marginalized communities in New Zealand. In each case, there are risks associated with the vision. For the inmate enterprises, the owners in the other businesses financed by the fund might not have the same ideals as Fred Braun; for K. T., the risk might be the loss of a competitive edge through becoming too successful. These risks are also increased because both Fred Braun and Karroll Brent-Edmondson have proceeded independently of other movement organizations that might support their work. Fred Braun has not associated his inmate program with other like-minded reform organizations. Similarly, even though Karroll Brent-Edmondson is heralded among Maori and Pacific Islander movement organizations, she has also pursued her objectives independently. Like other businesspeople discussed in this book, both have transferred to their social objectives the keen sense of individualism that they have applied to their business. Nevertheless, both of these cases demonstrate that it is possible to create successful businesses using the most marginalized members of society and in such a way that there are significant benefits for them.

K. T. FOOTWEAR

1954 Karroll Brent-Edmondson is born of a Maori mother and an absentee father of European origin.

1964 She becomes a ward of the state.

1971 She moves to Brisbane, Australia, to make a fresh start. Her formal schooling consists of the 10th grade.

1974 She opens a French restaurant in Brisbane, after being a self-employed industrial cleaner.

1990 Karroll Brent-Edmondson returns to Auckland from Brisbane.

1991 She starts K. T. Footwear with a work force of hard-core unemployed.

1991 She begins her lunch program. The company initially serves 800 hot meals per week. This is one of several programs whereby she and her firm assist children in need in the local community.

1993 New Zealand's second largest retail chain, The Warehouse, starts carrying K. T.'s shoes. Subsequently, they are picked up by other retail chains, including New Zealand's largest.

1996 Karroll Brent-Edmondson is honored by membership in the New Zealand Order of Merit. Previously, she had been named the Maori Business Woman of the Year, and her firm had been honored as the Small Business of the Year. Brent-Edmondson achieves a celebrity status in New Zealand, being called upon regularly for public appearances.

1996 K. T. Footwear is the fourth largest manufacturer of shoes in New Zealand, producing 900 pairs per day. Sales reach more than $3 million.

NOTES

Unless otherwise specified, quotes from the following employees and associates of Inmate Enterprises—Fred Braun, Helen Flanner, Brad Jones, Mike Keenan, Greg

Mussleman, Randy Reinhart, and Jesse Rodriguez—were taken from interviews conducted by the author in June 1995.

Unless otherwise specified, quotes from the following employees of K. T. Footwear—Arthur Bailey, Karroll Brent-Edmondson, Dave Murray, Russell Nathan, Keith Roberts, and Lewis Tange—were from interviews conducted by the author in January 1995.

1. In May 2000, N.Z.$1 purchased about U.S.$.48.

10

Wilkhahn

In the fall of 1996, Wilkhahn, a German company manufacturing high-quality office furniture and contract furniture, such as lounge seats for airports, was honored with the German Ecology Prize, a prestigious award that paid 500,000 deutsche marks (DM).[1] Wilkhahn has 614 employees and an annual turnover of 135 million DM, 50 percent of which is from exports;[2] the prize is one of many that it has received for its work on promoting sustainable, ecologically sound development. With the assistance of leading German ecologists, Wilkhahn began (in 1989) a process of restructuring the entire company and, a year later, hired two ecologists as permanent employees to ensure that the process of change continued. Each year the company undertakes a rigorous assessment of its "ecological balance," which identifies its production components and quantifies each type of waste and its disposal. The company continuously strives to reduce the quantity of its waste and to increase the amount that it recycles. Among its ecological accomplishments has been the reduction of waste water (not including sanitation facilities) to 100 cubic meters annually (or less than that of an average household) and the recycling of 20 of the 32 types of waste that result from its furniture production.

The driving force behind the production development and the ecological accomplishments of Wilkhahn has been Fritz Hahne, chairman of the company until 1994, when he retired at age 74.[3] Hahne was the second generation of his family to have a leadership role in the company begun in 1907 by his father and his uncle, Friedrich Hahne and Christian Wilkening. They were master carpenters who produced traditionally styled chairs under the company name of Wilkening & Hahne GmbH (changed in 1959 to its current name). Their products were much like those of many other family firms in the Eimbeckhausen region (near Hanover), a beautiful area of rolling hills and wooded valleys with a tradition for chair manufacturing dating from the middle of the eighteenth century. As Germany shifted toward war production in preparation for the Second World War and conscripted its male population into the military, these companies closed down. After the war, about 40 started producing again, but most failed to develop new products that would satisfy consumers, and by the late 1950s, only a handful remained in business.

Fritz Hahne took over as manager of the company in 1947 and worked closely with his cousin Adolf Wilkening, who was 15 years his senior. Unlike his father and uncle, who were in open conflict with each other, Fritz Hahne and his cousin worked well together. To insulate the company from family tensions, they formalized the corporate structure in 1958 and set up a five-person administrative board that included two outsiders. At that point, Fritz Hahne became the managing director (the company's chief executive), a post that he held until 1982 when he was appointed chairman of the board.

Although he had only limited experience with business prior to his entry into the company, Hahne was a curious and imaginative man with a willingness to experiment and to take risks. He modestly refers to his style as "management by accident" and candidly admits that he made his share of mistakes—such as having Wilkhahn produce sandboxes and tobacco pipes. However, he is philosophical about initiatives that did not work out, arguing that "if you try to go your own way, you'll make mistakes." In its transformation from a cottage industry to a modern corporation producing state-of-the-art furnishings, Wilkhahn (like so many other German companies) benefited from the postwar boom. But from the mid-50s, the socially innovative qualities of the company were apparent. Hahne was not satisfied with building basic chairs and tables; he searched for the means to create higher-value products. As he revealed: "In this area, there were many small companies producing chairs of the same type and at the same price. For me, it was important to be different." To realize that objective, he sought out avant-garde thinkers in architecture and industrial design. After the war, he joined a group called the Deutsche Werkbund (German Work League) that, since its founding in 1907, had attempted to reunite crafts production and art and had also addressed ecological issues in its design of products. This organization was the forerunner of the famous Bauhaus movement that emphasized the unity of form and function. In the 1950s, Professor Georg Leowald of the Advanced School of Arts and Crafts in Wuppertal and, particularly, the Ulm School of Industrial Design had an important influence upon Hahne. "I made the contact with Ulm and over the years became inundated with their ideas," he recalls. "It was more than designing products; it was a view of the world created by people with a vision." Wilkhahn's motto became: "First form, First function"—the first and second parts being interchangeable because form and function should be in balance with each other. From the early 1950s, Ulm argued that the goal of industrial design should be to increase durability and to decrease waste, a philosophy that was embraced at Wilkhahn. Ulm, in effect, became the training ground for the design department at Wilkhahn, and the influence became so strong that

Rudolf Schwarz, Wilkhahn's former director of public relations, jokes: "We still claim that we are Ulmed."

Although the emphasis on ecology and the restructuring of the company's production process did not come until much later, Hahne began to experiment as early as 1960 with recycling waste. He lamented the fact that "two-thirds of the wood cut to produce a chair ends up as waste." Together with Professor Roland Rainer of the nearby Advanced Technical High School of Hanover, he tried designing toys from the leftover wood. However, the workers preferred using fresh pieces to the leftovers, and the plan was dropped.

SOCIAL ORGANIZATION

During the sixties and seventies, much of Hahne's energy went into the social organization of the company. His egalitarian philosophy took root in the war when, for three years, he was a soldier on the Russian front. The war, Hahne recalls, was a defining moment in his life, and one that led to a turnaround in his social thinking. He had joined the Nazi youth movement at age 13 and participated enthusiastically in its activities. The Russian front, to which he was posted, gave him a lot of time to think about questions that were troubling him. During lulls in the fighting, he would have discussions with a fellow soldier (a medical doctor from Hanover whom he had befriended) about ideas that formed the foundation of the social philosophy that he would later apply at Wilkhahn.

We would lie under a truck, out of sight so our sergeant couldn't see us, and discuss issues at length. I was a boy of 20, in the prime of life, fighting in Russia. I had nothing against the people there, but I had to be there. If we had won the war, I would have ended up in Siberia as a guard; and if we had lost, I would have ended up in Siberia as a prisoner. Neither was desirable. I was caught *between the chairs* [the title of Hahne's autobiography].

Hahne was wounded in 1943 and consequently removed from a situation that he loathed into the relatively more humane environment of a clinic in Germany. At the end of the war, he became a prisoner first of the Americans and later of the French. Twenty-five years after, Hahne came across the notes that he had recorded during the war, and began to cry uncontrollably. "The question for me was: 'Why war?'" In retrospect, he felt that it was a horrible waste.

As a result of his war experience, Hahne developed a strong sense of identification with the employees of Wilkhahn. He felt that the system was unfair to them and, when the company had good years, he began an informal profit-sharing arrangement. Because of the war, he also developed a strong dislike for the military style of command and encouraged the practice at Wilkhahn that "no orders would be given without specifying the reasons." The company still maintains this practice because, as he stated, "I saw that others with whom I participated enjoyed this style of communication." His dislike of the command style of communication was also based on a strong reaction to his schooling. "My early years were certainly not enviable," he recalled in his biography (Hahne 1990, 25). "With no thoughtful consideration, the persons to whom I related tried to shape me as they wanted." He joked that even the Russian front with bombs falling around him was "better than the school at Hamelin" (which he attended at age 10).

During the 1960s, Hahne attended a series of seminars in the Advanced Management Academy in Bad Harzburg that introduced him to the Human Relations Movement in organizational behavior and, particularly, to approaches to the delegation of responsibility. "I began to take pleasure in belonging to a group in which people enjoyed being with each other." Hahne was not only interested in introducing changes in communication; he initiated a series of structural changes in the social organization of the company that institutionalized his egalitarian views. By North American standards, these changes would be quite radical, but within Germany where the law mandates a model for industrial democracy referred to as codetermination, the organizational restructuring Hahne introduced was not as leading-edge as his ecological policies (to be discussed). Nevertheless, the organizational changes and their relationship to Germany's legislative framework bear describing.

There are two pillars to this legislation that has been introduced in stages from 1946 until the present (Adams 1986; Bartolke et al. 1985; Knudsen 1994). First, every employer with at least five workers must have a Works Council, that is, a representative body of the employees that serves as an internal governance. Although the types of issues that are addressed and the effectiveness of the Works Councils vary, they are allowed to cover any matter not fixed in a collective agreement negotiated by a union representing the employees. In general, they serve as a sounding board for management initiatives, and in technologically advanced sectors of the economy, they have taken a leading role in developing policy for their firms (Knudsen 1994). Where employers have both Works Councils and unions, they usually collaborate with each other. The union negotiates industry-wide standards for such issues as pay and hours of work, whereas the Works Council applies these standards within each firm and deals with company-specific work issues. As compared to countries such as Canada and the U.S., Germany has had a relatively high degree of industrial harmony, as measured by days lost to work stoppages, for example (Adams 1995).

The second pillar of the German legislative framework is the right of employees to elect representatives to the board of directors, referred to as the "supervisory board." The representation varies from a parity structure between employees and management in the mining, iron, and steel industries, to a near-parity structure for companies of more than 2,000 employees, to having one-third of the board elected by employees in companies from 500 to 2,000 workers. Employers with fewer than 500 workers are not required to have employees on the board (Knudsen 1994).

Even though this legislation has established the predominant norms for German industry, Hahne still proved to be ahead of what was required. In the late 1950s, Wilkhahn established a Works Council to which employees throughout the company elected representatives to deal with company policy, and the chairperson elected by the Works Council became one of the members on the company's board. Wilkhahn was not required by law to have an employee representative on its board because it was a privately owned, limited company (and the law applied to publicly traded joint-stock companies). However, this was something that Hahne desired, and therefore it was implemented. Horst Knigge, the current chair of the Works Council, is a craftsman who has 40 years' seniority and who has been with the company since age 14. In addition to being represented on the Works Council, about 80 percent of employees at Wilkhahn (including both the tradespeople and the office staff) are unionized. The unions negotiate wage and benefit standards for each industry, and the Works Council, which also includes management representatives, deals with conditions of work in the company.

The next step in transforming the social organization of Wilkhahn occurred in 1971 when the company formalized its profit-sharing arrangements. Each year, half the profits are allocated to employees, and after allocation, 50 percent is divided equally and 50 percent is divided according to salary. By the standards of profit-sharing plans, 50 percent is an extraordinarily high allocation, and by those same standards, the distribution is relatively egalitarian. The employees' allocation is paid in shares, which after seven years can be sold internally, but only to other employees at an appraised value.[4] The employees' shares are held in a trust and are paid interest each year, the amount depending on the annual profits. Through this process, the employees accumulate an equity stake (amounting to about 30,000 DM and more for employees who have been in the plan since the beginning) and the company has a source of capital to finance investment. This arrangement is similar to that of the Mondragon worker cooperatives in the Basque region of Spain (Whyte and Whyte 1988).

As a group, the employees own about 30 percent of Wilkhahn, a stake that is gradually increasing as a portion of profits is allocated in shares each year. At present, Wilkhahn is planning to become a publicly traded company, so those employees who want to sell their shares can receive a fair value for them. However, listing the company publicly also poses a threat to Wilkhahn and what it stands for. As Hahne points out, "We have to try and balance two points of view: one, that the company doesn't get into the hands of outside capitalists; and another, that the employees can sell their shares at a fair market price."

The most recent change in the social organization of Wilkhahn has been the move to autonomous work groups and flexible work schedules, coinciding largely with the shift from a craft mode of production, which Wilkhahn maintained until about 1990, to an industrial mode with its coordination of specialized components. At Wilkhahn, there are only two levels of management: the first being a senior level consisting of the CEO (also referred to as the "president") and one vice president; and the second level consisting of 15 department heads. The work groups (operating within departments) are responsible for decisions within their unit, including financial and hours of work. Each work group has a speaker who participates with senior management in the planning process for the company, including production levels. This change was initiated by management but implemented by a special project group of the Works Council.

THE ECOLOGICAL PLAN

Much of the social restructuring at Wilkhahn was in place when ecological planning was initiated. Again, Fritz Hahne took the lead, pushing Wilkhahn toward making its relationship to the natural environment a priority. Influenced by the Club of Rome and the environmental concerns being expressed at the time, Hahne gained the support of the company's board and the Works Council for the environmental thrust. "I decided that ecology must be the major consideration in all that we do and that quick profit is no longer so important. I feel that the world is using up resources without asking questions about the consequences. We have to ensure that the next generation can live too."

There was nothing particularly original about Hahne's analysis (nor did he pretend that there was), but he was rare in his ethical stance and his singular determination to mobilize the resources of a successful corporation to put this philosophy into practice. By 1984, he established the moral tone for the ecological program when he stated: "At Wilkhahn, no two bricks will be laid on top of one another if this does not lead to a building with ecology and economy, aesthetics and human aspects as a common denominator" (Wilkhahn 1995, 15). Although the company had earlier taken some steps in this direction (for example, in the mid-80s, by investing 3 million DM in insulating its production halls), the major ecological changes have occurred in the 1990s. Consistent with the company's past practice, leading German ecologists were invited to give advice and to assist with the planning process. These included Rudiger Lutz, an architect and renowned futurologist, and Thomas Herzog, an award-winning advocate of environmentally friendly architecture. The Institute for Ecological Economic Research in Berlin was used as a resource, paid for by the state government of Lower Saxony.

The initial stage involved an evaluation of the entire production process in which all of the inputs or raw materials were analyzed, and both the products and the by-products of the company and their disposal were carefully evaluated. All the parts that went into production were given eco-numbers, specifying the nature of their materials, and these parts were then weighed and multiplied by the quantity used each year. The company was therefore able to classify all of its inputs and to determine how much of each of its materials was being used and for what purpose. The company's eco-balance sheet then analyzed each of the materials according to a series of environmental criteria. For example, the eco-balance sheet showed that ferrous metals, zinc diecastings, and aluminum (in several different forms) were among the raw materials being used in production. Each of these materials was then rated according to a series of environmental criteria such as recyclability, waste disposal, risk of hazardous incidents, and conformity with the law. Where there was insufficient information on an input, that too was noted. Subsequently, each residue of the production process was quantified and the method of disposal was recorded. Among materials sent to the waste dump, Wilkhahn's 1995 audit shows that there were 6,520 kilograms (kg) of lacquer sludge, 177 kg of fluorescent tubes, 120 kg of oil filters, and 6,569 kg of ash and dust (Wilkhahn 1995). Other residues—43,660 kg of scrap wood and 15,000 kg of shavings and sawdust—were recycled at a thermal power station to generate heat. In addition, 125,065 kg of residue were recycled in others forms; for example, 45,000 kg of scrap iron were sent to waste metal dealers for smelting, 740 kg of glass ended up with glass producers via bottle banks, 50,870 kg of cardboard and paper were recycled through cardboard and paper mills, and 8,170 kg of leftover fabrics and upholstery were sorted according to quality and used either for new yarns or for insulating boards and hard felt (the material used for the rear window ledges in cars).

The ecological practices outlined in the previous paragraph are in operation at Wilkhahn today. Most of the refuse is recycled externally, but some components such as organic waste are composted on the spot and used in the company's gardens. Cartridges that are used in printing and fax machines are returned to the supplier for refilling and are used again. Of 32 types of residue identified in the audit, 20 are either recycled or reused. The company is always endeavoring to reduce waste through such steps as using lacquer with a 7 percent solution (rather than 60–80 percent, as is usual); using glues with a minimum solution and eliminating glue altogether from newer products; giving leftovers of leather to another company that manufactures small animals for key tags and other similar items; and using low-energy bulbs throughout the premises. In selecting suppliers, Wilkhahn gives preference to those that have a recycling capacity. Otherwise, the company works with waste-recycling firms.

As a manufacturer of expensive furniture, Wilkhahn has to ensure that its products are packed carefully for transportation. The company received an award in 1995 for its returnable packaging system that includes a combination of reusable and recycled cardboard boxes and polyethylene sheeting. The sheeting is pressed into bales that are recycled into new sheets; the boxes are reused until they are too worn and are then recycled into new ones. Recently, for packaging, Wilkhahn has begun to use hemp, a material that is easily recyclable. To ensure that its trucks operate efficiently, the company makes arrangements with suppliers to pick up materials on the return end of a delivery. Also, during the 1990s Wilkhahn reduced the energy required for transportation to markets in southern Europe by increasing production in a factory it built in Spain in 1972. While ecologically sound, this practice also reduces employment in Wilkhahn's main plant.

The company's objectives to reduce its overall level of waste and to recycle or reuse as much as possible not only apply to residue but also to the actual products. Konrad Sander, one of the staff ecologists at Wilkhahn, argues that "there should be intelligent construction to convert existing products at the end of their lifetime to new products. The main goal of the future should be to design our products so that they can be reused first and then recycled if necessary." Initiatives that Wilkhahn has taken in line with this philosophy are to create chairs that are durable and to promote its refurbishing department as a service available to customers. "It is not a law of nature that we have to earn our money from producing new chairs," states Rudolf Schwarz. He points out proudly that some of the chairs that the company refurbishes were made in the 1950s.

In its product design, Wilkhahn is constantly striving to use materials that can be recycled. Wilkhahn's award-winning Picto line of adjustable swivel chairs, dubbed eco-chairs of the 90s by trade journals, is produced with a combination of materials that are 95 percent recyclable. These chairs also have releasable mechanical connections that make them easy to repair. The Picto line's use of recyclable materials has been applied to other products subsequently developed. The company's conference tables have tops veneered with native (rather than exotic) woods such as beech, ash, and cherry, or laminated with linoleum or melanin to increase durability.

Environmental consciousness has also been extended to the design of award-winning production pavilions, which were built in 1988 using the design of the world-renowned architect, Frei Otto. The design involved a tent-like structure of wooden hanging rafters. The tension-load construction minimized the use of material and provided excellent insulation. Four years later, production halls designed by architect Thomas Herzog received international awards. The bright airy halls are constructed of materials that are 85 percent recyclable. The front walls are completely glazed with insulation panels that reduce solar heat and radiation by 75 percent. The roofs, covered with plants, act both as additional heat buffers and as part of a system for collecting the rain. Through the use of drip plates, the rain is funneled off the roofs of the halls either to the ground or to a main drain that channels it into a stream flowing through the premises. For energy (solar heat and electricity), the halls are equipped with photovoltaic cells. However, the technology is as yet inadequate for such a large workplace and has been supplemented by a boiler room that utilizes the most modern state of heat engineering with computer-controlled heat circulation and waste heat recovery. Earth gas amounts to 35 percent of the energy utilization. The combination of these methods has made air conditioning unnecessary and has resulted in a high energy-utilization ratio. Wilkhahn has also invested in a wind-energy project that might yield long-term benefits. As Konrad Sander notes: "The objective is to progress by small steps that build upon each other."

The push for ecological restructuring at Wilkhahn came from the top with expert help from external consultants. However, for it to succeed, it had to elicit the cooperation of the employees, some of whom were involved in planning committees, including one committee dealing with staff communication. Initially, there were workshops for the employees, but now that the ecological direction of the company has been institutionalized, the issues are presented in a company newsletter and through messages on company notice boards in the various workstations. To mobilize the employees, there is an annual campaign to save energy, with prizes for the best suggestions. (The prizes—a weekend holiday on a North Sea island, a solar wristwatch, and a subscription to an ecological magazine—were selected for their ecological propriety.) In the beginning, there was some resistance from the employees. Asa Lennerling-Meder, who works in the export department, joined Wilkhahn at the time that the ecological program was being introduced. She states: "It is normal for people to resist. In the beginning people were uncertain, but since then they have been convinced that we are doing the right thing." She adds: "We have to take care of our resources. When you are working at Wilkhahn, you have to be aware of it; you have it in your blood, so to speak."

In every part of Wilkhahn, there are recycling bins that are divided into three sections: one for organic waste such as banana peel that is composted on the grounds; a second for recyclable material such as plaster or aluminum, napkins, and juice packages; and the third section for litter. This system of refuse disposal is part of the normal functioning of the company. The rest rooms have a "save water button," and the employees are expected to turn off the lights when they vacate their work space. The employees participate in these waste-recycling and energy-saving procedures with varying degrees of enthusiasm, but in general, there is a high level of cooperation.

At first, Wilkhahn was reluctant to promote its ecological initiatives as part of its marketing. The official view was that "ecology is regarded at the company as part of its identity and not as a means of image cultivation" (Wilkhahn 1995, 1). However, following the award of the German Ecology Prize, the most recent marketing materials emphasize Wilkhahn's environmental record, which, according to Asa Lennerling-Meder, sells well in European countries such as Hungary, the Czech Republic, Austria, Switzerland, and the U.K., but not in Arab countries such as Saudi Arabia and Bahrain. Although Konrad Sander would like to see ecology emphasized more in marketing, he realizes that "it is easier to use eco-marketing for products like The Body Shop's than for office furniture."

CONCLUSION

Less than a decade after it began its ecological program, Wilkhahn has received dozens of awards. The company is the main employer in the Eimbeckhausen valley; about 85 percent of the employees live a short distance from the plant and many go home to eat their lunch. The tradespeople at the company are well paid, averaging 50,000 DM plus profit sharing and benefits (including six weeks of holiday). Most of the postwar generation of workers have retired, and the average age of the current employees is 36. The employee turnover averages less than 1 percent each year. The absentee rate is only 3.4 percent, far less than the norm in Germany, and one of the factors gaining the company a national award in 1995 for providing a healthy workplace.

Essentially, Wilkhahn has succeeded in providing its employees with a high standard of living and a good-quality working life. Wilkhahn has been a consistently profitable company, profits averaging from 5 to 8 percent of sales over the past decade. Its office chairs sell on average for 1,400 DM, its tables for 3,000 DM, and its five-seat airport lobby chairs for 7,000 DM. The company, which sells through licensed dealers, faces fierce competition in some of its markets from low-price producers.

Although the company's ecological initiative is strongly entrenched, it remains to be seen how well it will fare once Fritz Hahne's influence ends. Hahne, who is now the honorary chairman of Wilkhahn, still makes his presence felt. He is viewed as the "grand old man of the company" and he is held in such high esteem that when he speaks at the annual general meetings, he easily captures the attention of the audience. His son Jochen, the third generation of the Hahne family to be involved in the company, is the finance director. Yet, as is usual in mature corporations, management opinion strongly influences company practice. Given its highly competitive market, questions inevitably get asked about the value of the investment in ecology. According to Rudolf Schwarz, "Some managers ask: 'Can't we wait?'"

Unlike its practices in industrial democracy, which are not inconsistent with the predominant norms for German industry as reflected in various laws that have been enacted since the end of the Second World War, Wilkhahn's ecological practices do not have legislative sanction and are therefore at greater risk. The typical CEO operating in Germany accepts the Works Council or employee representation on the board of directors because government legislation makes it normal. But Wilkhahn's ecological practices are extraordinary and they are costly at a time when competition from lower-priced producers is increasing. Therefore, unless the company's chief executive shares Hahne's values or the state introduces legislation that normalizes ecological standards in the same way as was done for employee participation in decision making, such innovations are always at risk. To institutionalize its ecological program, the company has taken some measures such as hiring staff ecologists and investing heavily in education of the employees. But without the type of leadership that Hahne provided as chairman of the firm, not only will the desire to continue innovating in this field be lost but also there are likely to be cutbacks in the initiatives taken to date.

Fritz Hahne recognizes the frailty of his innovations, but is determined to ensure that the tradition for ecological innovation will continue. For Hahne, the issue involves a principle that cannot be sacrificed. "The natural environment is the basis for life," he argues. "It is not for me to ask whether it is good, or not good, for the business." As he nears age 80, Hahne is an active member of Greenpeace and in elections votes for either the Green Party or the "socialists" (the German Social Democratic Party) to which he has belonged since 1960. He is cognizant of the finality of life, and jokes that he has been given extra years for the time that he lost during the war. In his remaining time, he is determined to see that the ecological course he has charted for Wilkhahn is not sacrificed to expediency. He has arranged for the buyout of two CEOs (in 1992 and 1995), because he felt that they lacked commitment to Wilkhahn's ecological agenda, and even though he is officially retired from the company, he meets regularly with senior management, the designers, and the chair of the Works Council. Hahne is doing everything within his power to ensure that senior management recognizes the importance of ecology, but he is not naive about the frailty of the innovations undertaken since 1989. "I've tried to do everything possible to ensure the ecological direction of the company," he states. "As long as I am alive, I will try to encourage management to support this wonderful philosophy. But if, in the future, management does not get the idea, at least I will be dead and will not have to see what has happened."

WILKHAHN

1907 Friedrich Hahne and Christian Wilkening start Wilkening & Hahne GmbH to manufacture traditionally styled chairs.

1920 Fritz Hahne is born.

1941 Hahne is sent to the Russian front. He is wounded and sent to a clinic in Germany for treatment.

1947 Hahne becomes a manager of Wilkhahn.

1950s Hahne is influenced by the Ulm School of Industrial Design and other avant-garde thinkers in architecture and industrial design.

1958 Hahne becomes the managing director of Wilkhahn. The company introduces a Works Council and an employee representative on the board of directors.

1960 Hahne begins experimenting with recycling industrial waste.

1960s He becomes caught up in the human relations school of organizational management.

1971 Wilkhahn introduces a radical profit-sharing plan, allocating 50 percent of its net income to the employees in the form of shares.

1982 Fritz Hahne steps down as managing director but remains as chairman until 1994.

1980s Wilkhahn starts investing in ecological improvements. Leading German ecologists are invited to give advice and to develop plans.

1990 Fritz Hahne publishes his autobiography, *Between the Chairs*.

1990s Wilkhahn starts introducing a major ecological redesign.

1994 Fritz Hahne steps down as chairman.

1996 Wilkhahn wins the prestigious German Ecological Prize.

1996 Wilkhahn has 614 employees and sales of 135 million DM, of which 50 percent is from exports.

NOTES

Unless otherwise cited, the quotes from the employees of Wilkhahn were from interviews by the author conducted in March 1995 and December 1996. Those interviewed were: Fritz Hahne, Asa Lennerling-Meder, Konrad Sander, and Rudolf Schwarz.

1. In May 2000, DM 1 purchased about U.S.$.44.

2. From the company's 1996 financial report.

3. Fritz Hahne's autobiography, *Between the Chairs,* and company documents are used as background material. The autobiography was translated from German by Rudolf Schwarz and Frank Keller.

4. If there are no purchasers within the company six months after the shares are offered, they can be sold to anyone.

11

An Interpretative Framework

At the end of the first chapter, I presented propositions that in this final chapter are used as an analytic tool for the case studies. The chapter will begin with a discussion of these propositions; I shall then present a model that seeks to explain the behavior of the businesspeople in the case studies and the meaning of their work.

PROPOSITION 1

The first proposition states that for businesspeople to be successful in introducing innovations, they must have control over their firm. In all eleven cases, when the innovation was introduced, the businesspeople were the principal owners and either chief executives or chairs of their boards of directors (or both in some cases). In other words, they had a privileged status that entitled them to act. Several of the businesspeople did not proceed with their agenda until they achieved the necessary control. Prior to moving ahead with his bold initiative, Spedan Lewis bought out the holding of his brother and then awaited the death of his aged father, because he feared that his father would have opposed his plans had he found out about them. Compared to Lewis, Gerard Endenburg had parents whose philosophy was more compatible with his, but he, too, waited until he had absolute control before moving ahead with the introduction of sociocracy. He had previously tinkered with Endenburg Electric's organization, but after taking control he moved more expeditiously. James John Harpell also took action following the death of his lifelong business partner in 1940, purchasing the company shares from his estate. The Roddicks (Anita and Gordon) were fortunate that a friend who holds about 25 percent of the stock (slightly less than their holding) is a passive investor who has supported their control. Therefore, even though it appears to be self-evident that control of the business is a prerequisite

for introducing major innovations, the businesspeople who were the subject of
this study were conscious of the importance of their proprietary rights.

In addition to proprietary rights, leadership skills are also needed in order to
gain the commitment of the employees and other key players such as senior management, union leaders, and investors (see Proposition 1). All of the people in
this study were skilled in leading their businesses and were generally perceived
as charismatic figures who were able to influence others strongly (Yukl 1981).
Their influence was enhanced because the plans that they promoted were based
upon idealistic and benevolent motives and they had relatively pliable work
forces that in most cases were not unionized. Nevertheless, not all found that
their employees were enthusiastic about what they were doing. Only about one-
third of the employees at Scott Bader favored the transfer of ownership to a trust,
in spite of the fact that Ernest Bader and his family were donating their shares
(Blum 1968). In reflecting upon the conversion of Baxi Heating, Phil Baxendale
(who sold the company for a fraction of its worth) recalls: "I made a big mistake
of thinking that it was self-evidently a good idea, that everybody would see it as
such."[1] At first, there was resistance from union representatives who felt threatened by Baxendale's plans.

Resistance, in some cases, came from investors and management. For example, after he became the chairman and managing director of Tullis Russell, David
Erdal had to convince 17 family members (as well as a number of trusts) who
held a stake in Tullis Russell that it was in their interest to convert the firm to
employee ownership. The task was made more challenging because the first merchant banker hired by the family members was hostile to employee ownership
and attempted to persuade them against it. However, Erdal had an inexorable
determination to see through the conversion and he wasn't acting in isolation, but
with the support of his uncle, Dr. David Russell, who, as the past chairman, had
considered a conversion to the John Lewis Partnership model. There was also a
family tradition of service to the community ("enlightened paternalism"), which
could have been violated if the company had been sold to either a competitor or
other investors.

Spedan Lewis also encountered resistance from shareholders when he started
introducing his reforms at the Peter Jones department store (prior to his takeover
of the entire corporation in 1929). Upon announcing his plans for profit sharing
at the 1918 general meeting, he bluntly stated: "The days when a lot of shareholders could stay at home doing nothing and take a very large proportion of the
earnings of a business are all over" (Lewis 1918a, 4).

PROPOSITION 2

The second proposition relates to the conditions under which these innovations will be sustained. As forceful leaders who were also the principal owners,
these businesspeople were able to obtain compliance from management. Some
(for example, Lewis, Bader, and Harpell) relied upon fear and intimidation. After

they introduced their innovation, all of the businesspeople hired management who would support it. It was understood that without managerial commitment, the likelihood was greatly reduced that the innovation would be sustained. However, once they relinquished control of the company, maintaining managerial commitment was more problematic. At Wilkhahn, even after Fritz Hahne stepped down as chairman, he has continued to monitor the performance of the top executives with respect to their commitment to the ecological innovations that he had encouraged. In 1992 and 1995, he arranged for the buyout of two successive CEOs because he doubted their commitment. In a brutally candid assessment of the innovator's dilemma, he states: "I've tried to do everything possible to ensure the ecological direction of the company. As long as I am alive, I will try to encourage management to support this wonderful philosophy. But if, in the future, management does not get the idea, at least I will be dead and will not have to see what has happened."

After the conversion of the firm to the Baxi Partnership, Phil Baxendale was also dissatisfied with the first managing director's commitment to the ideals. At least two of the innovators attempted to retain managerial compliance through legalistic methods. As he purchased firms for his inmate program, Fred Braun had to find people who would take them over and who also shared his ideals. But in order to increase the probability of a good match, he made one of the conditions support for the inmate program that he had fought to develop. Nevertheless, as someone in his sixties, he has recognized the vulnerability of his innovation. In the coming years, he must find a successor who will continue his commitment to gainful employment for inmates and who will also manage The Workman Fund that he created for investment in such businesses. Through his active involvement with the inmate enterprises, Braun has been able to monitor the agreement for the firms that he sold off. However, once his involvement ends, it is less likely that compliance will be enforced.

Ernest Bader endeavored to ensure compliance by writing into the constitution that he would be chairman for life and he would be followed in that position by his son Godric, whom he appointed as managing director in 1957. However, in his role as managing director, Godric Bader felt that this provision was inconsistent with the ideals of the Commonwealth and amended the constitution so as to discontinue his family's control. As the sole remaining family member in the firm, his role is largely symbolic and is also drawing to a close, as he is in his seventies.

The firms that were the subject of the case studies ranged from those in which the innovator is still in a leadership role (K. T. Footwear, The Body Shop, Inmate Enterprises, Endenburg Electric), to those in which the innovator has recently stepped aside (Wilkhahn, Allied Plywood, Baxi, and Tullis Russell), to a group in which the innovator disengaged earlier from a leadership role (Harpell, the John Lewis Partnership, and Scott Bader). It is this last group that is most vulnerable because the innovators are dead and the management that they appointed has ceased to be involved. It has been suggested by Zald and Ash (1966) that under such circumstances, organizations with charismatic leaders are more likely than others to experience a drop-off in commitment, because the loyalty is to the leaders rather than their ideas. These cases do not lend themselves to testing this proposition because all the leaders were charismatic.

Whereas there is insufficient evidence to assess the impact of leadership style, the data indicate that market factors are an important influence on the ability of these firms to sustain their innovations (Proposition 2). James John Harpell's innovation has ceased to exist because of market factors—one of the worker cooperatives that he set up closed in 1975 and the other in 1996. The latter firm is still operating as a subsidiary of another company that purchased it, but without the innovative qualities initiated by Harpell. Market factors have also affected the innovations at Scott Bader. In order to compete effectively in the market, Scott Bader has recruited managers externally who have the appropriate experience for a chemical products' manufacturer operating internationally. In their study of the firm, Hadley and Goldsmith (1995, 185) state that this change has drawn the company "closer to the predominant models of organization prevailing in conventional industry."

The influence of market forces is found not only where the innovator has ceased to be involved for a lengthy period of time but also in firms in which the innovation is relatively recent. At the Baxi Partnership, the glut in the market for the company's signature product led to static sales and profits that were declining as a percentage of sales. Under the circumstances, employees have been reluctant to hold onto company shares that were allocated to them, and the company has centralized management to a greater degree.

Unlike Baxi, Allied Plywood has been able to maintain strong profits, but the company's executives are always conscious of the vulnerability of the firm's ESOP in the face of an increasingly competitive market that now includes such retail giants as Wal-Mart and Home Depot. Gene Scales, the secretary/treasurer at Allied Plywood, states: "The ESOP can only work if the company increases its profits. If the profits don't increase, the company is likely to go public because that is the only way to raise enough money to pay people off."

Therefore, market forces are critical to the sustainability of these innovations. Lewis and Bader attempted to protect their innovations by locking the company's shares into a permanent trust. That arrangement provides protection against a takeover of these companies, but their survival is ensured only if they meet the measure of the market.

Market forces are of importance not only once the innovator ceases to be involved but also during the formative period when the innovator is providing active leadership to the company. The financial performance of The Body Shop reinforced its social marketing strategy and made available financing for activities that have a more peripheral relationship to marketing, for example, the Eastern European Relief Drive or the Brazilian Healthcare Project. Anita and Gordon Roddick were cognizant of the vulnerability of their innovation to market forces and therefore resorted to conservative financial management. The company is completely free of debt and is even in a net cash position. In early 1996, plans were abandoned to repurchase all outside shares and to go private—a step that would have allowed the Roddicks to put their shares in trust like the John Lewis Partnership and thereby increase the likelihood that The Body Shop's social agenda would be preserved beyond their tenure. The repurchase would have required borrowing in excess of £250 million and would have made the company dependent upon financial institutions—something that they have sought to avoid.

The relationship to the market has also played heavily at K. T. Footwear. During its first two years, the company came perilously close to sinking because of large losses. Through the support of the owner of New Zealand's second-largest retailer, who identified with Karroll Brent-Edmondson's social agenda, K. T. was able to get its shoes into the market and sales expanded rapidly. Part of the company's success is due to its solidarity with the most vulnerable members of New Zealand society—its so-called underdog status. As it has expanded and become a major force in the New Zealand shoe industry, it is not clear that the public will relate to K. T.'s products in the same way.

Therefore, the evidence is strong that market forces influence the likelihood that the innovations will be sustained not only after the innovator departs from the company but also while the innovator is still involved. Nevertheless, these data should not be interpreted to mean that nothing else matters. Market factors affect the degrees of freedom, yet within similar market constraints, there is room for innovation or social risk taking of the type undertaken by these businesspeople.

This second proposition also suggests that there is a tendency independent of market forces for the innovative quality to be lost. Essentially, this is the Weberian thesis that over time organizational routines subsume the innovative drive (Weber 1947). This thesis can be interpreted in two ways: first, that the drive to continue innovating becomes lost once the innovator ceases to be involved; and second, there is a tendency over time toward greater conservatism (Zald and Ash 1966). Each of these interpretations will be discussed in turn.

With respect to the former, there is strong evidence from the case studies that the drive to continue innovating weakens once the innovator departs. The three firms from which the innovator departed earliest—John Lewis, Scott Bader, and Harpell—lost their drive toward continued social innovation once the innovator moved on. In fact, in all of the firms in this study, innovation is followed by consolidation. That's not to say that there is one major innovation that occurs suddenly and then nothing subsequent to that. Rather, in most cases, prior to the major innovation, there is a period of experimentation where ideas ferment and are tested. Endenburg spent about 14 years working out the practices related to sociocracy before taking the final step of having the company owned through a trust. The same can be said for Spedan Lewis, who formulated his plan for the company between 1914 and 1929, when he placed his shares into a trust. Ed and Phyllis Sanders experimented with an ESOP for five years before deciding to sell in total to the employees. "Management by accident" is the way that Fritz Hahne referred to his approach, to emphasize its experimental quality. Although the ecological direction of the company took off in the 1990s, significant steps were taken in that direction during the preceding decade.

The experimentation prior to the major innovation can also be interpreted from a social reinforcement perspective. Even though the businesspeople are driven by their ideals, they are also pragmatists who are sensitive to the impact of change upon their business. The financial impact on the firm acts as a reinforcer for the innovative direction. Social responsibility became the trademark of The Body Shop, in part, because the Roddicks believed in it and, in part, because it was perceived as boosting sales. Nevertheless, it would be an oversimplification to argue that these businesspeople's actions are only determined by the financial performance of their firms. In spite of declining financial performance in the 1990s, Phil Baxendale stuck with the essentials of the Baxi Partnership. Similarly, Karroll Brent-Edmondson continued with her lunch program for children in need and her dream to have a work force of people on the margins of New Zealand society, even though for the first two years her firm was close to bankruptcy and she would have lost her hard-earned savings.

Therefore, the case studies indicate that prior to a major innovation, there is a process of experimentation that is reinforced by positive business results. The innovators also receive social reinforcement (ego rewards) for their initiatives. Karroll Brent-Edmondson has become a national figure in New Zealand, and has received the New Zealand Order of Merit in recognition of her work. Anita Roddick has become an international celebrity, the leading symbol of New Age Business. An 85-year-old Ernest Bader was referred to as "a saint of a man" as he sat in the gallery of the British House of Commons in 1976, and he also received an honorary doctorate from the University of Birmingham, even though his formal schooling ended at age 12. Wilkhahn was recently honored with the prestigious German Ecology Prize in recognition of its environmental accomplishments, an award of which Fritz Hahne is extremely proud.

Both the performance of the company and the recognition received by the businesspeople serve to reinforce the innovative direction and to overcome doubts that might exist during the formative period. However, once the innovation is adopted, the institutional arrangements are altered to conserve it. This process is akin to what Lewin (1947) described as unfreeze > change > refreeze. Other organizational change theorists (for example, Hinings 1989; Kanter 1992) use different terminology, but also acknowledge that following a major change, there is a process of consolidation.

The Weberian thesis can also be interpreted to mean that over time there will be change toward the predominant norms; in other words, not only will innovating cease but, in addition, the innovation will gradually be eroded and the firm will become conventional in its behavior. At Harpell Printing, as noted, the change in organization toward the predominant norms resulted from market factors. Scott Bader provides a better test of this thesis in that even though the company's business performance has been strong, over time there has been some erosion of the ideals that Ernest and Godric Bader encouraged. For example, the ratio of highest to lowest salary has increased because external managers with the appropriate skills want pay that is commensurate with the market. Moreover, as the research of Hadley and Goldsmith (1995, 182) suggests, since 1971 when Godric Bader stepped aside as managing director, a "managerialist culture" has developed. Even though the democratic institutions that Ernest Bader put in place have withstood this culture, there are indications that senior management would like some changes in that regard as well.

Spedan Lewis took a radical step with respect to the ownership arrangements of the company (to be discussed more fully in the next section), but unlike Bader, his reforms with respect to pay ratio and decision making were more modest. His reforms were not intended to challenge management's right to earn the market rate or its right to operate the business. Rather he sought to ensure that none of his employees was impoverished, that they would benefit from the success of the company through a bold profit-sharing scheme that typically involved the distribution of 45 percent of the net income, and that through the governance, management would have to communicate with employee representatives, be accountable to them, and be responsive to their concerns. Lewis referred to this arrangement as a "constitutional monarchy," as if he was drawing the standards of his firm in line with those of British political democracy (Lewis 1954, 11). Arguably, the standard falls short because the British people elect their prime minister, whereas at the John Lewis Partnership neither the employees nor their representatives elect their "chairman." Rather, he is appointed by his successor after consultation with selected senior management.

However, unlike Bader's bold initiatives at his company, where employees elected half of the representatives on the company's board of directors and the employee-elected community council had an influential role in decision making, Lewis's reforms have not been eroded over the years. This might be because Lewis's reforms did not depart as substantially as Bader's from the predominant norms for industry. Unlike the executives at Scott Bader who were brought in after Godric Bader's departure, those at John Lewis adapted well to the structures. In part, this may have been because they were recruited from within; but more likely, there was a recognition that managerial authority was still sovereign and there were advantages to working with employee representatives in the governing councils and to learning of employee concerns through the communication committees before they festered into major grievances. During the First World War when Spedan Lewis began introducing some of these practices, their departure from predominant norms would have been quite fundamental. By modern standards in Western Europe, his reforms are more in line with norms. In other words, with respect to its governance, the changes that Spedan Lewis introduced in the period between 1914 and 1929 might have been viewed as a harbinger of future events. Like Robert Owen's educational reforms, the standards for industry in Western Europe, in particular, have caught up.

Therefore, once these businesspeople have left their firms, the innovative drive that they initiated subsides and over time the innovations may be eroded. This is most likely to happen where a company encounters financial difficulties, but can also occur because new management with more conventional views does not support the innovation. Where the innovation represents a fundamental departure from existing practices, it would appear to be at greater risk than when the reform is more modest.

SOCIAL MOVEMENT ACTIVITIES

It would be naive to believe that the innovations in one particular firm would endure forever. Therefore, aside from the impact on the lives of individuals who are part of these firms (something that should not be trivialized), the significance of these innovations is their role in related social movements. That is, to what extent do they have an influence outside of the innovator's firm?

None of these businesspeople was content to simply innovate in their own firms; they were also creating a model for others to emulate. These movement activities were manifest in different ways. Many wrote books describing their innovation (for example, Gerard Endenburg, Anita Roddick, Spedan Lewis, Fritz Hahne, and James John Harpell). Some utilized television and public speaking to get out the message (for example, Karroll Brent-Edmondson, Anita Roddick, Ernest Bader, and Gerard Endenburg). Although he is consulted at legislative hearings in the U.S. that deal with corrections' issues, Fred Braun has tended to shun publicity because he remains concerned about a public reaction to his work. In the U.S., and particularly in Kansas where Braun operates, the public favors a more punitive response toward inmates. Nevertheless, Braun is slowly building up an infrastructure that he hopes will sustain his work beyond his involvement. Although he maintains some connections with other inmate-reform organizations, he has also operated quite independently, much as he did when he had conventional business interests.

Ernest Bader also created movement organizations (Demintry and, subsequently, the Industrial Common Ownership Movement) that would encourage firms to develop common ownership. Similarly, the Roddicks have taken a leading role in setting up movement organizations that would extend their work, for example, Business for Social Responsibility and the New Academy of Business.

These businesspeople have also associated themselves with existing movement organizations, often taking a leading role. After hesitating at first because he felt that his ideas were too radical, Spedan Lewis joined and eventually became a vice president in the Industrial Co-Partnership Association, an organization of British businesspeople who promoted such concepts as codetermination and profit sharing. During the 1930s, James John Harpell developed strong links with the Antigonish Movement in Atlantic Canada and actively promoted cooperatives through his publishing operation. As ecology became his passion, Fritz Hahne became involved in the Green Party in Germany. Following the conversion of his firm to the Baxi Partnership, Phil Baxendale became the chairman of Job Ownership Ltd. (an organization that promoted employee ownership and was founded by Robert Oakeshott and Jo Grimond, the former leader of the British Liberal Party). David Erdal, who has thrown himself with passion into promoting employee ownership in the U.K. and other parts of Europe, succeeded Baxendale as chairman. Ed Sanders also took a role in the employee ownership movement in the U.S., assisting in lobbying for legislation that would provide incentives for small businesspeople like himself to convert their firms to employee ownership. One piece of legislation, enacted in 1984 (two years after Sanders converted his company to employee ownership), became known as the Sanders provision, in recognition of his contribution.

PROPOSITION 3

The third proposition suggests that under relatively stable social circumstances, the social innovations aligned with reformist movements are more likely to have an impact than those that depart fundamentally from predominant norms. The innovations described in these case studies and the related social movements presented particular challenges to the predominant norms, but all operated effectively within a capitalist framework and their challenges could be integrated within the system. Nevertheless, each innovation had the potential to change business norms in a significant manner and each had broader implications for social change. In illustrating these points, the innovations will be classified as follows: ownership, decision making, and relationship to the community.

a. Ownership

With respect to ownership, the case studies looked at three basic approaches: first, the transfer of shares from the innovator and family members to a trust that is intended to hold them permanently, as in the John Lewis Partnership, the Scott Bader Commonwealth, and Endenburg Electric; second, cooperative arrangements as in the worker cooperatives developed by James John Harpell and the common ownership approach of Ernest Bader; and third, employee share-ownership, as in Allied Plywood, the Baxi Partnership, and Tullis Russell (the latter two combining employee ownership with ownership by a trust).

Although the companies that were owned through a trust operated effectively within a capitalist framework, this approach contains within it the seeds of a different concept of an economy, because such corporations operate without shareholders—shareholders being a basic feature of a capitalist corporation. By transferring shares to a permanent trust, a closely held family firm is transformed into social property not owned by anyone. The arrangement is analogous to a nonprofit corporation. Such companies are not guaranteed survival in a competitive market, but they are relatively immune from takeover by other firms, because there are no shares that can be purchased. Therefore, they either sink or swim on their own merits. Since they tend to be self-financing, relying largely on the reinvestment of their earnings for development, growth is likely to be slower than in a dynamic capitalist firm, which can easily attract external investment. A company owned through a trust is likely to have a small debt load. In addition, management is not under pressure to satisfy external shareholders by paying out substantial dividends, and therefore that portion of the net income can be used to supplement the income of employees. There is no guarantee that senior management will operate equitably in that distribution. Not having external shareholders gives senior management a relatively free hand unless the other employees are organized either through a union or through the governance of the company. All of the companies using the trust involved employees in the governance, but these ranged from the John Lewis Partnership, where employee influence was modest, to Scott Bader and Endenburg Electric, where the intent was to strike relative equality between management and employee influence.

It would be an understatement to say the trust arrangement used by Lewis and Bader has not captured the mainstream of the business community. It has been taken up by a small number of businesspeople, primarily in the U.K. (see chapters 2 and 3) and in Germany where Ernst Abbe set up the Carl Zeiss *Stiftung* in 1888 (Volkmann 1966; Oakeshott and Schmid 1990). These are endowed firms (Cornforth et al. 1988) that rely upon the goodwill of people to give away wealth that would normally be transferred to their families. Where businesspeople are inclined to be generous with their wealth, the more usual practice is a gift to a foundation that makes donations to projects in the community. In other words, even though a portion of their wealth is transferred to a trust, their business interests remain conventional. It is also possible for a business to be owned through a trust that utilizes its revenues to support projects in the community. Since 1964, 92 percent of the stock in Robert Bosch, the huge German multinational, has been owned through a trust (the Robert Bosch *Stiftung*) that donates funds to humanitarian projects (Heuss 1994). Unlike the John Lewis Partnership, the dividends accruing to the shares in the trust are used for charitable donations rather than profit sharing with the employees.

The transfer of a company's ownership to a trust does not necessitate a gift. Gerard Endenburg was gradually reimbursed from the company's revenues for his holding in Endenburg Electric and Phil Baxendale received some compensation (albeit very partial) when he established the Baxi Partnership Trust. Receiving reimbursement would be a more attractive arrangement for small business owners who are not wealthy but who desire to protect their company against external takeover by having the shares held in a trust. Even under those circumstances, the strengths of this form of ownership would still pertain. However, for the average businessperson exiting from a firm, ownership of the company's shares through a permanent trust does not receive consideration. The businesspeople in these case studies who were proponents of the trust involved themselves in activities to promote this approach, but the concept departs too fundamentally from the norms and has been undertaken by only a handful of firms (including some large corporations). However, these experiments are important because if there were to be a major crisis in the capitalist system, it is possible that this model would receive more serious consideration.

Neither the worker cooperative promoted by James John Harpell nor the common ownership approach encouraged by Ernest Bader has had a major impact on the business culture. Like ownership through a trust, this approach challenges the association between shares and voting rights by adopting the democratic principle of one worker/one vote (Ellerman 1990). It is a radical concept dating back to the middle of the nineteenth century that has never attracted a large following either in the business community or among organized labor. As noted, there are only 1,400 common ownership firms in the U.K., primarily micro enterprises. Although Harpell's Press Co-operative took a leadership role in Canada's worker cooperative movement, there are only about 300 such firms, generally small enterprises (Quarter 1992; 1995). With some exceptions (for example, the Mondragon group in the Basque Region of Spain [Whyte and Whyte 1988] and some large worker cooperatives in the Emilia Romagna region of northern Italy [Earle 1986]), the worker cooperative has remained a small, alternative form of enterprise outside the mainstream of the economy.

By comparison, employee share-ownership has achieved greater cultural penetration, in part, because it retains the notion of the shareholder, albeit one that is also an employee of the company. Therefore, it is more consistent with the culture of capitalism. Most cases of employee ownership involve only a minority of a company's stock (Blasi and Kruse 1990). The cases considered in this book are more fundamental, because they either involved the entire company (Allied Plywood) or a substantial portion of the company (the Baxi Partnership and Tullis Russell) with the remainder either in a trust or in the process of distribution. All of these cases overcame a fundamental obstacle to employee share-ownership in that payment to the original owners was made through company revenues. In the cases of Allied, Baxi, and Tullis Russell, procedures were used whereby the owners could sell their shares to an employee trust (an ESOP in the U.S. and an ESOT in the U.K.) with tax benefits to both the owners and the company. (These trusts differed from those discussed above in that they were simply mechanisms to transfer shares from the original owners to the employees rather than a permanent device for holding the original owner's shares and thereby eliminating individual shareholders from the ownership of the company.)

The employee share-ownership movement in the U.S. has become a significant force, being promoted by such organizations as the National Center for Employee Ownership, the ESOP Association, and the Center for Economic and Social Justice. According to Corey Rosen, the director of the National Center for Employee Ownership, ESOPs (not including other types of employee ownership) embrace about 9,500 firms with 10 million employees.[2] About half of these ESOPs involve the sale of a family business and about half of that group are majority-owned by the employees. Allied was one of the earliest examples, its founders Ed and Phyllis Sanders selling the company in total to the employees by 1982. The movement in the U.K. and Canada (where employee share-ownership was promoted in a report released by the Toronto Stock Exchange in 1986) bears many of the same features of that in the U.S., but is not as strong.

Majority or total employee ownership is still not a concept with broad acceptance in the business community—unless the company is under threat of closure. More often than not, employee share-ownership is a financing mechanism whereby companies take advantage of the tax credits associated with the transfer of a small portion of their stock to their employees (Rosen 1986). It is also viewed as a mechanism for building greater commitment to the corporation on the part of the employees through having them share in the benefits of capital, although there is no compelling evidence that share-ownership per se creates that commitment (Blasi and Kruse 1990).

There is also, however, a transformative vision associated with employee share-ownership of creating a more equitable distribution of wealth. Louis Kelso, the controversial founder of the ESOP, viewed it as the centerpiece of a movement for economic democracy and touted the ESOP as "the Trojan Horse for democratizing American capitalism" (Kelso and Kelso 1986, 53). Ed and Phyllis Sanders embraced this vision and lobbied for the legislation that would make it easier for retiring owners to transfer their firm to their employees. Phil Baxendale pushed this legislative framework in the U.K. and, in a similar vein, David Erdal argued that "Employee ownership is a very little used mechanism for redistributing wealth, and part of what I want to explore is how far it can be used." Erdal recognized that redistributing wealth through employee ownership is a long-term strategy. One of the difficulties in pursuing wealth redistribution in this manner is that employee owners, unlike capitalists with greater wealth accumulations, tend to liquidate their equity when the opportunity arises; in essence, they use it as income that is needed to supplement other earnings rather than as investment capital. Moreover, stocks represent a relatively small portion of wealth (Rosen 1991). Therefore, the ideal of redistributing wealth may not be attainable through employee ownership. Also, unless the ownership package includes a trust that controls the company (as in Tullis Russell and Baxi), an employee-owned company is always vulnerable to sale (for example, to earn a profit for the shareholders or to attract more investment).

Nevertheless, there is a better fit between employee share-ownership and the culture of capitalism than either the transfer of ownership to a trust or the creation of worker cooperative. Employee share-ownership represents a modest reform of capitalism, with the long-term objective of achieving some wealth redistribution if the problems associated with that ideal can be overcome. Ownership through a trust or a worker cooperative represents a more fundamental departure from the predominant norms in that both of these approaches greatly reduce the influence of capital (Schumacher 1973). For that reason, neither of these approaches has had much appeal.

b. Decision making

The same pattern—integration of practices involving a small modification of norms and the marginalization of more radical approaches—is evident in the decision-making innovations as well. All of the businesspeople who innovated around ownership arrangements also introduced approaches to decision making that, in varying degrees, enhanced employee influence. The Industrial Common Ownership Movement that Ernest Bader helped to start in the U.K. was designed to promote the development of democratic workplaces, largely by creating an alternative radically different in design from conventional businesses. Gerard Endenburg's goal was similar to Bader's. He applied himself, however, not only to the design of a democratic workplace but also to a detailed strategy for converting existing organizations to that design. At first, Endenburg's movement activities were confined to the Netherlands, but more recently, he has attempted to promote sociocracy internationally. However, he is handicapped because his home base is a small country whose primary language is rarely used elsewhere.

Sociocracy, like the other innovations, includes both modest modifications to existing norms for decision making and a transformative vision of a democratic workplace. As noted in chapter 4, Endenburg used an unusual combination of Quaker principles (derived from his earlier education) and cybernetics (from his training as an engineer) to involve employees in decision making from the basic production unit to the highest levels of organization. The decision-making circle, the election of representatives, and achieving consent were central tenets derived from Quaker thought; and the interlinking of decision-making circles at different levels of the organization was derived largely from cybernetics as a way of facilitating the flow of information up and down the organizational hierarchy. Endenburg did not argue that hierarchy could be eliminated in large organizations. Rather, he attempted to create processes to counteract the effects of hierarchy by allowing for employee participation in decision making at all levels of an organization and for the representatives at each level to interrelate.

Endenburg was also successful in having the Dutch government enact statutes for incorporating sociocratic firms, thereby legitimating the organizational form that he was promoting. Yet he acknowledges that even though representatives of hundreds of companies have attended workshops and about 40 companies have prepared statutes based upon sociocracy, only two owners have adopted the entire model and transferred their shares to a trust, thereby neutralizing the control of capital. In other words, those aspects of sociocracy that can most easily be grafted onto the existing company structure are most likely to be used.

c. Relationship to the community

As with ownership and decision making, the innovations in this category range from those that can be easily integrated into the capitalist system to others that represent a more fundamental challenge. James John Harpell's critique of monopoly control of banking and insurance posed a fundamental challenge to capitalism. Since he was a leading publisher during the 1930s, his critique was taken seriously (as reflected in the libel charges against him). However, that part of his work had little impact. He proved more effective as an adult educator in creating correspondence courses for industrial workers, and he also organized study clubs, credit unions, and other community institutions. While these were invaluable to the community and were in line with the broader thrust of the Antigonish Movement that he assisted, unlike his critique of monopoly control of capital, they could be integrated within the existing economic system.

Karroll Brent-Edmondson put her energy into creating opportunities for people on the margins of the labor force in New Zealand—the Maoris and other Pacific Islanders. This work is part of a broader movement for social justice for members of these groups. By creating a successful business with employees from these groups (and particularly in an industry in decline), and by becoming a public figure speaking out on behalf of the members of such groups, Brent-Edmondson has strengthened these movements. Brent-Edmondson's strategy does not purport to change the dynamics of business, but rather the face of the work force. If it becomes widespread, her work will represent an important reform.

The same could be said of Fred Braun's inmate-reform work in Kansas and other parts of the U.S. Through the three firms that he started to employ inmates and the additional firms in which his Workman Fund has invested, he has created the seeds of a movement, but a movement that has deliberately focused on one important issue and not on all aspects of inmate reform.

It is interesting to speculate why Braun has been able to proceed with a reformist agenda at a time when there is a punitive attitude toward criminals. He is an established businessman in Kansas, who is well connected within the Republican Party. Through the inmate enterprises, he is also providing a private-sector strategy in tune with government-cutback sentiments in conservative political circles in Kansas. He is not profiting from the inmate businesses and, in fact, has placed his own money at risk in order to set them up. Moreover, a central part of his justification for the inmate enterprises is that he is reducing recidivism, increasing the probability that inmates will become gainfully employed, and saving the taxpayers' money. Therefore, even though his innovations have a strikingly reformist character to them and run counter to the punitive attitudes toward inmates reflected in such spectacles as chain gangs, in other respects, they are compatible with the overall culture.

Karroll Brent-Edmondson and Fred Braun are part of the movement for corporate responsibility that includes Anita Roddick among its leaders. There is an obvious paradox about Roddick—she is an outspoken, irreverent critic of the corporate world, who is also the CEO of a large, successful corporation that mushroomed from nothing in less than 20 years. Roddick's critique derives credibility from The Body Shop's strong support for an array of social movements dealing with such concerns as ecology, human rights, fair trade, and banning animal testing. These activities are the basis for the company's marketing strategy and, therefore, a way to earn money for shareholders. Nevertheless, The Body Shop has a legitimate entitlement to undertake social marketing because, unlike many other firms using this approach, the promotions are a reflection of a substantial investment of finance and personnel in related causes.

There is also a broader vision related to the movements with which The Body Shop has aligned itself. The work of those movements remains on the fringe, whereas The Body Shop, as a mainstream corporation (albeit with a paradoxical role), is able to generate revenues to assist their challenge to the status quo. It is a highly unusual posture for a large corporation, but one that has proven effective both for The Body Shop and the movements it supports.

Until recently, Wilkhahn has shunned social marketing even though it has built up a strong record as an environmentally friendly corporation. However, with the receipt of the prestigious German Ecological Prize, the company has begun to promote its accomplishments. Fritz Hahne also has endeavored to ensure that Wilkhahn retains its commitment by establishing an ecology department and, as noted, by attempting to ensure that the CEO shares his ideals.

Relative to the norms for companies in industrial production, Wilkhahn is pushing the limits of ecological responsibility. Wilkhahn, in a role somewhat analogous to New Lanark, has become a leading example of what is possible for a business to accomplish ecologically at the same time as it functions effectively in the market. The success of the business is extremely important for these initiatives to have credibility.

PROPOSITION 4

The fourth proposition looks at the relationship between the state and the movements associated with the businesspeople in this study. It suggests that under particular circumstances the liberal-democratic state can be responsive to social movements that challenge the predominant norms and that it serves an important role in legitimizing innovation.

The businesspeople who were the subject of this book proceeded independently of the state, but its influence upon their activities was manifest in many ways. Fred Braun's inmate program was the only innovation that impinged directly upon the public sector. He became involved through a task force initiated by the governor of Kansas, and the legislative framework for his activities came from the Prison Industries Enhancement Act sponsored by Senator Charles Percy. Even though his was a private-sector initiative, it depended upon collaboration with the state corrections' authority.

None of the other innovations was directly associated with the public sector, but there still was an interaction with the state. For example, when Wilkhahn mounted its ecological program, the state government of Lower Saxony defrayed a portion of the cost for assistance from outside experts. Similarly, K. T.

Footwear received grants from the government of New Zealand for training the hard-core unemployed that were hired. The businesspeople who sought to innovate with respect to the ownership of their firms (Spedan Lewis, Ernest Bader, and James John Harpell) used legislation enacted by the state. The movement that Bader founded also lobbied successfully for legislation on the incorporation of common-ownership firms. Similarly, Gerard Endenburg was able to gain government approval for legislation that would permit employers to incorporate as sociocratic corporations. Part of the reason for Endenburg's success was that in the Netherlands as in Germany, there is already a tradition for the state sanctioning codetermination models in the workplace.

The state also has a tradition for making tax incentives available to particular types of business initiatives. Ed Sanders's work was important in that regard, because he and the employee-ownership movement in the U.S. helped to gain tax assistance for small business owners who wanted to sell their holding to an ESOP. Phil Baxendale and David Erdal played a similar role in the U.K.

Anita Roddick's relationship to the state has been primarily as a critic, in that she has aligned herself with nongovernment organizations that have challenged state policies on human rights. James John Harpell had a similar role in relation to the banking and insurance monopolies in Canada. These are only some of the examples that could be cited.

Essentially, the state has an important role in sanctioning innovative practices and in legitimating and integrating them into the predominant norms. But not all movement organizations are treated equally in that regard. Business organizations are often much more influential than organizations representing the poor, for example. However, the innovators who are the subject of this book may also have had the advantage of being businesspeople and, therefore, having the anomalous status of belonging to a privileged group at the same time as they associate with movements challenging the predominant norms. This point is made by Gavin Grant, the general manager of Public Affairs at The Body Shop, in reference to that firm's movement activities: "It confuses the hell out of people who think, 'You're a skin and hair corporation. What are you doing organizing people from the South Pacific against nuclear testing?'" Quite often, The Body Shop provides logistical support for social organizations such as Amnesty International, Greenpeace, and some lesser-known groups. Grant states proudly: "What we have done is to provide a platform for social activism."

UNDERSTANDING THE INNOVATORS

It is not difficult to understand why social movements attempt to integrate the contribution of such businesspeople as are discussed in this book. The dynamic of social movements is to marshal evidence in support of their challenge to the predominant norms. The innovations undertaken by these businesspeople and their promotion of that work are an important part of that evidence. Another issue is why these businesspeople have used their firms as a laboratory for social innovation rather than limiting themselves to a conventional role. To address this issue, I present a social humanistic model (see figure below).

The model uses three types of explanatory factors—initial motivation, background influences, and reinforcing circumstances. The first explanatory factor is derived from existentialism. The social humanistic tradition views the capacity to respond to injustice as something that is part of the contradictions in the human condition, that is, the lack of instinct in humans and the recognition that improvements in the quality of life come from betterment of the social environment (Fromm 1941; 1966; 1970). Within this model, agency is inherent to the human condition. However, the direction taken by the human desire to improve the quality of society is learned through culturally patterned responses. Depending upon the patterns of acculturation, individuals can find different and,

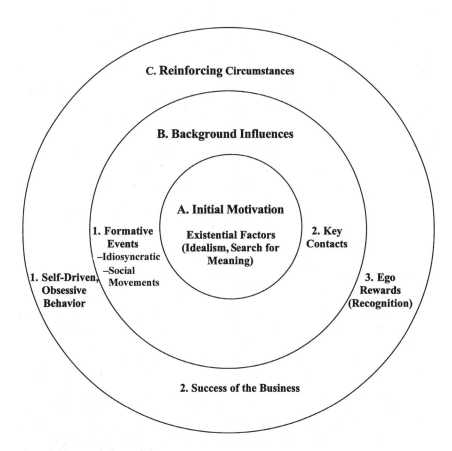

A social humanistic model.

indeed, competing outlets for such existential desires as freedom and justice. This means that even innovators such as those in the case studies bear the imprint of the predominant cultural patterns. They have departed from the norms for businesspeople in investing much of their energy in projects that improve the quality of the workplace and the surrounding community, yet in many other respects their behavior is normative. They are entrepreneurs with a keen sense of individualism, who believe that obstacles notwithstanding they can make a difference. In this case, the difference pertains to the social characteristics of the business and its relationship to its community rather than conventional business criteria.

However, even though the predominant norms have influenced these businesspeople, they have also been subject to other important influences. In distilling the information from the case studies, it is possible to discern two explanatory factors—formative events and key contacts (see figure on p. 179). Formative events involve both idiosyncratic factors that are unique to one person and social movements that have a broader influence. For example, Spedan Lewis's social innovations started shortly after he had suffered a serious riding accident that necessitated a lengthy recuperation (at age 24, about five years after he entered the family business). Fred Braun was moved toward inmate reform after a mid-life crisis precipitated by his wife's decision not to support his aspirations to become a politician. He had no past history with inmate reform, but he was a religious man who felt that he should give something back to society. "It is the obligation of people who do well to share what they have," he stated. For Fritz Hahne, being a soldier on the Russian front during the Second World War had a sobering impact upon him and caused a profound reaction against the values that he had held during his adolescence as a member of the Nazi youth movement. As a result of his war experience, he developed a strong identification with the employees of Wilkhahn and humanitarian values that sustained him in his leadership. For Karroll Brent-Edmondson (a Maori who grew up as a ward of the state), there was a strong sense of identification with people on the margins of New Zealand society. She was determined to apply her business acumen (honed for about 20 years in Australia) to help the members of this group. James John Harpell, the product of a poor farm family, also had a strong identification with people of similar circumstances that was strengthened by the Great Depression and the Antigonish Movement that arose at that time. During their formative years, Gerard Endenburg, Anita and Gordon Roddick, and David Erdal were strongly influenced by alternative value cultures that they transferred to their business endeavors. Endenburg's parents were part of a communal culture in the Netherlands, and during the Second World War, he was sent to a Quaker boarding school where he acquired his basic ideas about decision making and group processes. Anita and Gordon Roddick and David Erdal were influenced by the youth culture of the 1960s and attempted to apply to their businesses values that they acquired during that period. Erdal was the fourth generation of a proud family business that served the community of Markinch (north of Edinburgh). After a rebellious youth that included joining the Trotskyist movement and going to China, he entered the family business, but was always searching for a way in which he could fuse his idealism and concern for the gross inequalities in modern capitalism with his role in leading a sizable corporation. "I was looking for ways of redressing the wrongs being done by the system to ordinary people. The revolution was the first idea. This [employee ownership] is trying to produce a very similar end effect, but in a way that works and is evolutionary rather than revolutionary." If Erdal had not become acquainted with employee ownership, it is likely that he would have found another outlet for his idealism. Again, there was an element of chance in his adoption of the employee-ownership agenda. Like Erdal, the Roddicks were products of the youth culture, but of middle-class rather than patrician roots. They were caught up with the social movements of the day and sought an approach to business that was consistent with their values. Aligning the business with nonprofit, social organizations and using that alignment as a form of marketing allowed them to express their social values through the business.

In addition to a formative event, key contacts were important. For Phil Baxendale, contacts that included Spedan Lewis's nephew (Peter Lewis) and Robert Oakeshott of Job Ownership Ltd. made him aware of models in successful companies that he could apply to his own firm. For the Sanders, the key contact was with Norman Kurland, a Washington attorney who was a leading advocate of ESOPs. Both Sanders and Baxendale were searching for solutions, and therefore, it was not simply fortuitous that they encountered people who assisted them. David Erdal was not seeking to enter the family business, but the request from his uncle, Dr. David Russell, who was looking for a successor was critical to the direction he took. Contacts were important both during the formative stage where an innovative plan was being developed and also after the innovation was underway. Had Karroll Brent-Edmondson not contacted Stephan Tindall, the head of the second-largest retailer in New Zealand, her dream of a business consisting of employees on the margins of society would have ended in bankruptcy at an early point. Similarly, the loan that the Roddicks received from longtime friend Ian McGlinn to open the second outlet was critical to their success.

In addition to a formative event and key contacts, there was reinforcement for the innovative direction (see figure on p. 179). Two types of circumstances—success of the business and ego rewards such as recognition—have been referred to earlier in this chapter. Even though these businesspeople were highly self-directed, they were also cognizant of how their innovation affected their business and how others were responding to their initiative. However, self-driven behavior of the type engaged in by these businesspeople has a self-reinforcing character to it. In all cases, their innovation took on obsessional proportions; it was not simply something that they did on top of their business activities but something to which they applied themselves with missionary zeal.

The social humanistic model seeks to explain why these businesspeople have become innovators and have challenged some of the predominant norms for business, but it does not address the significance of their contribution to related social movements. Assessing that impact is problematic because these movements would have proceeded had they not been involved. That is not to say that individual leaders, such as these businesspeople, are insignificant. But rather, it is important not to create a romantic illusion about the impact of one individual's work. Although Robert Owen made an immense contribution to the movements of social justice during the nineteenth century, all of these movements had many other proponents. Moreover, unlike the people in this book, Owen was operating during a period when major social changes were occurring.

Brinton (1965) uses an agricultural metaphor to analyze the role of leaders of revolutionary movements. He draws an analogy to gardeners, arguing that their individual talents are important but that, in order for them to be effective, they require fertile soil. The context for this book differs from those that Brinton analyzed. There is a tendency in revolutionary movements to thrust someone into a command position who can speak on behalf of the movement—a tendency that both romanticizes and aggrandizes the importance of the leader.

None of these businesspeople is associated with revolutionary movements. Rather, they are participants in social movements that are attempting to change the organization of business and society during a relatively stable social period. Those who have taken a leading role in developing movement organizations (for example, Gerard Endenburg's Sociocratic Center in the Netherlands, Ernest Bader's Industrial Common Ownership Movement in the U.K., and Fred Braun's Workman Fund in the U.S.) are associated with relatively weaker groups. However, while these movement organizations might be seen as unique, they are also part of a broader movement for social justice in the workplace and society.

This discussion, therefore, begs the question of how to assess the contribution of these businesspeople. With respect to social movements, it is difficult to determine the impact of an individual. In assessing themselves, however, these businesspeople have transferred the individualistic logic that they have utilized in leading their businesses to their role as social innovators. Fred Braun highlights this point of view when he states: "I still believe that one guy can change the system—if he goes about it the right way, busts his ass, and is lucky." Ernest Bader was so convinced that the common ownership approach he promoted as a "third way" between communism and capitalism would succeed that he told his son Godric (whom he convinced to take over as managing director) that if he carried on he'd receive a knighthood. Spedan Lewis was also convinced that the Partnership model he created at his firm was the way of the future, referring to it on the cover of his 1954 book (*Fairer Shares*) as "perhaps the only alternative to communism."

This keen sense of the power of the individual was important in sustaining the work of these businesspeople. To borrow Brinton's metaphor, however, within their own firms, they had fertile soil—in part, because they owned them and were charismatic figures who could move others. As owners, they had a legitimate entitlement to innovate, and their skill, determination, leadership qualities, and noble intentions made it likely that others would cooperate with them. However, outside of their businesses, those conditions did not apply. Spedan Lewis could, if he desired, place his shares in the company into a trust so that his employees could benefit from the dividends. But he was an outlier in the business world, and there was not much receptivity to the idea on the part of others. Toward the end of his life, Lewis recognized that there was a lack of interest in the Partnership model. A 1957 letter to his successor Bernard Miller indicates that he still held out hope: "There seems to me to be still a real chance that I may live to see our experiment burst into a sudden blaze. But in the meantime it has been something of a disappointment" (Lewis 1957, 1). By 1960, the disillusionment was apparent: "The experiment embodied in the John Lewis Partnership has come too late to have perhaps some value," he stated (Lewis 1960b, 448). Max Baker, one of the senior management team who worked closely with Lewis, recalled: "It was a vision that inspired him and he sacrificed a lot for it, not least his own family. . . . He thought that he would blaze a trail that others would be inspired to follow. It didn't happen and he died (in 1963) a bitterly disappointed man" (Baker 1985, 114).

Essentially, Lewis did not appreciate that the individualistic logic that had served him well as businessman was less useful in his movement activities, because broadly based social movements do not turn around one individual. This logic prevented him from recognizing that he was one of many "social" actors who were both inspired by movements for workplace betterment and, at the same time, were adding to those movements—in Lewis's case through creating the John Lewis Partnership, writing about it, and promoting the idea in other ways. Lewis, as noted, was not the first businessman to donate his shares to a trust that controlled the company. Ernest Abbe did that in 1888 at the German optical parts manufacturer Carl Zeiss (Volkmann 1966), and James Eagan followed suit in 1923 at the American Cast Iron Pipe Co. in the U.S. (Cleghorn 1995). Nor were Lewis's ideas about profit sharing and involving employees in decision making one of a kind. He was far ahead of the norms for the First World War period when he started introducing these ideas, but there was a tradition that preceded him and would have had some influence on his thinking. In his writings, Lewis acknowledges the work of Robert Owen but not the contribution of others. In that regard, he typifies the attitude of the businesspeople in these case studies—a striking degree of individualism, of initial optimism, and of faith that they can change society. While these attitudes sustained them in their innovations, they are based on a fallacy that inevitably leads to the type of disappointment that, in their final years, plagued Spedan Lewis and Ernest Bader and to which Phil Baxendale also refers. Yet, ironically, all of these businesspeople have made important contributions to movements for betterment of the workplace and society. Not only have the employees of their firms benefited from their work but they have also inspired other businesspeople with their innovations.

In conclusion, while these businesspeople provide sustenance for social movements and are embraced by them for their contributions, as social actors, the movements to which they are contributing also influence them. It is possible that any one of these innovations will at some point become predominant, but it will not occur because of the work of one person. However, without believing in their own power to change the workplace, it is doubtful that these businesspeople would have embarked upon their innovations. Their individualism is important to motivate them, but it also creates a false consciousness that inevitably leads to disappointment and disillusionment.

There is not a simple formula to discern the impact of these social actors on movements to improve the quality of the workplace. Over the years, one or more of these innovations could become part of the predominant norms and, if that were to occur, it is possible that some of these businesspeople will be acclaimed as major social leaders, much as was Robert Owen in the nineteenth century. While the idea of using the workplace as a laboratory to innovate did not originate with them, they are following a noble tradition that will undoubtedly inspire others to do the same.

NOTES

1. All quotes for which a source is not cited are based upon interviews with the author, which were part of the case studies discussed in chapters 2 through 10.

2. Personal communication, March 1998.

References

Adams, Roy. 1986. Two policy approaches to labour-management decision-making at the level of the enterprise. In *Labour-management co-operation in Canada,* ed. Craig Riddell, 87–107. Toronto: University of Toronto Press.

Adams, Roy. 1995. A pernicious euphoria: 50 years of Wagnerism in Canada. *Canadian Labour & Employment Law* 3–4: 321–355.

Altenberg, Lee. 1990. An end to capitalism: Leland Stanford's forgotten vision. *Sandstone and Tile: Stanford Historical Society* 14(1): 8–20.

Anagnostelis, John. 1982. An appreciation of Ernest Bader. *The Reactor* (March): 6–7.

Bader, Ernest. 1943. *Letter to employees: Proposed community.* 4 November, Wollaston, U.K.: Scott Bader. Photocopy.

———. 1947. A message from our chairman. *The Catalyst* May: 2, 6.

———. 1948. Letter. *The Catalyst* 3(1): 3–4.

———. 1957. Cultivating friendship with sympathetic firms: Best & Lloyd of Birmingham. *The Catalyst* (December): 3–4.

Baker, Max. 1985. Interview. In *John Spedan Lewis: 1885–1963,* ed. Hugh Macpherson, 104–115. London: John Lewis Partnership.

Bartolke, Klaus, Walter Eschweiler, Dieter Flechsenberger, Michal Palgi, and Menachem Rosner. 1985. *Participation and control.* Spardorf, Germany: Verlag René F. Wilfer.

Baxendale, Phil. 1984. From participation to partnership. Preston: Baxi Partnership. Photocopy.

———. 1994. Baxi Partnership founder's vision. Preston: Baxi Partnership. Photocopy.

Baxi Partnership Ltd. 1995. Annual report & accounts: 1994/95. Preston, U.K.: Baxi Partnership.

Bell, Daniel. 1960. *The end of ideology.* New York: Free Press.

Blasi, Joseph, and Douglas Kruse. 1990. *The new owners.* New York: HarperCollins.

Blum, Fred. 1968. *Work and community: The Scott Bader Commonwealth and the quest for a new social order.* London: Routledge & Kegan Paul.

Bradley, Keith, and Saul Estrin. 1986. *The success story of the John Lewis Partnership: A study of comparative performance.* London: Partnership Research Ltd.

———. 1988. *Does employee ownership improve company performance? The Case of the John Lewis Partnership.* London: Partnership Research Ltd.

Bradley, Keith, and Simon Taylor. 1992. *Business performance in the retail sector: The experience of the John Lewis Partnership.* Oxford: Clarendon Press.

Briggs, Asa. 1961. *A study of the work of Seebohm Rowntree, 1871–1954.* London: Longmans.

Brinton, Crane. 1965. *The anatomy of revolution.* New York: Vintage.

Brohawn, Dawn. 1994. Value-based management: A framework for equity and efficiency in the workplace. In *Curing world poverty: The new role of property,* ed. John Miller, 189–211. St. Louis: Social Justice Review.

Callison, Herbert. 1989. *Zephyr Products: The story of an inmate-staffed business.* Washington: American Correctional Association.

Carnegie, Andrew. 1901. *The gospel of wealth and other timely essays.* New York: The Century Co.

Carroll, William. 1997. Social movements and counterhegemony: Canadian contexts and social theories. In *Organizing dissent: Contemporary social movements in theory and practice,* ed. William Carroll, 3–38. Toronto: Garamond Press.

Case, John. 1995. *Open-book management.* New York: HarperBusiness.

Cleghorn, John S. 1995. The work of justice: The quest for moral common ground in the authority relations of work. Ph.D. dissertation, Emory University, Ga.

Cohen, Carl, ed. 1967. *Communism, fascism, and democracy.* New York: Random House.

Cole, G. D. H. 1966. *The life of Robert Owen.* Hamden, Conn.: Archon Books.

Cole, Margaret. 1969. *Robert Owen of New Lanark.* New York: Augustus M. Kelley.

Corina, John. 1996. Letter regarding the *New Dictionary of National Biography.* 9 September, n.p.

Cornforth, Chris, Allan Thomas, Jenny Lewis, and Roger Spear. 1988. *Developing successful worker co-operatives.* London: Sage.

Donnachie, Ian, and George Hewitt. 1993. *Historic New Lanark: The Dale and Owen industrial community since 1785.* Edinburgh: Edinburgh University Press.

Earle, John. 1986. *The Italian co-operative movement.* London: Unwin Hyman.

Ellerman, David. 1990. *The democratic worker-owned firm: A new model for east and west.* Boston: Unwin Hyman.

Endenburg, Gerard. 1988. *Sociocracy: The organization of decision-making.* Rotterdam: The Sociocratic Center.

Engels, Friedrich. 1959. Socialism: Utopian and scientific. In *Marx & Engels: Basic writings on politics & philosophy,* ed. Lewis Feuer, 68–111. New York: Anchor Books.

Entine, Jon. 1994. Shattered image. *Business Ethics* September/October, 23–28.

———. 1995a. Rain-forest chic. *Report on Business* October, 41–52.

———. 1995b. The Body Shop: Truth & consequences. *Drug and Cosmetics Industry* 156 (2 February), 54–64.

Erdal, David. 1995. *Tullis Russell Group Limited: Case study.* Markinch: Tullis Russell. Photocopy.

Flanders, Allan, Ruth Pomeranz, and Joan Woodward. 1968. *Experiment in industrial democracy.* London: Faber and Faber.

Friedman, Kathy. 1994. Capital credit: The ultimate right of citizenship. In *Curing world poverty: The new role of property,* ed. John Miller, 133–149. St. Louis: Social Justice Review.

Fromm, Eric. 1941. *Escape from freedom.* New York: Holt, Reinhart, Winston.

———. 1966. The application of humanist psychoanalysis to Marx's theory. In *Socialist humanism,* ed. Eric Fromm, 228–245. New York: Doubleday.

———. 1970. *The sane society.* New York: Fawcett.

Gamson, William. 1975. *The strategy of social protest.* Homewood, Ill.: Dorsey Press.

Gillespie, James. 1965. Towards freedom in work. *Anarchy* 47(1): 5–32.

Gleisser, Marcus. 1965. *The world of Cyrus Eaton.* New York: A.S. Barnes and Co.

Gray, Brian. 1995. Chief executive's report. Preston, U.K.: Baxi Partnership.

Hadley, Roger, and Maurice Goldsmith. 1995. Development or convergence? Change and stability in a common ownership firm over three decades, 1960–89. *Economic and Industrial Democracy* 16: 167–199.

Hahne, Fritz. 1990. *Between the chairs.* Translated by Frank Keller and Rudolf Schwartz. Bad Munder, Germany: Wilkhahn.

Harpell, James John. 1906a. Improper and extravagant management of a number of Canadian life insurance companies. Toronto: Garden City Press.

———. 1906b. The rights of the policyholders and the benefits from properly regulated insurance. Toronto: Garden City Press.

———. 1908. Canadian banking and insurance under Hon. W. S. Fielding, Finance Minister. Toronto: Garden City Press.

———. 1911. *Canadian national economy.* Toronto: MacMillan.

———. 1926. *Garden City Press: Its purpose and location.* St. Anne-de-Bellevue, Quebec: Garden City Press.

———. 1932. The world's greatest crooks. *Journal of Commerce,* October edition.

———. 1935. *The New Deal vs the old system of exploitation.* St. Anne-de-Bellevue, Quebec: Garden City Press.

———. 1936. *Arts and Crafts: A co-operative community of student workers.* St. Anne-de-Bellevue, Quebec: Garden City Press.

———. 1937. *The dawn of a new era.* St. Anne-de-Bellevue, Quebec: Garden City Press.

———. 1942. *The creation and maintenance of opportunities for employment.* St. Anne-de-Bellevue, Quebec: Garden City Press.

———. n.d.a. *The Study Club of St. Anne-de-Bellevue.* St. Anne-de-Bellevue, Quebec: Garden City Press.

———. n.d.b. Letters from a business man to a student of economics. St. Anne-de-Bellevue, Quebec: Garden City Press.

———. n.d.c. The Pan American Home-Builders. St. Anne-de-Bellevue, Quebec: Garden City Press.

Hasselmann, Erwin. 1971. The impact of Owen's ideas on German social and co-operative thought during the nineteenth century. In *Robert Owen: Prophet of the poor,* ed. Sidney Pollard and John Salt, 285–305. London: Macmillan.

Heuss, Theodor. 1994. *Robert Bosch: His life and achievements.* New York: Henry Holt & Co.

Hinings, Christopher. 1989. *The dynamics of strategic change.* New York: Blackwell.

Hoe, Susanna. 1978. *The man who gave his company away: A biography of Ernest Bader, founder of the Scott Bader Commonwealth.* Wollaston, U.K.: Scott Bader.

Hook, Sydney, ed. 1958. *Determinism and freedom in the age of modern science: A philosophical symposium.* New York: NYU Press.

Jenkins, J. Craig. 1983. Resource mobilization theory and the study of social movements. *Annual Review of Sociology* 9: 527–53.

John Lewis Partnership plc. 1996. Report and accounts. London: John Lewis Partnership.

Jones, Mick. 1982. The end of an era. *The Reactor* (March): 1.

Kanter, Rosabeth. 1992. *The challenge of organizational change: How companies experience it and leaders guide it.* New York: Free Press.

Kelsey, Jane. 1995. *The New Zealand experiment: A world model for structural adjustment?* Aukland: Auckland University Press and Bridget Williams Books.

Kelso, Louis, and Mortimer Adler. 1958. *The capitalist manifesto.* New York: Random House.

Kelso, Louis, and Patricia Hetter Kelso. 1986. *Democracy and economic power.* Cambridge, Mass.: Ballinger.

Knox, Paul. 1995. Nobel prize puts Pugwash on map. *Globe and Mail,* 14 October, 1.

Knudsen, Herman. 1994. *Employee participation in Europe.* London: Sage.

Kruse, Douglas. 1993. *Profit-sharing: Does it make a difference?* Kalamazoo, Mich.: Upjohn Institute for Employment Research.

Kurland, Norman. 1994. Economic justice in the age of the robot. In *Curing World Poverty: The new role of property,* ed. John Miller, 61–74. St. Louis: Social Justice Review.

Lager, Fred. 1994. *Ben & Jerry's: The inside scoop.* New York: Crown.

Lewin, Kurt. 1947. Frontiers in group dynamics. *Human Relations* 1: 5–41.

Lewis, John Spedan. 1918a. Minutes of the 18th annual ordinary general meeting, Peter Jones, Ltd., 26 April.

———. 1918b. To my fellow-employees of Peter Jones, Ltd. *The Gazette* March, 1–5.

———. 1928. Letter to the Industrial Co-partnership Association. London: 12 January. Photocopy.

———. 1929. Letter to the Industrial Co-partnership Association. London: 18 November. Photocopy.

———. 1931. Letter to the Industrial Co-partnership Association. London: 16 September. Photocopy.

———. 1948. *Partnership for all.* London: Kerr-Cross.

———. 1954. *Fairer shares.* London: Staples.

———. 1957. Letter to Bernard Miller. 23 March. Photocopy.

———. 1960a. Communications from former chairman. *The Gazette* 13 August, 677–78.

———. 1960b. Significance of our own experiment. *The Gazette* 11 June, 448.

Liebig, James. 1994. *Merchants of vision.* San Francisco: Berrett-Koehler.

Lloyd-Davies, Martyn. 1985. Interview. In *John Spedan Lewis: 1885–1963,* ed. Hugh Macpherson, 88–93. London: John Lewis Partnership.

Long, Russell. 1984. Proceedings and debates of the 98th Congress, second session. *Congressional Record,* 29 June, 6.

Lynn, Constance. 1985. Interview. In *John Spedan Lewis: 1885–1963,* ed. Hugh Macpherson, 122–27. London: John Lewis Partnership.

MacPherson, Ian. 1979. *Each for all: A history of the co-operative movement in English Canada, 1900–1945.* Toronto: MacMillan.

Mannheim, Karl. 1952. *Essays on the sociology of knowledge.* New York: Routledge & Kegan Paul.

———. 1953. *Ideology and utopia.* New York: Harcourt, Brace and World.

Manuel, Frank. 1969. Toward a psychological history of utopias. In *Studies in social movements,* ed. Barry McLaughlin, 370–399. New York: The Free Press.

Marx, Karl, and Friedrich Engels. 1968. *The communist manifesto: With an introduction by A. J. P. Taylor.* Harmondsworth, U.K.: Penguin.

May, Paul. 1985. Interview. In *John Spedan Lewis: 1885–1963,* ed. Hugh Macpherson, 58–75. London: John Lewis Partnership.

McCarthy, John. 1977. Resource mobilization and social movements. *American Journal of Sociology* 82: 1212–1241.

McCarthy, John, and Mayer Zald. 1973. *The trend in social movements in America: Professionalization and resource mobilization.* Morristown, N.J.: General Learning Press.

McLaren, David. 1983. *David Dale of New Lanark.* Milngavie: Heatherbank Press.

McLellan, David. 1997. *Engels.* Sussex: The Harvester Press.

McWhirter, Douglas. 1991. Employee ownership: Performance and prospects. In *Understanding employee ownership,* ed. Corey Rosen and Karen Young, 43–73. Ithaca, N.Y.: ILR.

Miller, Bernard. 1985. Interview. In *John Spedan Lewis: 1885–1963,* ed. Hugh Macpherson, 20–43. London: John Lewis Partnership.

Morris, Aldon, and Carol McClurg Mueller, ed. 1992. *Frontiers in social movement theory.* New Haven, Conn.: Yale University Press.

Murphy, Annie. 1994. The seven (almost) deadly sins of high-minded entrepreneurs. *INC.* 16(7) (July), 47–51.

National Center for Employee Ownership. 1995. *Theory O: Creating an ownership style of management.* Oakland, Calif.: National Center for Employee Ownership.

Oakeshott, Robert. 1978. *The case for workers' co-ops.* London: Routledge and Kegan Paul.

———. 1994. *The winding road to "x" efficiency: The first ten partnership years at Baxi.* London: Partnership Research Ltd.

Oakeshott, Robert, and Felix Schmid. 1990. *The Carl Zeiss Stiftung: Its first hundred years of impersonal ownership.* London: Job Ownership Ltd.

O'Sullivan, Edmund. 1990. *Critical psychology and critical pedagogy.* New York: Bergin & Garvey.

Owen, Robert. 1857. *The life of Robert Owen, written by himself.* Vol. 1. London: Effingham Wilson, Royal Exchange.

———. 1969. *A new view of society.* Harmondsworth, Middlesex: Penguin.

Pateman, Carole. 1970. *Participation and democratic theory.* London: Cambridge University Press.

Piven, Frances Fox, and Richard Cloward. 1992. Normalizing collective protest. In *Frontiers in social movement theory,* ed. Aldon Morris and Carol McClurg Mueller, 301–325. New Haven, Conn.: Yale University Press.

Pollard, Sidney. 1971. Introduction. In *Robert Owen: Prophet of the poor,* ed. Sidney Pollard and John Salt, vii–xi. London: Macmillan.

Poole, Lorna. 1992. Cradle of the partnership: John Spedan Lewis and Peter Jones Ltd. *The Gazette,* 22 August, 743–44.

Quarter, Jack. 1992. *Canada's social economy: Co-operatives, non-profits and other community enterprises.* Toronto: James Lorimer.

———. 1995. *Crossing the line: Unionized employee ownership and investment funds.* Toronto: James Lorimer.

Quarter, Jack, and Jo-Ann Hannah. 1989. From worker buyouts to conversion strategies. In *Partners in enterprise: The worker ownership phenomenon,* ed. Jack Quarter and George Melnyk, 59–84. Montreal: Black Rose.

Queen's Bench. 1993. The Body Shop International plc vs. Channel Four Television Company Limited, 30 July.

Reijmer, Annewiek, and Georges Romme. 1994. *Sociocracy in Endenburg Electric.* Rotterdam: The Sociocratic Center.

Robertson, Alex J. 1971. Robert Owen: Cotton spinner: New Lanark, 1800–25. In *Robert Owen: Prophet of the poor,* ed. Sidney Pollard and John Salt, 145–165. London: Macmillan.

Roddick, Anita. 1991. *Body and soul.* New York: Crown.

———. 1994a. Spirituality and service. Littlehampton: The Body Shop International. Photocopy.

———. 1994b. Corporate responsibility. Littlehampton: The Body Shop International. Photocopy.

———. n.d. Bringing your heart to work with you. Littlehampton: The Body Shop International. Photocopy.

Roddick, Gordon. 1994. Letter to *Business Ethics* subscribers. Littlehampton: The Body Shop International. Photocopy.

Rosen, Corey. 1986. How employee ownership plans work. In *Employee ownership in America: The equity solution,* ed. Corey Rosen, Katherine Klein, and Karen Young, 13–39. New York: Lexington.

———. 1991. Employee ownership, performance, prospects, and promise. In *Understanding employee ownership,* eds. Corey Rosen and Karen Young, 1–42. Ithaca N.Y.: ILR Press.

Sanders, Edward. 1978. Letter to Hon. Russell B. Long, Chairman, Senate Finance Committee. 17 July, Washington, D.C. Photocopy.

Schumacher, E. F.. 1973. *Small is beautiful.* New York: Harper & Row.

Scott Bader. 1987. Constitution. Wollaston, U.K.: Scott Bader.

———. 1996. Annual report 1995. Wollaston, U.K.: Scott Bader.

Scott, Mary. 1995. Lost and found: After an over-hyped launch and near-death experience, *BSR* is back. *Business Ethics* 9(4) July/August, 22–23.

Siler, Charles. 1994. Body Shop marches to its own drummer. *Advertising Age* 10 October, 4.

Skocpol, Theda. 1979. *States and social revolutions.* London: Cambridge University Press.

Slater, Robert. 1996. *Soros: The life, times and trading secrets of the world's greatest investor.* New York: Irwin.

Soros, George. 1995. *Soros on Soros: Staying ahead of the curve.* New York: Wiley.

———. 1997a. Interview with Michael Ignatieff. *CBC Television,* 1 November.

———. 1997b. The capitalist threat. *The Atlantic Monthly,* February, 45–58.

Spayde, Jon. 1995. 100 visionaries. *Utne Reader,* January/February, 54–81.

Stack, Jack. 1992. *The great game of business.* New York: Doubleday.

Stranz, Walter. 1973. *George Cadbury: An illustrated life of George Cadbury, 1839–1922.* Aylesbury, Bucks, U.K.: Shire Publications, Ltd.

The Body Shop. 1995a. Annual reports and accounts. Littlehampton, U.K.: The Body Shop.

The Body Shop. 1995b. The Body Shop social statement 95. Littlehampton, U.K.: The Body Shop.

Thurow, Lester. 1996. *The future of capitalism.* New York: William Morrow.

Tribunal du travail. 1982. Decisions du Commissaire du travail et du Tribunal du travail, Imprimerie coopérative Harpell c. Syndicat québécois de l'Imprimerie et des communications, section locale 145, 2 March, 1982, File No. T82–225.

Tullis Russell. 1996. Report & accounts for the period from incorporation to 31 March, 1996. Markinch, Scotland: Tullis Russell.

Vallance, Aymer. 1909. *William Morris: His art, his writings, and his public Life.* London: George Bell and Sons.

Vernon, Anne. 1958. *A Quaker business man: The life of Joseph Rowntree, 1836–1925.* London: Allen & Unwin.

Vincent, Paul. 1984. Historique de l'Imprimerie coopérative Harpell. Montreal: n.p. Photocopy.

Volkmann, Harald. 1966. Ernst Abbe and his work. *Applied Optics* 5: 1720–1731.

Wall, Joseph F., ed. 1992. *The Andrew Carnegie reader.* Pittsburgh, Penn.: University of Pittsburgh Press.

Webb, Sidney, and Beatrice Webb. 1921. *The consumers' co-operative movement.* London: Longmans.

Weber, Max. 1947. *The theory of social and economic organization.* New York: The Free Press.

Whyte, William F., and Kathleen Whyte. 1988. *Making Mondragon.* Ithaca, N.Y.: ILR.

Wilkhahn. 1995. Wilkhahn green: A company in the process of change. Bad Munder, Germany: Wilkhahn.

World Health Organization. 1995. *World health statistics annual 1994.* Geneva, Switzerland: World Health Organization.

Young, Arthur. 1981. *Cost impact of using inmate labor in a manufacturing environment.* Kansas City, Kan: Department of Corrections.

Yukl, Gary. 1981. *Leadership in organizations.* Englewood Cliffs, N.J.: Prentice-Hall.

Zald, Mayer, and Roberta Ash. 1966. Social movement organizations: Growth, decay and change. *Social Forces* 44 (March): 327–40.

Index

Abbe, Ernst, Carl Zeiss company trust, 17
Adler, Mortimer, *Capitalist Manifesto*, co-
author, 67–68, 70
Airflow Development, 47. *See* Wilson,
Connor
Allied Plywood: "Allied's form of socialism", 76; and Bob Shaw, president,
74–79; and Ed and Phyllis Sanders,
owners, 72, 74, 81; and Gene Scales,
vice president, 74–78; and
Washington, D.C. area, 72–73, 77;
cash-flow constraints on ESOP,
80–81; chronology, 82; corporate
culture of, 78; employee benefits
70–71; employee dependence on
company performance, 76, 80, 82n;
employee gains through ESOP, 70,
74–77; employee owned, not managed, 71, 79–81; employees' traditional roles, 80; ESOP as benefit
plan, 69, 79; ESOP as employees'
benefit, 70–71, 75, 77; ESOP as
retirement "vehicle", 80; ESOP liabilities, 76. (*See also* ESOP); expansion pressures, 77–78; fixed and
variable compensation, 77; flexible
labor costs and layoffs, 78; formal
accountability, 80; incentives for

employee longevity and productivity,
69, 75, 77; open-book management,
79; original board of directors, 78;
origins, 67, 72–74; pressure to
increase profits, 76; profit-sharing
difficulties, 77; repurchase of ESOP
liabilities, 81; sale of company, transfer of management, 72, 74–75;
Sanders' legacy, 75, 81; shareholders' meetings, 79; traditional management practices, 78; transfer of
ownership to employees, 79, 81; 25
percent security, 73, 76; vesting
employees, 70, 75; wholesale build-
ing-supply business, 72–73; year-end
bonus, 77. *See also* Sanders, Ed and
Phyllis
Antigonish Movement: and James John
Harpell, 106; and *Masters of their
Own Destiny,* 106

Bader, Ernest: and Demintry, 46; and
Scott Bader Fellowship, 36; and
Scott Bader, importer, 34, 41; and
social justice, 36; and strike of 1948,
36, 41; bargain with workers Quaker-
style, 42; commonwealth as social
property, 35, 37; comparison with

NOTE

I would like to thank Jorge Sousa and Richard DeGaetano for preparing this index.

ABOUT THE AUTHOR

JACK QUARTER is a professor at the Ontario Institute for Studies in Education of the University of Toronto, where he specializes in the study of workplace democracy, cooperatives, nonprofits, community development, the social economy, and social investment. His recent books include *Canada's Social Economy: Co-operatives, Non-Profits and Other Community Enterprises; Crossing the Line: Unionized Employee Ownership and Investment Funds*; with Paul Wilkinson, *Building a Community Controlled Economy: The Evangeline Cooperative Experience*; and coedited with Uriel Leviatan and Hugh Oliver, *Crisis in the Israeli Kibbutz* (Praeger).